Battle Born Nevada: People, History and Stories

By Don Lynch and David Thompson

A Publication of
The Grace Dangberg Foundation, Inc.

A DANGBERG HISTORICAL PUBLICATION

The Grace Dangberg Foundation was established in 1982 by the late Grace Dangberg, a distinguished Nevada historian and granddaughter of Carson Valley pioneers. The Foundation was created to improve the study of history by young people through the publication of books and the support of research.

Publisher: The Grace Dangberg Foundation, Inc.

Authors: Don Lynch and David Thompson

Editor: James H. Bean

Title: BATTLE BORN NEVADA: People, History and Stories

Library of Congress Catalog Number: 93-079470

ISBN 0-913205-20-6

Revised Second Printing 1998

Printed by Gilliland Printing, Inc. Arkansas City, Kansas

FOREWORD

The words "battle born" in the title of this new history book describe the beginning of the state of Nevada. Congress granted statehood to Nevada during the Civil War. Nevada could provide the money and the political support President Lincoln needed to free the slaves and to establish civil rights for everyone. This valuable support to Lincoln gave statehood to Nevada more than 20 years ahead of the other Mountain States. The full title, *BATTLE BORN NEVADA: People, History and Stories*, refers to people and stories because this is more than just a history book. It also deals with Nevada's economic and social conditions along with its history. The specific wording for this title was suggested, during a group discussion, by Gary and Jennifer Blake, graduates of Carson High School, 1991 and 1992.

The first edition of *BATTLE BORN* had two authors, Don Lynch and David Thompson. Lynch is a writer for the Dangberg Foundation. Thompson is president of the Foundation. His research led to the first edition of *BATTLE BORN* and contributed to the second edition. Lynch revised and added new content to the previous book, the first edition of *BATTLE BORN* which has been used in Nevada schools for the past four years. The Foundation trustees agreed that after four years, new material would be needed in a second edition that would reflect some of what has happened in our rapidly growing Silver State.

James Bean, trustee of the Dangberg Foundation, edited all material and contributed substantially to this new edition. Bean is director of the Foundation and a former director of curriculum and instruction for the State Department of Education.

Susan Bean, Foundation editorial assistant, using publishing software designed and composed the pages.

We hope you enjoy the book.

Denise Dangberg

Denise Dangberg, Vice President
The Grace Dangberg Foundation, Inc.

iii

ACKNOWLEDGEMENTS

A number of people gave us invaluable assistance in writing this history book.

Phillip Earl, curator of the Nevada Historical Society. His knowledge of the Nevada history was especially helpful.

Verne Horton in Carson City is responsible for the original artwork of the attractive cover and the sequence of matching color pages that introduce the chapters.

Jean Ford caused me to see the importance of women in history. We feel this edition of *BATTLE BORN NEVADA* reflects the importance of women from the earliest days in Nevada history.

Eugene Moehring, professor of history at the University of Nevada in Las Vegas and author of *Resort City in the Sunbelt*, graciously gave of his time to read and react to the first printing our history book.

Here are the names of other contributors who were especially helpful in obtaining information and pictures:

Susan Bean, Page layouts of this book
Tim Dunn, Photo editor at Reno Gazette Journal
Doug Driesner, Nevada Bureau of Mines
Kim Morgan, Nevada Legislative Counsel Bureau, Legal Division
Andy Harvey, Nevada Legislative Counsel Bureau, Legal Division
Bryan Kaiser, Bureau of Business and Economic Research, UNR
Guy Rocha, Nevada State Archivies, for his knowledge and information
　　　　　on the Portuguese people

Finally, scores of people freely interrupted their time to help us obtain information and photos.

D.L.

TABLE OF CONTENTS

Historical Events

10,000 - 5,000 B.C.
Oldest Indian Sites

1855
Treaty with Shoshone

1860
Pyramid Lake War

1866
Peace Between Paiutes and Whites

1870-1890
Indian Reservations Created

1886
Indian Courts Established

1887
Congress Passed Dawes Act

1889
Wovoka's Ghost Dance Movement

1901
Stewart Indian School Established

1924
Congress Made Indians U.S. Citizens

1934
Congress Passed Wheeler-Howard Act

Chapter One

The Indians

The Indians

The first people, later called Indians, came to North America over a land bridge from Asia. They developed a way of living by gathering various foods and hunting and fishing.

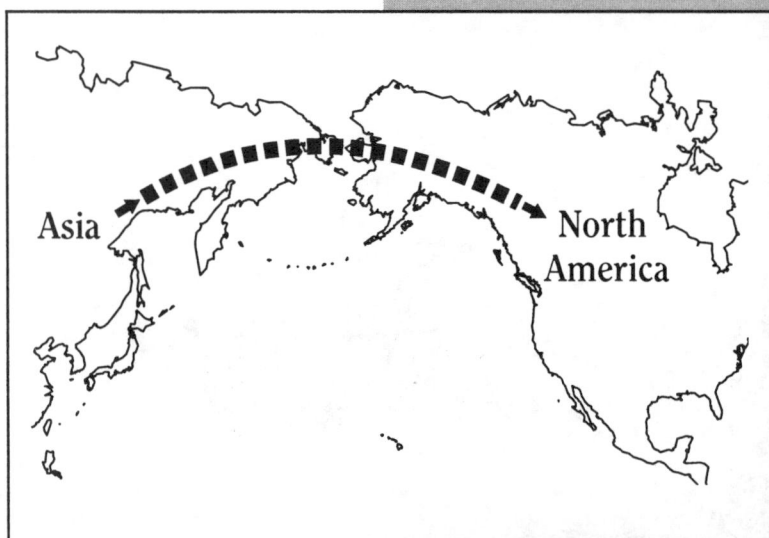

Their way of living, customs and traditions were interwoven in a delicate way with the land on which they lived. Then came a different people, intruding into the Indians' way of living. The intruders brought things the Indians had not dreamed of and ideas which were strange to their ways. The Indians' reaction to the intruders is a story of events, including wars, treaties, and reservations. The Indian way of living had changed forever.

Land Bridge from Asia. *In prehistoric times, before the rising oceans covered it, this land bridge was used by ancient ancestors of the American Indians to migrate from Siberia to North America.*

Before the first white people arrived, American Indians were the only people who lived in Nevada. For thousands of years they led a wandering life in small groups of families, or bands. These Native Americans left no written histories for us to read. We know about them through the discoveries of archaeologists. The writings of early explorers, trappers, soldiers, and other intruders who passed through the Great Basin also told of the Indians.

The Great Basin is an area bordered on the east and west by high mountain ranges and on the north and south by high plateaus. The mountains and plateaus are so high that rain and snow water, which fall into the Great Basin, cannot drain into the ocean. Rain, snow water, and rivers drain into swamps called sinks, or into lakes like Pyramid Lake and Walker Lake, or into the ground.

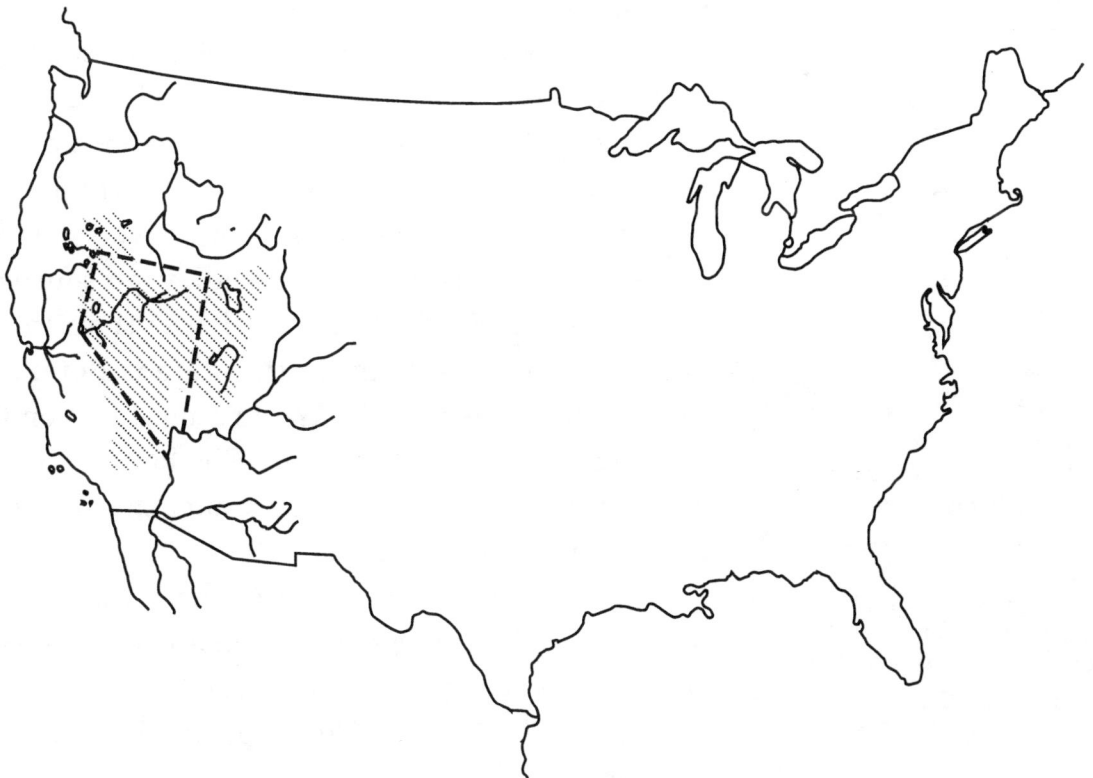

Nevada in the Great Basin

Cross Section of Basins and Ranges

(Altitudes Are Approximations)

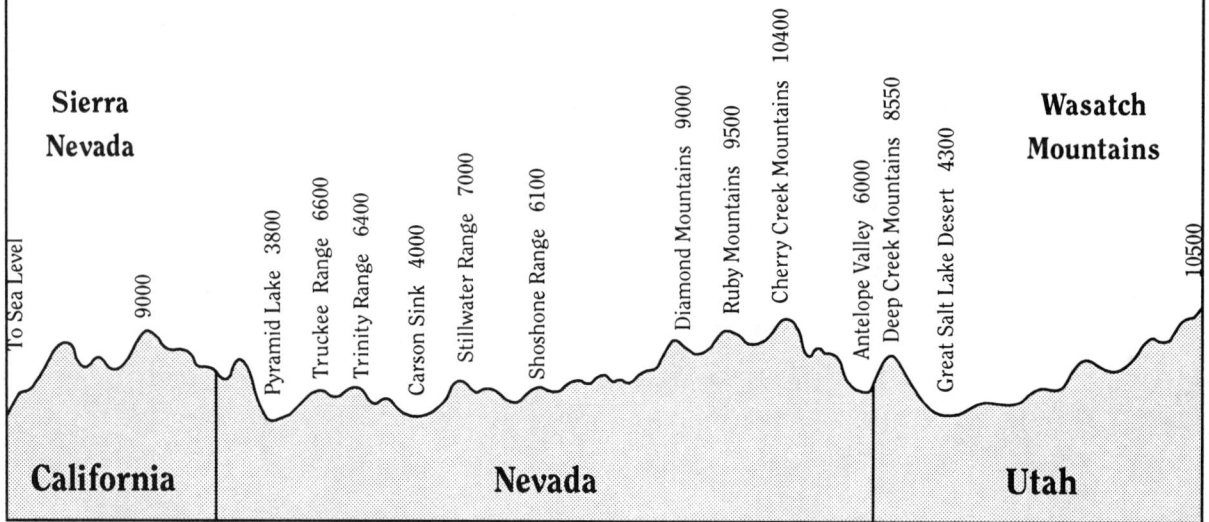

Sierra
Nevada

Wasatch
Mountains

To Sea Level

9000

Pyramid Lake 3800

Truckee Range 6600

Trinity Range 6400

Carson Sink 4000

Stillwater Range 7000

Shoshone Range 6100

Diamond Mountains 9000

Ruby Mountains 9500

Cherry Creek Mountains 10400

Antelope Valley 6000

Deep Creek Mountains 8550

Great Salt Lake Desert 4300

10500

California

Nevada

Utah

Cross-section of Basins and Ranges. This west to east cross-section of the state was drawn at about the 40th parallel. It shows that the state gradually becomes higher as one travels east over rows of valleys and mountains toward the Rocky Mountains.

Ichthyosaurs Used to Live in Nevada. Fossil remains of the huge marine reptile, ichthyosaur, may be seen at the Berlin-Ichthyosaur State Park, 23 miles east of Gabbs. These fish-lizards, up to 50 feet in length, lived in ocean water but surfaced to breathe. They were here 225 million years ago, when Nevada was covered with ocean waters.

The Great Basin covers most of Nevada and extends into parts of Utah, Oregon, and California. Both the highest and the lowest points in the lower 48 states lie within the Great Basin. Mt. Whitney, in California, towers 14,496 feet above sea level, while Death Valley lies nearby at 280 feet below sea level.

In Nevada, the mountains generally run north and south. The highest are in the northern part of the state, some reaching over 10,000 feet high. The valley basins are about 4,500 feet above sea level. In general, the mountains and valleys in southern Nevada are 2,000 to 3,000 feet lower than in the north. The highest point in the state is Boundary Peak at 13,140 feet in the White Mountains on the California and Nevada border. The lowest point is at the southern end of Nevada where the elevation is 490 feet above sea level.

The earliest places, or sites, where the Indians lived in the Great Basin date from about 9,000 B.C. One place where they lived, worked, and died was discovered in 1933 at Tule Springs in southern Nevada.

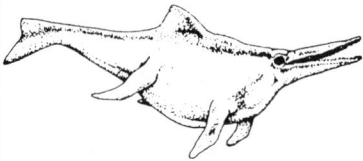

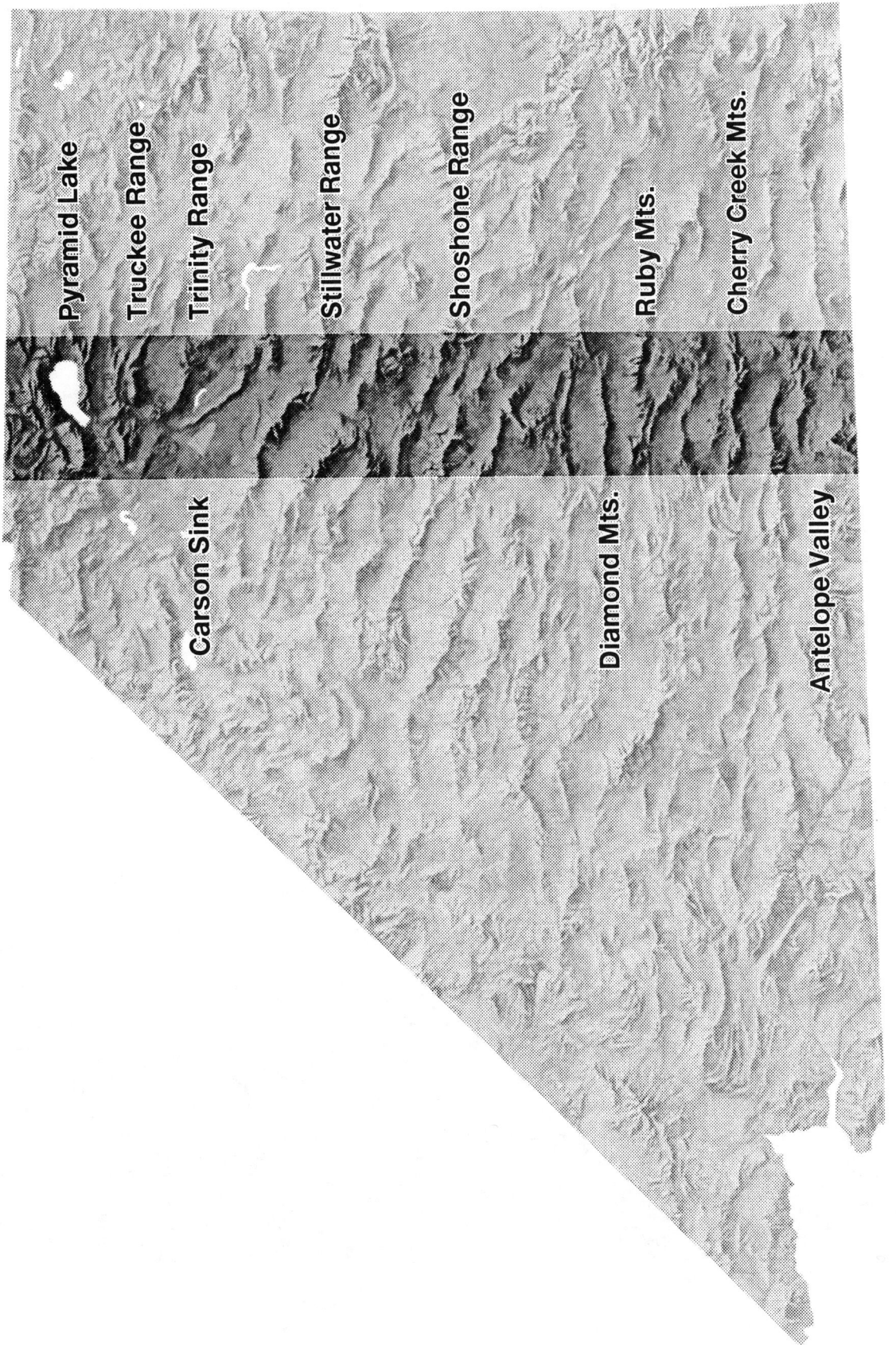

Pyramid Lake

Truckee Range

Trinity Range

Stillwater Range

Shoshone Range

Ruby Mts.

Cherry Creek Mts.

Carson Sink

Diamond Mts.

Antelope Valley

Physical Features of the Great Basin

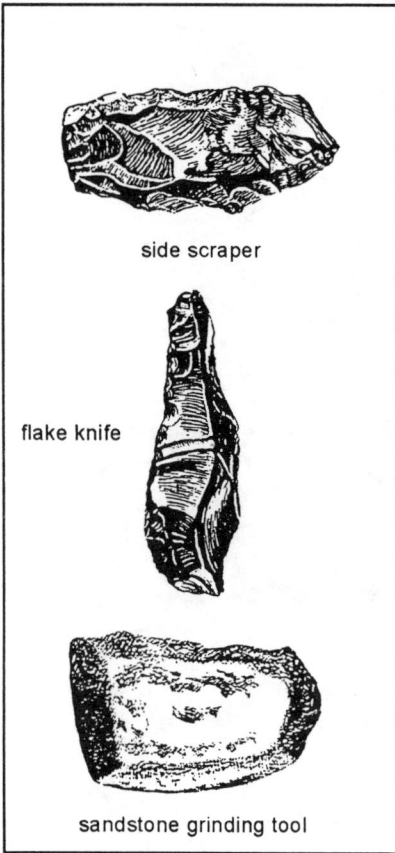

side scraper

flake knife

sandstone grinding tool

Prehistoric Artifacts

Archaeologists who dug or excavated this site discovered manmade things called artifacts. These artifacts are most often stone grinders, stone knives, and arrowheads. They are found at locations throughout the state of Nevada.

Ancient Lifeways

The earliest Nevadans developed a prehistoric culture in the Colorado River area of southern Nevada as early as 3,000 B.C. The Anasazi, or "ancient ones," learned to grow crops in the rich, muddy soil left by flood waters and, later, how to use irrigation. Their crops were corn, beans, and squash for food, and cotton for clothing.

At first they lived in caves. Then they built pit houses and later constructed mud dwellings. They learned to weave baskets from willows and to make pottery from clay. Using bows and arrows, they hunted deer, rabbits, and bighorn sheep.

Prehistoric Anasazi Village. *The Anasazi Indians in southern Nevada developed a sophisticated prehistoric culture. They grew crops along river beds and produced food surpluses that they stored. This permitted them to stay in one area and build fortified villages where they could protect themselves from nomadic, predatory Indians. The Anasazi dominated southern Nevada until they mysteriously disappeared from the region in about 1150 A.D.*
Courtesy of Nevada State Museum

As they grew more advanced, they built scores of mud villages along the Virgin River and Muddy River valleys. About 1150 A.D., they disappeared. No one knows why. It is thought they may have migrated eastward into Utah, Arizona, and New Mexico.

The Anasazi were soon replaced by the Southern Paiute Indians, who were hunters and gatherers, skillful at living in the barren desert climate. The Paiutes were migratory, depending on their knowledge of the weather and the land to survive. They understood the delicate balance of nature and knew how to live in harmony with their environment. They remained and were the Indians living in southern Nevada when the first white men came into the state.

Today there are four major tribal groups in Nevada: the Washo, Shoshone, Northern Paiute, and Southern Paiute Indians. Except for the two Paiute groups, all of these tribes speak different languages. At the beginning of the nineteenth century, the early 1800s, these tribes were living the same way as their ancestors had lived for the past thousand years. Bands of families moved from place to place. They followed the seasons as food became available. Many of the bands had names indicating their main food, such as cui-ui eaters (a fish), trout eaters, rabbit eaters, ground squirrel eaters, and so on.

The Indian bands and tribal groups had certain territories over which they roamed for food. The territories had no boundaries like our modern counties and states. They had no government structure but lived in accordance with their customs passed along for generations. Decisions were made by the elders and other important men and women of the tribe. They didn't have elections, and they didn't have the levels of government that we have.

Indian Tribes. *This map shows where each of the Nevada Indian tribes lived as of about 1863. Note that the approximate tribal areas are related to the different geographical areas of the Great Basin and overlap the state boundaries.*

Wickiup Construction. The small inset photo shows the frame of the wickiup. The completed wickiup, covered with woven grass, stands in the background. A sunshade is held up by poles at the left. Woven baskets, jugs, and a bowl hang from the sides of the wickiup.
Courtesy of Special Collections, University of Nevada Reno Library Margaret M. Wheat Collection

Shoshone Winter Tepees

Seasonal Migrations

The Indians had to move constantly to hunt and gather food. Many of the Indians built temporary shelters, called wickiups, out of grass, tules, cattails, sagebrush, willows, or pine boughs. Large willow branches were placed in a circle, and the tops were bent over to form a dome. The poles were then covered with brush or grass to keep out most of the wind and cold. The shelter was warmed in the winter with a small fire, and there was an opening on the top to let the smoke out. When the Indians moved to another area in search of food, they left the old wickiups and built new ones wherever they camped.

In eastern Nevada, the Shoshone Indians built tepees instead of wickiups. The summer tepees were made of interwoven rushes and willow branches. Their winter tepees were made of hides sewed together.

The most important food gathering done by the migratory Indians was the pine nut harvest from the pinon pine trees. Long poles were used to knock the pine cones from the branches of the pinon pines to the ground. The women and children collected the cones and separated the nuts which were then put in baskets to be carried when they moved or stored near the camp until they were ready to be eaten.

After the nuts had been separated from the cones, they were roasted in their shells. The women ground them between stones. Then, they separated the crushed shells from the nuts by tossing the mixture in a winnowing basket. The tossing fanned out the lightweight shells, and the pine nuts remained to be put into cooking baskets. Sometimes they were eaten whole, and sometimes they were ground into flour. The flour was used to make a thick soup or porridge.

Pine Nut Harvest. *Washo Indian women harvest a crop of pine nuts from a pinon grove. The sticks are used to knock down the cones which burst open when ripe. The pine nuts are gathered and winnowed in large flat trays, called winnowing baskets, then carried back to camp in the larger baskets.*
Courtesy of Nevada Historical Society

Basket Maker. Dat-so-la-lee, the famous Indian basket maker, stands beside her masterpieces of **degikup** -- finely coiled and braided fiber baskets of elegant design. She became well known for the great beauty and superb craftmanship of her baskets.
Courtesy of Nevada Historical Society

Dat-so-la-lee's Masterpieces
Courtesy of Nevada Historical Society

The Indian women cooked in baskets woven from natural fibers with such skill that they were watertight. They were so tight they would hold the mixture of pine nut flour and water. A fire made of sagebrush and greasewood was used to heat a number of rocks. The rocks heated in the fire were put into the mixture until it began to boil. If the mix that cooked was thick enough, it could be scooped up and plunged into cold water to make a loaf of pine nut bread.

To the Indians of Nevada, the pine nuts were as important as wheat or other grain is to us. It was a food that could be stored for future use. When bad weather interfered with hunting and fishing, a supply of pine nut food could make the difference between life and death.

The Indians celebrated the pine nut harvest with dances and parties. The Washo Indians held their celebration at Double Springs, in Douglas County. A pine nut dance was an all-night affair which started at sunset. Shoulder to shoulder, the Indian dancers formed a tight circle around a pinon tree. When the Man-Who-Knows-Many-Songs started to sing, the dancers began moving in unison to their left with a slow, shuffling step.

The Indians always knew where and when the next food was ripening. As they moved from region to region, the men hunted while the women dug roots and gathered seeds, berries, and nuts. The women kept the family possessions, such as baskets and water jugs which were light and durable, and carried their babies on their backs. In the winter, when they had to stop harvesting and hunting, the tribe lived off the food the women had gathered and saved. The women repaired their homes and prepared new harvesting and house-hold equipment for the coming year.

Hunting and Fishing

Hunting was another main source of food. The Indians hunted with stone weapons and moved on foot. They had no horses until the arrival of the white intruders. The antelope, deer, and mountain sheep were extremely important to the Indians. These larger animals were hunted by herding them along rock walls and into a pen. There they were killed with rocks, spears, and arrows. The Indians used every part of the animal to provide food or some other necessity of life. Various portions were used to make clothing, footwear, tools, weapons, ornaments, string, and rope.

The Indians also had a more powerful weapon which they used to kill larger animals and to kill human enemies. It was the "atlatl" and dart. The atlatl was a wooden, hand-held catapult which increased the range, speed, and force of the short spear, or dart, that it threw. The dart had a point of carefully chiselled flint rock or glass-like, black obsidian.

The Atlatl and Dart.
This southern Nevada Indian is ready to kill man or beast with his throwing tool. The deadly combination of spear and sling was popular for hundreds of years in the Great Basin, until it was replaced by firearms.
Courtesy of Southwest Museum of Los Angeles

Making arrows and dart points was a man's job. The points were carefully made by chipping (also called knapping). Hunters would often fashion points while they waited for their prey along game trails. Two of the sources of projectile points were near Steamboat Springs, in Washoe County, and near Tule Springs, in Clark County. There, hunters could find beautiful and superior sinter and basalt rock.

Smaller animals, such as rabbits and ground squirrels, were trapped by snares or nets, killed, and then skinned. Rabbits were abundant in the Great Basin desert. They were hunted in large community drives. Each family in the band contributed a net made of woven hemp. The mesh of the net was designed to be just large enough to catch a rabbit behind the ears when it tried to force its way through. Some of the Indians stretched the nets out across a wash, or dry river bed, while the others fanned out in the desert, forming a moving wall to frighten the rabbits into running toward the nets. The captured rabbits were clubbed to death and skinned. The meat was then either roasted and eaten or dried for storage as winter food.

The rabbit pelts -- the skin and fur -- were cut into strips, sewn together, twisted into ropes, and hung up to dry. When they were completely cured, the ropes of soft fur were woven with cordage into a soft cape which could be worn over the shoulders during the day and used as a blanket at night. An adult's blanket required about one hundred rabbit skins, while a child's blanket needed only about forty.

In the fall, birds such as mudhens (coots) were also hunted in drives similar to those which have been described. They were skinned before roasting, and the Indians used their feathers to make warm blankets and capes.

The Rabbit Drive. *Indians with clubs stand by a large woven net stretched across a dry creek bed, while other Indians beat the brush to drive the rabbits into the trap. A successful hunt produced food and clothing for the hunters and their families.*
Courtesy of Nevada State Museum

Rabbitskin Robes.
Worn by Washo Indian couple John and Wama Anthony, in about 1920, these robes were warm and luxurious.
Courtesy of Nevada
Historical Society

The Indians also fished to get food. Pyramid and Walker lakes, Lake Tahoe, and the rivers throughout Nevada provided a variety of fish to those patient enough to spear or net them. If they weren't eaten immediately, the fish were dried on a rack and then stored for winter use. The dried fish could also be ground with stones into a meal and cooked to make a nourishing soup.

Spear Fishing. Fishing with a spear required great individual skill, cunning, and ability. The Indians also used nets and traps to catch fish.
Courtesy of Library of Congress

Intrusions and Changes

For thousands of years before the white intruders appeared, the Indians of Nevada had a culture that was ideally adapted to their natural situation. Because they were largely self-sufficient, these Indian bands were able to live as social and economic units. They were free of the white man's complex, modern society. This Indian life was shattered, however, when the white civilization came into Nevada.

The First Whites

The first white men, with their guns and horses, burst into the settled ways of the Indians like "men from Mars." To the Indians, the whites looked strange and acted even stranger. They possessed material things beyond the wildest dreams of the native Nevadans. Tragically, it was going to take less then two generations -- only about 40 years -- for the white intrusion to almost completely change the Indians' way of life.

The Indians generally stayed away from the whites. This was easy in the first years of contact, when the white trapping parties were small and didn't stay long. The overland emigrants presented a different problem. Their cattle, mules, and horses ate up most of the grass along the California Trail, and the emigrants cut and burned almost all the wood for fuel. Game animals were either hunted down or fled. The Indians along the Humboldt River in particular were hurt by the intrusion of the whites. The whites destroyed the delicate ecological balance the Indians had with their environment and cut off their regular food supply.

Black Rock
Desert

Quinn *River*

Winnemucca

Elko

California

Trail

Humboldt

Lovelock

Battle
Mountain

River

River

Pyramid
Lake

Humboldt
Sink

Ruby   Valley

Carson
Sink

Central Overland Trail

Reno

Truckee River

Williams
Station

Carson River

Central Overland Trail

Lake
Tahoe

Carson
City

Reese

Duck Creek Range

Steptoe Valley

Spring Valley

Walker River

Walker
Lake

N

W   E

S

Muddy River

Virgin River

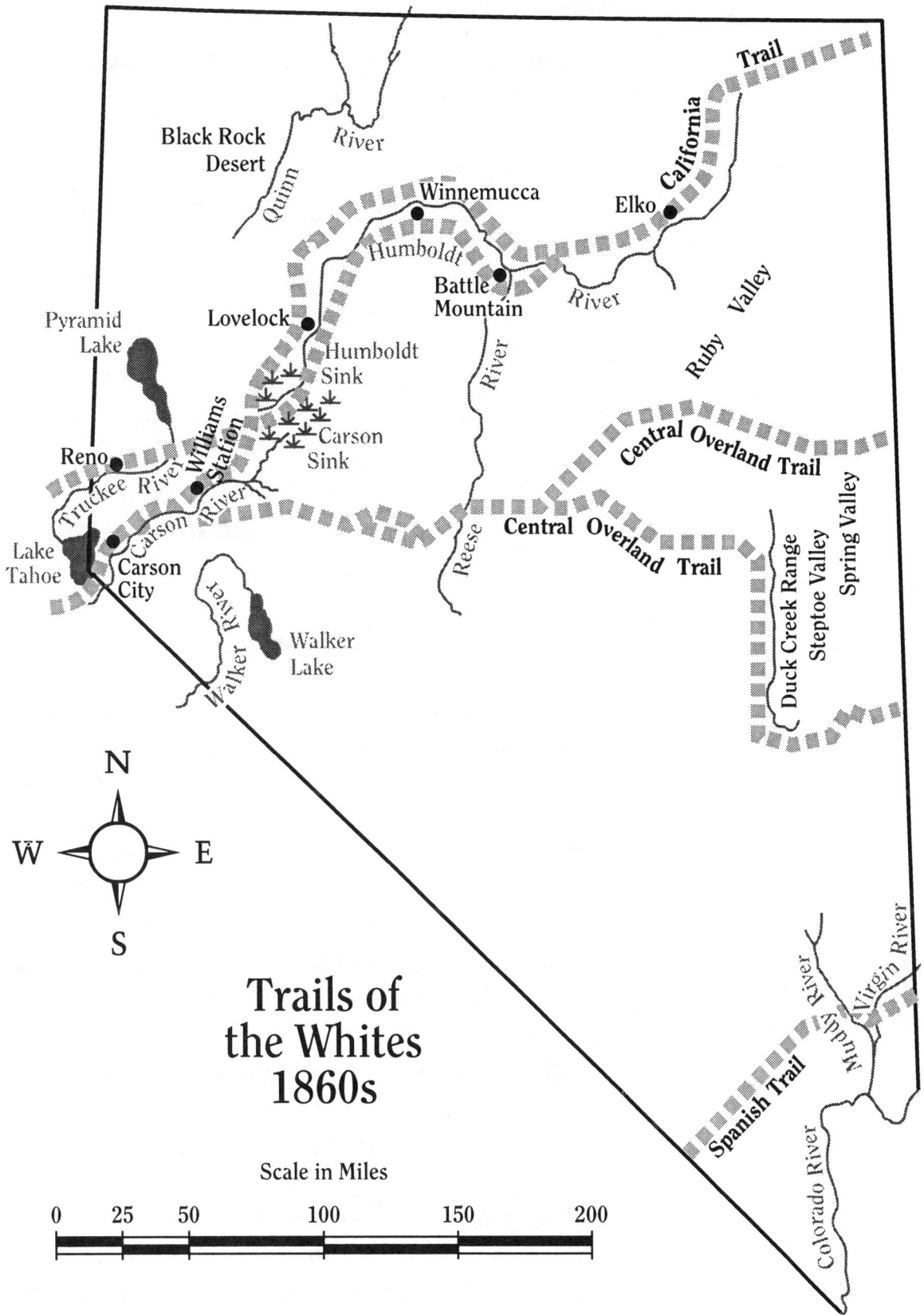

Trails of
the Whites
1860s

Spanish Trail

Colorado River

Scale in Miles

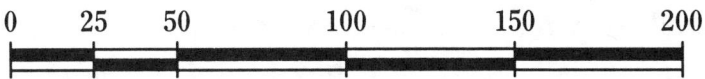

0   25   50   100   150   200

Strife on the Roads

Armed conflict soon followed along the California Trail. Thousands of emigrants, on their way to California, came along the Humboldt River with their cattle, oxen, horses, and mules. This gave the Indians the opportunity to take animals from the white intruders for food or to ride. Captured horses gave the Indians great mobility and speed which they had not had before. Ambushes of small parties of travelers provided the Indians with firearms, which could also be acquired by bartering with the travelers. Unscrupulous station keepers along the California Trail sometimes worked with local Indians to attack and rob small parties of emigrants, and they provided favored Indian bands with guns and ammunition.

The first battle in Nevada between the Indians and the whites was fought at the Humboldt Sink, October 4, 1833. The Indians were defeated by a party of white fur trappers who had firearms which these Indians had never seen before.

Both Indians and emigrants retaliated against each other when acts of violence and thievery took place. The innocent were murdered when the guilty could not be found. Along the Humboldt River section of the California Trail, white men and Indians fought and killed each other in bloody conflicts that lasted through the 1850s and into the early 1860s.

William Hickman was a pioneer of Utah who traveled overland to California in the fall of 1851. In his autobiography, *Brigham's Destroying Angel*, he gave a horrifying description of the slaughter on the trail. He wrote that his party was traveling along the Humboldt River when they began to see burned wagons and human remains. There were skeletons of men, women, and children. They had all been scalped, and their hair hung from the nearby brush.

Some of the men in Hickman's party wanted to stop and hunt the Indians, but the party continued on. Then they met a wagon train coming back that had started ahead of them. They had fought the Indians for several days, lost nearly half of their livestock, and twelve or thirteen of their men. Hickman wrote:

They advised us to turn back, assuring us there was no show to get through. We thought differently, and some of the boys laughed at them. Finding out we were determined they turned to go with us, but told us they had traveled and fought Indians all day only three days before. As we journeyed, with the new company in our rear, all at once there was a dash, a hoot and a yell from the brush about three hundred yards off. The train was halted; twenty-five of my men in less than a minute had their guns, about half of us mounted our horses, telling at the the same time the other company to remain still and take care of the teams.

We popped them right and left until all were out of sight. I flew around on my horse to see the boys, fearing I had lost some of them, but all were safe. Two were slightly wounded. All swore they would scalp the Indians, and have a war dance over their scalps. I told them to do as they pleased.

They got thirty-two scalps off of the Indians killed on the ground, and what gave my men increased anger, one of the Indians was found with the scalps of two women, cured and dried, and another had the scalp of a child, I should think not more than three or four years of age. I need not tell you -- you may guess the feeling that existed.

Both the Indians and the whites tried to stop the reprisals. On August 7, 1855, a Treaty of Friendship between the United States and the Western Shoshone Indians of northeastern Nevada was signed. However, Congress failed to ratify or officially recognize the treaty. Indian Agent Garland Hurt and other government officials had promised the Indians food and gifts as part of the peace agreement. The food and gifts were never delivered as promised. Many Shoshones became embittered, and heavy attacks by Indians on the overland emigrants followed. The majority of these fights took place along the Humboldt River.

The Goshute Indians, a branch of the Western Shoshone tribe, lived in eastern Nevada along the Central Overland Route. After 1859, when large numbers of emigrants began to pass through the Goshute territory, the Indians found it difficult to feed themselves. In the spring of 1860, the Goshutes attacked a number of Pony Express stations along the route. In 1863, Goshute Indians, led by Chief White Horse, attacked and burned seven overland mail stations. Captain S.P. Smith and units of a California volunteer cavalry defeated the Ghoshutes in a series of fights at Duck Creek, Spring Valley, and Steptoe Valley. The Goshute War was over by autumn, 1863.

By 1862, the United States was in the middle of its Civil War. The Indian attacks along the Humboldt and Central Overland Route, opened four years earlier, threatened the security of the transcontinental telegraph lines and the overland mail. Because this was a concern to the whole nation, the United States Army sent strong forces from California to bring peace to the region.

Throughout 1862, the Indian raiding parties, as well as peaceful bands of Indians along the Humboldt, were attacked by soldiers and driven from the area.

On January 29, 1863, troops commanded by General Patrick E. Connor made a forced march in the middle of winter into Idaho. The soldiers attacked a large, hostile Indian encampment across the frozen Bear River in Cache Valley, Idaho, and defeated the Indians completely. This battle broke the power of the Shoshone tribes of northeastern Nevada and effectively ended the problem of Indian raids along the California Trail. The Western Shoshones formally made peace on October 1, 1863, when twelve chiefs and principal men of the Indian tribe signed a treaty with the United States at Ruby Valley, in Elko County. This treaty, later ratified by Congress, brought the war with the Western Shoshones to a close.

General Patrick E. Connor (1820-1891). *General Connor decisively defeated the last hostile bands of Shoshone Indians in the Great Basin at the battle of Bear River in Idaho in 1863, ending the attacks upon emigrants traveling along the California Trail.*
Courtesy of Church of Jesus Christ of Latter-day Saints

War and Peace with the Paiutes

Some time after the defeat of the Indians on the Humboldt in 1833, Chief Truckee, the tribal leader of the Northern Paiutes, told his people to live in peace with the whites. After that, there were good relations between the Paiutes and the whites for many years. Sarah Winnemucca, daughter of the great Chief Winnemucca, remembered, "We lived together and were as happy as could be. There was no stealing, no one lost their cattle or horses ...."

After a number of years of peace, Chief Winnemucca, who followed Chief Truckee as the leader of the Northern Paiutes, signed a Treaty of Friendship with the white settlers in 1855. The treaty provided that Paiute tribal justice would punish Indians who killed or robbed the whites. It also provided that white men who killed or stole from the Indians were to be punished by the settlers' government. The treaty disapproved of random acts of revenge, or getting even. Although the treaty was not ratified by Congress, the Indians and the settlers both lived up to it.

Chief Winnemucca. *Posing for a portrait in about 1880-1882, Chief Winnemucca dressed to show both religious and military authority. He wore a fur hat topped with feathers and the tunic of a U.S. Army officer. In his nose, he wore a carved and decorated wooden plug to show rank and distinction.*
Courtesy of Nevada Historical Society

Nevada Population Prior to the 1859 Silver Rush

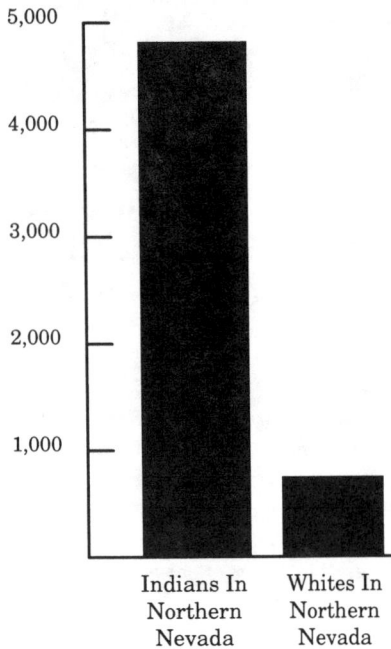

(Chart: bar graph with vertical axis marked 1,000; 2,000; 3,000; 4,000; 5,000. Two bars: "Indians In Northern Nevada" reaching near 4,800, and "Whites In Northern Nevada" reaching near 700.)

This kept relations friendly between the Indians and the settlers, but not for very long. Soon the discovery of rich silver deposits on the Comstock Lode in northern Nevada upset the friendly, peaceful relations.

The silver rush changed everything. Even though the Indians of northern Nevada were never many in number (less than 5,000 at this time, counting both Paiute and Washo Indians), they still outnumbered the whites more than five to one. The rush to the silver mines of the Comstock in 1859 drastically changed the racial balance.

Thousands of white settlers poured into western Nevada in the spring of 1859, and they just kept coming. They didn't know or care about the 1855 Treaty of Friendship with the Paiutes. They didn't live up to the terms of the treaty. Worst of all to the Indians, the white settlers moved onto lands the Indians had understood was their own territory.

The Pyramid Lake War

The stage was set for trouble. Early in May of 1860, several white men at Williams Station, on the big bend of the Carson River, kidnapped some Indian girls. In retaliation, the Indians burned the station and killed the white men there. Then, Major William Ormsby and other settlers organized a volunteer militia force and marched to Pyramid Lake. On May 12, the white force was ambushed. Ormsby and many of his force were killed. The leader of the Indians in this battle was Numaga, a relative of the main Paiute leader, Chief Winnemucca. This was a great victory for the Paiutes, but it was only temporary.

Major William Ormsby. *A businessman and pioneer of Carson City, Major Ormsby led a volunteer force of white miners and settlers into a disastrous defeat in the first battle of the Pyramid Lake War in 1860. Northern Paiute warriors ambushed Ormsby and his party along the Truckee River, killing him and many of his men.*
Courtesy of Nevada Historical Society

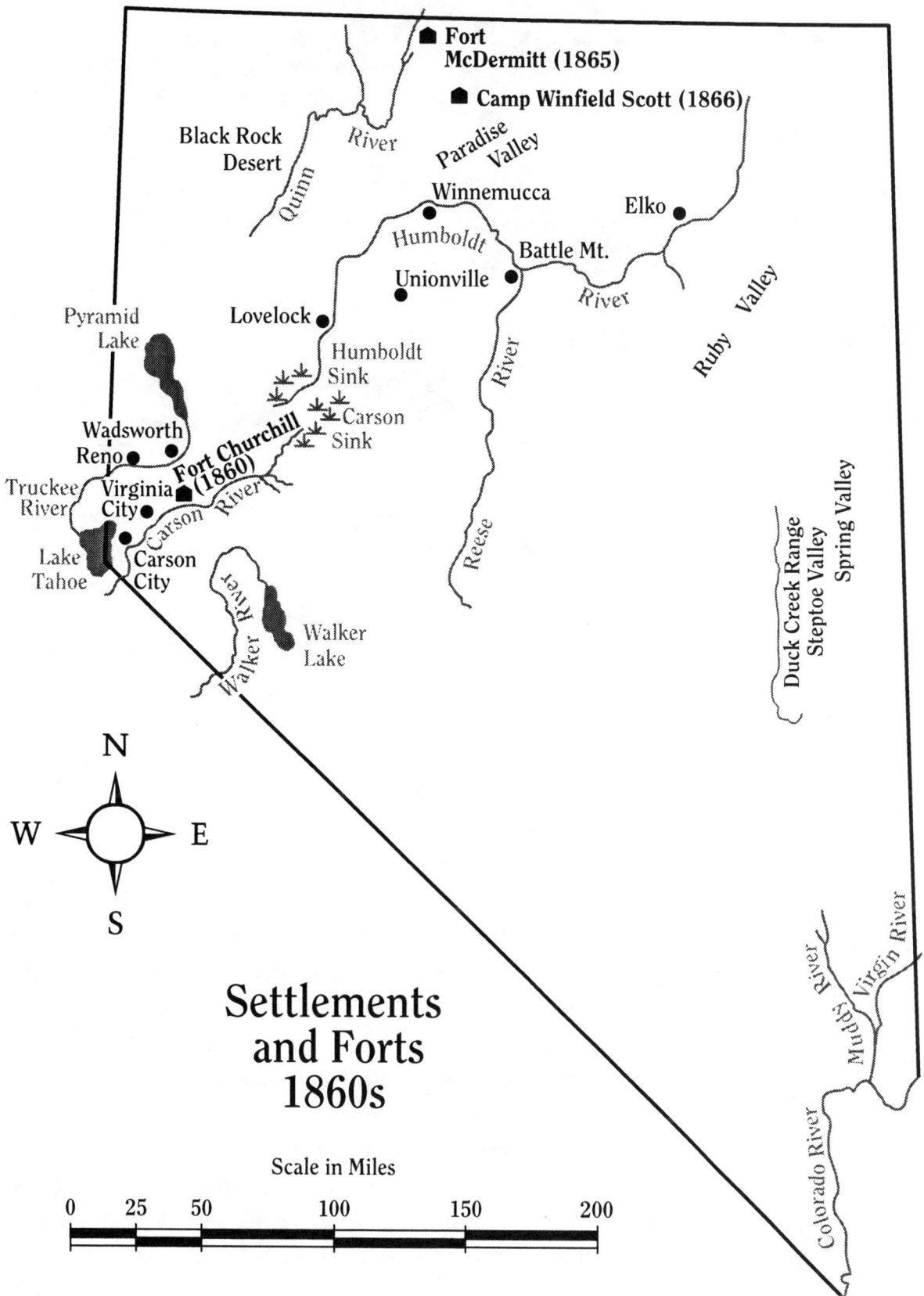

Settlements and Forts 1860s

■ Fort McDermitt (1865)

■ Camp Winfield Scott (1866)

Black Rock Desert

Quinn River

Paradise Valley

Winnemucca

Elko

Humboldt River

Battle Mt.

Unionville

Ruby Valley

Pyramid Lake

Lovelock

Humboldt Sink

River

Carson Sink

Wadsworth

Reno

Fort Churchill (1860)

Truckee River

Virginia City

Carson River

Reese River

Duck Creek Range

Steptoe Valley

Spring Valley

Lake Tahoe

Carson City

Walker River

Walker Lake

N
W   E
S

Colorado River

Muddy River

Virgin River

Scale in Miles

0   25   50   100   150   200

Fort Churchill, about 1861. *Established in 1860, Fort Churchill was the first permanent military base in Nevada.*
Courtesy of Nevada Historical Society

After the defeat of the Ormsby expedition, the white community organized a military force of more than 500 men from California, commanded by Col. John C. Hays. These men engaged the Paiutes in a skirmish on June 2, 1860, at Pyramid Lake, near the scene of the Ormsby disaster. The Paiutes withdrew to the north. Later, in 1860, the U.S. Army built Fort Churchill on the Carson River to keep peace in the territory.

On May 25, 1862, Governor James W. Nye met with the principal Northern Paiute Indians, including Winnemucca and Numaga. They met in the big bend of the Truckee River near the present town of Wadsworth. This meeting united the whites and most of the Northern Paiute Indians in a policy of peace. As a sign of peace and friendship, the Indians and the whites exchanged gifts.

Numaga, whose name meant "Giver" because of his generosity towards others, gave away his war cap trimmed with eagle plumes, his tomahawk, and a magnificent bow with arrows and quiver. These articles had been worn by Numaga in all his battles and are now on display in the Nevada State Museum.

Numaga was a tragic figure. Though he was a constant advocate of peace, he led his warriors in victorious battles against the whites knowing they would eventually take over Indian lands. During a tribal council, he told his people:

You would make war upon the whites. I ask you to pause and reflect. The white men are like the stars over your heads. You have wrongs, great wrongs, that rise up like those mountains before you; but can you, from the mountain tops, reach and blot out those stars? Your enemies are like the sands in the bed of your rivers; when taken away they only give place for more to come and settle there. Could you defeat the whites in Nevada, from over the mountains in California would come to help them an army of white men that would cover your country like a blanket. What hope is there for the Paiute? From where is to come your guns, your powder, your lead, your dried meats to live upon, and hay to feed your ponies with while you carry on this war? Your enemies have all of these things, more than they can use. They will come like the sand in a whirlwind and drive you from your homes. You will be forced among the barren rocks of the north, where your ponies will die; where you will see the women and old men starve, and listen to the cries of your children for food. I love my people; let them live; and when their spirits shall be called to the Great Camp in the southern sky, let their bones rest where their fathers were buried.

Numaga died of tuberculosis in 1871 at Wadsworth and was greatly mourned by Indians and whites alike.

Chief Numaga. *This Northern Paiute chieftain was known for his generosity. Although he led his warriors to victory in battle during the 1860 Pyramid Lake Indian War, he was a constant advocate of peace.*
Courtesy of Nevada Historical Society

War at Black Rock, Paradise Valley and Quinn River

Paiute Chief "Black Rock Tom" was the leader of hostile Indian bands in the northwest corner of Nevada. He refused to keep the peace that had been agreed upon by Numaga and Winnemucca in their meeting with Governor Nye. Trouble began early in 1865 with attacks on the Black Rock stretch of the National Wagon Road. Fighting spread to Paradise Valley in April and to the Quinn River Valley in August.

Lt. Col. Charles McDermit, the commander of the Military Department of Nevada, led the Army troops against the Indians. He was ambushed and killed on the Quinn River, August 6, 1865.

Black Rock Tom was captured and shot on August 11, near Unionville. The hostile Indian bands were broken up after January, 1866, ending warfare between the Northern Paiutes and the whites.

Fort Churchill had been set up in 1860. It was followed by Fort McDermit in 1865, Camp Winfield Scott in 1866, and other posts to protect travelers on the California Trail. The Army abandoned these forts late in the nineteenth century, and some of them became Indian reservations.

Reservations and Modern Indian Life

After the Indian Wars were over, the U.S. Government wanted the Indians to give up their wandering way of life. They wanted the Indians to stay in one place and raise livestock and be farmers. Areas of land, called Indian reservations, were set aside as places for the Indians to live and farm. The rest of the land -- all but the reservations -- would be given to the white people. The government would help the Indians with food and clothing until they learned how to farm successfully.

The first reservation in Nevada was set up at Ruby Valley, but it was soon abandoned. Other permanent reservations were established at these locations: Pyramid Lake (1860), Walker Lake (1860), Camp Murray and Moapa (1872), Duck Valley and Carlin Farm (1877), and Fort McDermit (1889). Many years later, after the Tribal Reorganization Act in 1934, Indian colonies were formed wherever they were needed in Nevada cities.

The Indians, who had been used to their life of freedom for thousands of years, did not like the reservations. Instead of moving there, they took jobs working for white people. They worked as farm laborers and household domestics on the farms, and at cutting wood in the cities. There was plenty of wood cutting work for the Indians. By 1862, the miners on the Comstock needed a lot of wood. They used timbers from the Sierra forests in the mines and firewood cut from the pinon trees to power their machinery. The Indians also sold pine nuts to the whites. The white people loved pine nuts. Selling them became a big business for the Indians. They could buy more food with the money from the nuts than the nuts themselves could provide.

Unfortunately, once the ecological balance between the Indians and the land was broken, the Indians' way of life was gone forever. Hunting was ruined because the game was gone. Almost all the pine nut trees had been cut down. Ranchers cut the grass before it ripened to yield the seed the Indians had used for food. The good land that was fertile was taken by the white settlers for their farms and towns. All this caused a crisis in the Indian way of life.

In 1887, The Indian Allotment, or Dawes Act, provided for giving pieces of reservation land to individual Indians. The Indians could then own and farm their own farms. Gradually, over a period

WOVOKA
The Paiute prophet, Wovoka, who died in 1932, lived near Yerington and became the most famous of Nevada Indians. He taught his followers a Ghost Dance which, he said, God had given to him. He said God had instructed him to tell his people to "... be good, love one another, do not fight, and live in peace with the white man." Thousands of Indians in western tribes began dancing Wovoka's Ghost Dance. Among the Sioux Indians, the Ghost Dance caused so much excitement that it confused and frightened the U.S. Army officials and Indian agents. Their fears apparently set the stage for the U.S. Army to kill 146 persons, who were Ghost Dance followers, at Wounded Knee Creek in South Dakota on December 29, 1890.
Courtesy of Nevada Historical Society

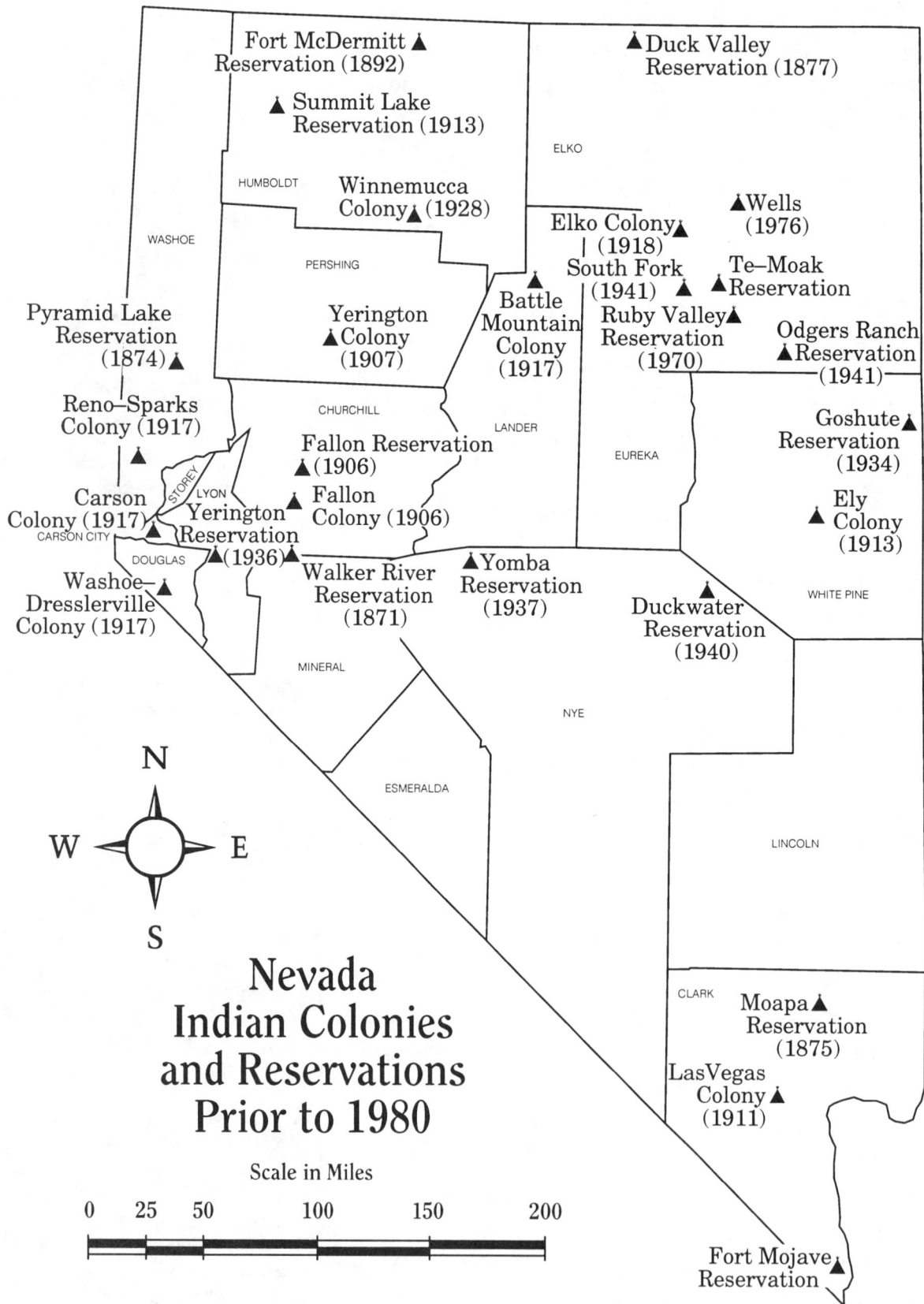

Fort McDermitt ▲
Reservation (1892)

▲ Duck Valley
Reservation (1877)

▲ Summit Lake
Reservation (1913)

ELKO

HUMBOLDT

Winnemucca
Colony▲ (1928)

WASHOE

Elko Colony▲
| (1918)

▲Wells
(1976)

PERSHING

South Fork
(1941)

Te–Moak▲
Reservation

Battle
Mountain
Colony
(1917)

Ruby Valley▲
Reservation
(1970)

Yerington
▲Colony
(1907)

Pyramid Lake
Reservation
(1874)▲

Odgers Ranch
▲Reservation
(1941)

Reno–Sparks
Colony (1917)

CHURCHILL

LANDER

Goshute▲
Reservation
(1934)

EUREKA

Fallon Reservation
▲(1906)

Carson
Colony (1917)

STOREY

CARSON CITY

LYON

Yerington
Reservation
▲(1936)▲

Fallon
Colony (1906)

Ely
▲ Colony
(1913)

DOUGLAS

Washoe–
Dresslerville
Colony (1917)

▲Yomba
Reservation
(1937)

Walker River
Reservation
(1871)

Duckwater
Reservation
(1940)

WHITE PINE

MINERAL

NYE

N

W   E

S

ESMERALDA

LINCOLN

Nevada
Indian Colonies
and Reservations
Prior to 1980

CLARK

Moapa▲
Reservation
(1875)

LasVegas
Colony ▲
(1911)

Scale in Miles

0   25   50   100   150   200

Fort Mojave▲
Reservation

of about 50 years, most of this land was sold into white ownership. This meant that even more of the Indian land was taken over by whites. Finally, in 1934, the Tribal Reorganization Act ended the policy of allotting reservation land to individual Indian ownership.

When the wandering tribes of Indians were forced to live on the reservations, the tribal leaders worked to establish self-government and to educate their children. This has become the modern way of life for most Indians in Nevada.

The first Indian schools were established at Pyramid Lake in 1878 and at Walker River in 1882. The Stewart Indian School was founded and located just south of Carson City in 1891. Indian boys and girls from all across the United States were sent to the Stewart School. The Indians learned the white man's ways. They wore the white man's clothing and spoke the white man's language. Many of the Indian schools taught vocational skills such as farming, the use of farm machinery, and homemaking skills.

With their own tribal government, the Indians had their own tribal police and, in 1886, their own Court of Indian Offenses. Congress passed an act expressing appreciation for the services of Indians in World War I. In 1924, Indians were made U.S. citizens; and, in 1932, they were made subject to local laws. Most laws applying only to Indians were swept away.

The present form of government for Indians in Nevada is based upon the Tribal Reorganization Act, or Wheeler-Howard Act of 1934. This provided for the tribes to be self-governing under their own constitutions, or corporate charters, approved by the Congress of the United States. It also enabled the tribes to purchase additional land for their reservations and colonies. These documents are the basis for tribal affairs in Nevada today.

First Graduating Class, 1901. Indian scholars at the Stewart Indian School in Carson City pose with their diplomas in this turn-of-the-century portrait. Richard E. Barrington, a Washo Indian, occupies the central seat of honor. He would later become a prominent businessman in California and Nevada.
Courtesy of Nevada Historical Society

Vocational Training, 1915. Young Indian women at the Stewart Indian School learned cooking skills and mastered the intricacies of the sewing machine under the watchful eye of their teacher. Many Indian students rebelled against being sent to Stewart Indian School.
Courtesy of Nevada Historical Society

A Visit with Sarah Winnemucca

Sarah Winnemucca was a famous Indian woman. She was the daughter of Chief Winnemucca who led the Northern Paiute Indians in war and peace during the worst years of conflict. Sarah was an educated woman who spoke to large crowds in San Francisco, Baltimore, Boston, and other cities telling people about the problems of the reservation system.

Imagine yourself listening to Sarah Winnemucca tell you about her life as the daughter of a great Indian chief. Here are some of the things she said:

The chief's tent is the largest tent, and it is the council-tent, where everyone goes who wants advice. In the evenings the head men go there to discuss everything, for the chiefs do not rule like tyrants; they discuss everything with their people, as a father would in his family. Often they sit up all night. They discuss the doings of all, if they need to be advised. If a boy is not doing well they talk that over, and if the women are interested they can share in the talks. If there is not room inside, they all go out of doors, and make a great circle. The men are in the inner circle, for there would be too much smoke for the women inside. The men never talk without smoking first. The women sit behind them in another circle, and if the children wish to hear, they can be there too. The women know as much as the men do, and their advice is often asked. We have a republic as well as you. The council-tent is our Congress, and anybody can speak who has anything to say, women and all.

The chiefs do not live in idleness. They work with their people, and they are always poor for the following reason. It is the custom of my people to be very hospitable. When people visit

Sarah Winnemucca (1844-1891). *The first Paiute Indian to write an account of her people, Sarah spoke to large crowds at lectures in major cities. She tried to educate the public on the problems of the reservation system. In this photograph from 1883, Sarah wears a star-spangled gown with several tiers of patterned fringe. Ornamented moccasins, leggings, and a handsome necklace complete the attire she wore for the lecture circuit. The purse is made of velvet, fringed with beads, and embroidered with a figure of Cupid.*
Courtesy of Nevada Historical Society

them in their tents, they always set before them the best food they have, and if there is not enough for themselves they go without.

The chief's tent is the one always looked for when visitors come, and sometimes many come the same day. But they are all well received. I have often felt sorry for my brother, who is now the chief, when I saw him go without food for this reason. He would say, "We will wait and eat afterwards what is left." Perhaps little would be left, and when the agents did not give supplies and rations he would have to go hungry.

At the council, one is always appointed to repeat at the time everything that is said on both sides, so that there may be no misunderstanding, and one person at least is present from every lodge, and after it is over, he goes and repeats what is decided upon at the door of the lodge, so all may be understood. For there is never any quarrelling in the tribe, only friendly counsels. The sub-chiefs are appointed by the great chief for special duties. There is no quarrelling about that, for neither sub-chief or great chief has any salary. It is this which makes the tribe so united and attached to each other, and makes it so dreadful to be parted. They would rather all die at once than be parted.

When it is publicly known that there is a young marriageable woman, any young man interested in her, or wishing to form an alliance, comes forward. But the courting is very different from the courting of the white people. He never speaks to her, or visits the family, but endeavors to attract her attention by showing his horsemanship, etc. As he knows that she sleeps next to her grandmother in the lodge, he enters in full dress after the family has retired for the night, and seats himself at her feet. If she is not awake, her grandmother wakes her. He does not speak to either young woman or grandmother, but when the young woman wishes him to go away, she rises and goes and lies down by the side of her mother. He then leaves as silently as he came in. This goes on sometimes for a year or longer, if the young woman has not made up her mind. She is never forced by her parents to marry against her wishes. When she knows her own mind, she makes a confidant of her grandmother, and then the young man is summoned by the father of the girl, who asks him in her presence, if he really loves his daughter, and reminds him, if he says he does, of all the duties of a husband. He then asks his daughter the same question, and sets before her minutely all her duties. And these duties are not slight. She is to dress the game, prepare the food, clean the buckskins, make his moccasins, dress his hair, bring all the wood, -- in short, do all the household work. She promises to "be himself" and she fulfills her promise. Then he is invited to a feast and all his relatives with him. But after the betrothal, a tepee is erected for the presents that pour in from both sides.

Our boys are introduced to manhood by their hunting of deer and mountain-sheep. Before they are fifteen or sixteen, they hunt only small game, like rabbits, hares, fowls, etc. They never eat what they kill themselves, but only what their father or elder brothers kill. When a boy becomes strong enough to use larger bows made of sinew, and arrows that are ornamented with eagle-feathers, for the first time, he kills game that is large, a deer or an antelope, or a mountain-sheep. Then he brings home the hide, and his father cuts it into a long coil which is wound into a loop, and the boy takes his quiver and throws it on his back as if he was going on a hunt, and takes his bow and arrows in his hand. Then his father throws the loop over him, and he jumps through it. This he does five times. Now for the first time he eats the flesh of the animal he has killed, and from that time he eats whatever he kills but he has always been faithful to his parents' command not to eat what he has killed before. He can now do whatever he likes, for now he is a man, and no longer considered a boy.

Many years ago, when my people were happier than they are now, they used to celebrate the Festival of Flowers in the spring. I have been to three of them only in the course of my life.

Oh, with what eagerness we girls used to watch every spring for the time when we could meet with our hearts' delight, the young men, whom in civilized life you call beaux. We would all go in company to see if the flowers we were named for were yet in bloom, for almost all the girls are named for flowers. We talked about them in our wigwams, as if we were the flowers, saying, "Oh, I saw myself today in full bloom!" We would talk all the evening in this way in our families with such delight, and such beautiful thoughts of the happy day when we should meet with those who admired us and would help us to sing our flower-songs which we made up as we sang. But we were always sorry for those that were not named after some flower, because we knew they could not join in the flower-songs like ourselves, who were named for flowers of all kinds.

I will repeat what we say of ourselves. "I, Sarah Winnemucca, am a shell-flower, such as I wear on my dress. My name is Thocmetony. I am so beautiful! Who will come and dance with me while I am so beautiful? Oh, come and be happy with me! I shall be beautiful while the earth lasts. Somebody will always admire me; and who will come and be happy with me in the Spirit-land? I shall be beautiful forever there. Yes, I shall be more beautiful than my shell-flower, my Thocmetony! Then, come, oh come, and dance and be happy with me!" The young men sing with us as they dance beside us.

I was a very small child when the first white people came into our country. They came like a lion, yes, like a roaring lion, and have continued so ever since, and I have never forgotten their first coming. My people were scattered at that time over nearly all the territory now known as Nevada. My grandfather was chief of the entire Piute nation, and was camped near Humboldt Lake, with a small portion of his tribe, when a party travelling eastward from California was seen coming. When the news was brought to my grandfather, he asked what they looked like? When told that they had hair on their faces, and were white, he jumped up and clasped his hands together, and cried aloud, -- "My white brothers, -- my long-looked for white brothers have come at last!" He immediately gathered some of his leading men, and went to the place where the party had gone into camp. Arriving near them, he was commanded to halt in a manner that was readily understood without an interpreter. Grandpa at once made signs of friendship by throwing down his robe and throwing up his arms to show them he had no weapons; but in vain, -- they kept him at a distance. He knew not what to do. He had expected so much pleasure in welcoming his white brothers to the best in the land, that after looking at them sorrowfully for a little while, he came away quite unhappy. But he would not give them up so easily. He took some of his most trustworthy men and followed them day after day, hoping in this way to gain their confidence. But he was disappointed, poor dear old soul!

Verne Horton

Historical Events

1826 - 1827
Jedediah Smith Expedition

1828
Peter Ogden Expedition into Great Basin

1843
John C. Fremont Began Mapping of Transcontinental Route

1844
Wagon Train Used Emigrant Gap

1846
Donner Party Tragedy

1848
Gold Discovered at Sutter's Mill

1848
Treaty Signed with Mexico

1852
Las Vegas Springs Way Station

1859
Silver Ore Discovered

1860
Pony Express Started

Chapter Two

Trailblazers and Emigrants

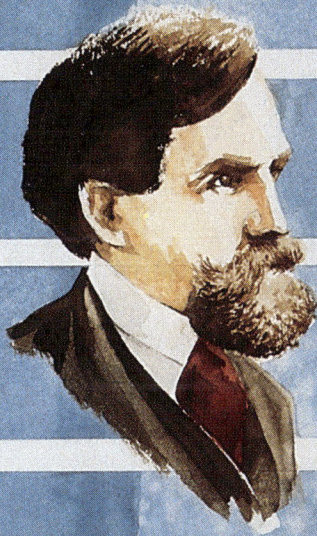

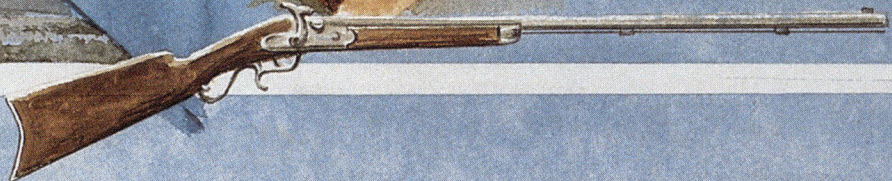

Trailblazers and Emigrants

Nevada first came to the attention of the nation because it was such a difficult area to cross in order to reach the rich agricultural land and gold fields of California. It was the blazing of these trails in the early 1800s that gave Nevada its start. These paths of the trappers and explorers, first traveled on foot, were later crossed by pack trains carrying furs, minerals, and supplies; then by wagons and stagecoaches; and finally by railroads. In the twentieth century, the pattern has continued with the development of highways and airways.

Keith Fay

The first descriptions of the Great Basin came from the reports of trapping expeditions. The fur trappers were businessmen who hunted beaver and otter for their pelts. The pelts were very valuable. There was a great demand for the fashionable hats they would make. The trappers were called "mountain men" because they set their traps in the streams and rivers of the Rocky Mountain region. The trappers were always looking for the best ways across the Great Basin. This hunt for travel routes made them explorers and trailblazers. Geographers had hoped and even believed that there was a river flowing across the Great Basin through California to the Pacific Ocean. On some maps the river was actually drawn in and named "San Buenaventura." Of course, the explorers discovered that there was no such river.

During their explorations, the trappers discovered the Humboldt River, Carson River, Carson Sink, Walker Lake, and many other geographical features of the Great Basin in Nevada.

The most lasting work of these trapper-explorers was the trails they blazed because they became the wagon trails used by pioneers and the highways of today. They established three main routes across Nevada: the southern route, the central route, and the northern route. Here is how they were discovered.

The Southern Route

The southern route is the oldest of the three main routes across Nevada. There were four trailblazers who contributed to the route through southern Nevada.

Francisco Garces was the first of these explorers. In 1775-1776, he traveled across the area that is now the southern boundary of Nevada.

N
W   E
S

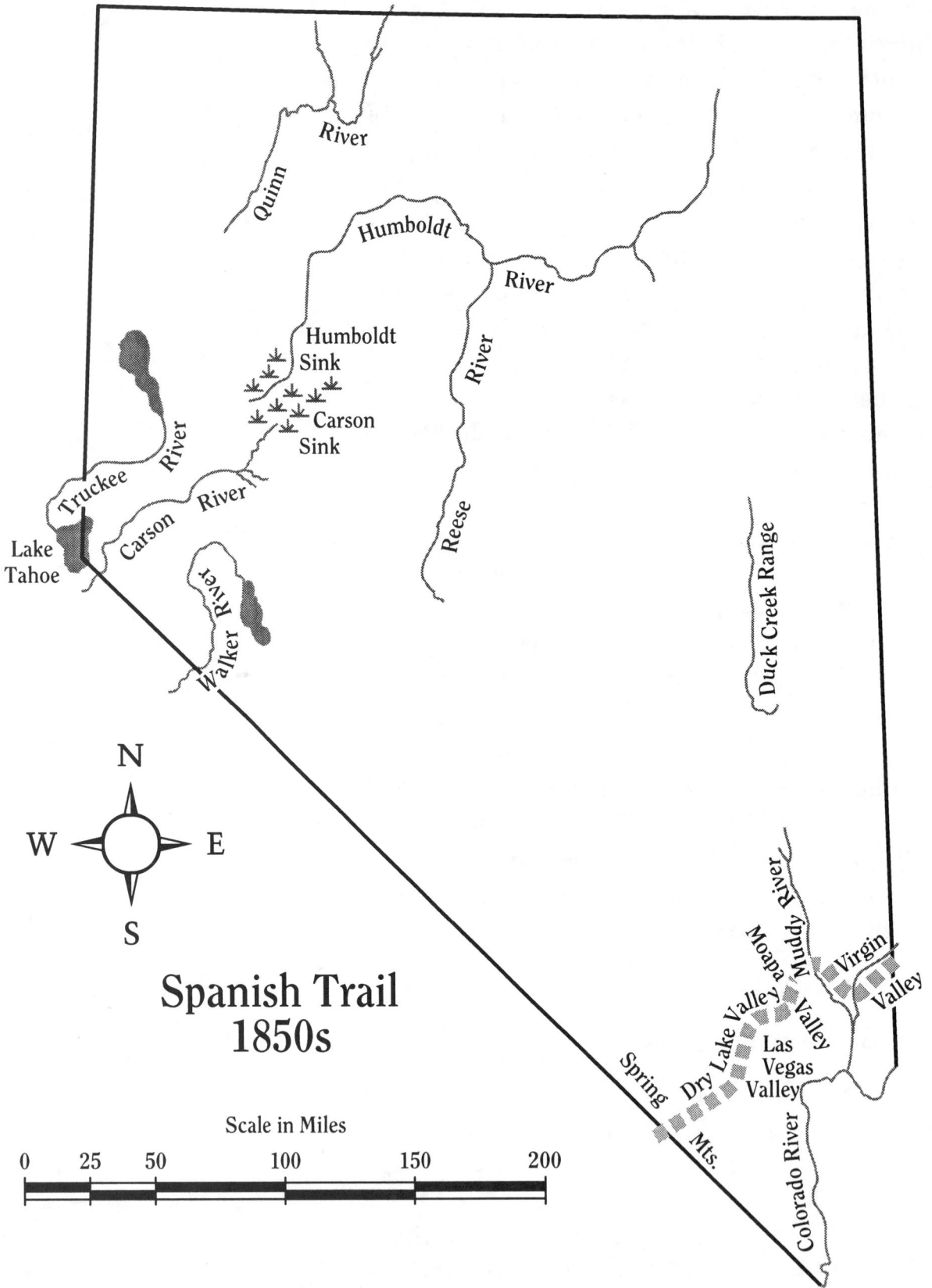

Spanish Trail
1850s

Scale in Miles

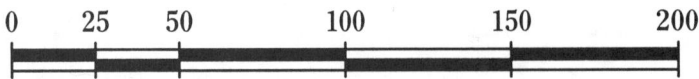

0   25   50   100   150   200

Quinn

River

Humboldt

River

Humboldt
Sink

Carson
Sink

River

Reese

Truckee

River

Carson   River

Lake
Tahoe

Walker River

Duck Creek Range

Moapa Valley

Muddy River

Virgin

Valley

Dry Lake Valley

Las
Vegas
Valley

Spring

Mts.

Colorado River

Garces was a Spanish friar of the Franciscan Order. He was looking for an overland route to travel between the cities of northern New Mexico and the missions and harbors of southern California. Garces is credited with being the first white man in recorded history to enter Nevada.

Fifty years later, Jedediah Strong Smith, the famous western explorer, was the next white man to come into Nevada. He was a member of the North American Fur Company; and, in 1826, he led a fur-trapping expedition west across the southern tip of Nevada. He traveled along the Colorado River into California, where he spent the winter hunting and trapping. The next spring, Smith and his men returned eastward over Ebbets Pass, crossing the Great Basin from west to east.

Antonio Armijo was the third of the southern trailblazers. In 1829-1830, he led a trading expedition from Santa Fe, New Mexico, to Los Angeles, California, crossing Nevada near present-day Las Vegas. Armijo was the first man in history to find a trade route across the American southwest. It was known as the Spanish Trail.

A teenage boy, Rafael Rivera, who was a scout for Armijo, was the first non-Indian to enter the Las Vegas Valley. He also, apparently, discovered the route that became the Spanish Trail.

On Christmas Day in 1829, Rafael wandered away from the caravan and got lost in the Virgin River country. He was gone for nearly two weeks, but had plenty of food and supplies with him. He went down the Virgin River to the Colorado River and down the Colorado until he ran into Black Canyon, with steep cliffs and raging rapids. From there, he turned up the Las Vegas Wash and camped near the present location of Henderson, on top of the mesa where the Southern Nevada Vocational Center is now located.

Jedediah Strong Smith (1799-1831). A native of New York, Smith was the first American trailblazer to cross Nevada. He discovered the southern route across Nevada in 1826, and the central route in 1827. Four years later, Smith was killed by Comanche Indians on the Cimarron River in Kansas.
Courtesy of Nevada Historical Society

From this mesa, he viewed the entire Las Vegas Valley with its springs and lush meadows.

He returned to the Colorado River, rode up the Virgin River and rejoined the caravan. It was after Rafael's discovery of this route that caravans began to travel through the Las Vegas Valley over the central part of the Old Spanish Trail.

William Wolfskill and George C. Yount were the next of the southern trailblazers. It was the very next year, during the winter of 1830-1831, that they led a pack train of mules, laden with fine wool blankets from Santa Fe, over the newly discovered Spanish Trail to southern California. They traded the blankets for California mules and then sold the mules in New Mexico. After that, the Spanish Trail became a regular trade route.

Finally, it was the Mormons who really established travel across southern Nevada. The Spanish Trail from Sante Fe to California was long, hazardous, and expensive to use. After the Mormons emigrated to Utah in 1847, they pioneered a new route between Salt Lake City and Los Angeles. They used the Nevada section of the Spanish Trail as part of the new road. This new route was called the Mormon Trail. Congress encouraged the improvement of this route by awarding a contract to carry the mail between the two cities. Monthly service began in 1853. Today, the Mormon Trail is a freeway, Interstate Highway 15. Thousands of people traveling between southern California and Utah use it every year.

The Central Route

Jedediah Smith, the southern trailblazer, was also the first person to use the central route across Nevada. He found it during his fur-trapping expedition of 1827. The journey was so hard, however, that he lost his notes and maps and barely survived.

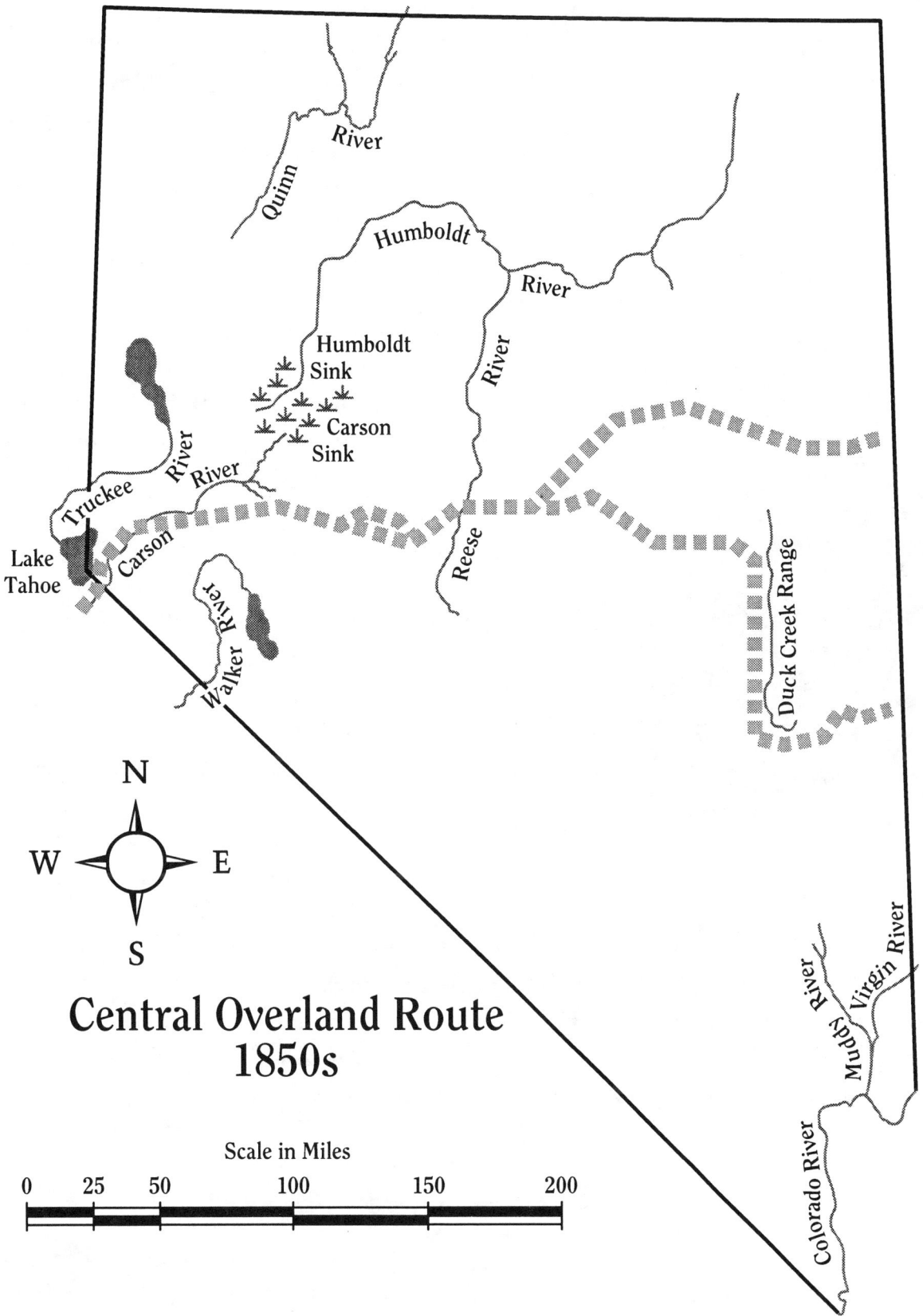

Quinn

River

Humboldt

River

River

Humboldt
Sink

Carson
Sink

River

Truckee

River

Carson

River

Reese

Duck Creek Range

Lake
Tahoe

Carson

Walker River

N

W E

S

Central Overland Route
1850s

Muddy River

Virgin River

Colorado River

Scale in Miles

| 0 | 25 | 50 | 100 | 150 | 200 |

Smith reported that he traveled for 20 days from the Sierra Nevada mountains of California to the Great Salt Lake. Sometimes he went two days without water, crossing sandy deserts with no sign of vegetation. Only one horse and one mule survived, Smith wrote, "...which were so feeble & poor that they could scarce carry the little camp equipage which I had along, the balance of my horses I was compelled to eat as they gave out."

Twenty-seven years later, in 1854, John Reese and four soldiers discovered a new and shorter route across Nevada between Salt Lake City and the Carson River. Until 1859, this new route was used mostly by cattlemen driving livestock between Carson Valley and Salt Lake City.

In May and June of 1859, U.S. Army Captain James Hervey Simpson surveyed a new wagon road along the route used by the cattlemen. This new route was almost 300 miles shorter than the much-traveled northern route across the Great Basin. This central route was also known as the Central Overland Route and was used by the Pony Express to carry the mail. The transcontinental telegraph line, completed in 1861, followed the same route. Then, overland stage coaches carrying mail began using it in 1862. The central route became a favorite of overland emigrants until the completion of the transcontinental railroad in 1869. It was one of the first interstate highways in the nation, known as the Lincoln Highway. It is now U.S. Highway 50.

John D. Reese (1808-1888).
Reese was a merchant from Salt Lake City who built Mormon Station, the first roofed house in Nevada, during the summer of 1851. In 1854, Reese and a squad of soldiers discovered the Central Overland Route, which was later surveyed in 1859 by U.S. Army Captain James H. Simpson.
Courtesy of Nevada Historical Society

The Northern Route

The northern route was the famous California Trail, traveled by nearly all the wagon trains of emigrants going to California. It is now a freeway,

Interstate 80, running from Chicago to San Francisco. Originally, this route across Nevada was pioneered by Peter Skene Ogden, a member of the Hudson's Bay Company of Canada. In 1828, Ogden led a fur-trapping expedition into the Great Basin to search for beaver pelts. In the fall, he found the Humboldt River (later named by John Fremont). About the river, Ogden wrote in his *Snake Country Journal*:

> *I had not advanced more than four miles when a fine large stream apparently well lined with willows was in sight. So glad was I to see it, that at the risk of my life over swamps, hills and rocks I made all speed to reach it, and the first thing that presented itself was a beaver house, apparently well stocked. A most pleasant sight to me and I hope it will repay us for all the trouble and anxiety it has caused me to reach it.*

In following the Humboldt River, Ogden discovered two important facts. First, the river did not flow west into the Pacific Ocean, like the mythical San Buenaventura. Instead, it emptied into a sink, which had no outlet. Second, some Indians in the area already possessed guns and horses. Armed and mounted Indians had not been seen in the Great Basin before. They may have obtained their horses and guns when a number of Jedediah Smith's trappers were ambushed and murdered in the summer of 1828. In journal entries in May of 1829, Ogden reported numerous encounters with Indians but no violence. The Indians followed the trappers, stealing some of their traps and disturbing the beaver. Once, more than 200 Indians came up to Ogden's camp. They were equipped with rifles and ammunition. Ogden and the Indian chief made peace, Ogden

Peter Skene Ogden (1794-1854). *Peter Ogden was a Canadian-born fur trapper for the Hudson's Bay Company. He discovered the Humboldt River in 1828 and pioneered much of what later became the California Trail. He made the first known north-south crossing of the Great Basin in 1829-1830. Ogden, Utah, is named after him.*
Courtesy of Nevada Historical Society

giving the Indians a "foot of tobacco," and the Indians giving Ogden a land otter. Ogden wrote, "More daring and bold Indians seldom or even have I seen, they requested to be allowed to come into the camp but this I refused."

Ogden led a second fur-trapping expedition across Nevada in 1829-1830. This time he traveled from north to south. He explored the Humboldt River more thoroughly and discovered another river and a lake, which were later named after Joseph Reddeford Walker.

Three years later, in 1833, Joseph Walker led a fur-trapping expedition which traveled down the Humboldt River. His band had trouble with Indians. Unlike the Indians encountered by Ogden's trappers five years earlier, many of these Indians apparently had never seen firearms. An eye witness named Zenas Leonard described an experience. In his diary for September 4, he wrote that the Indians were all around in the high grass in every direction. About 900 Indians marched directly toward the camp singing and dancing with glee. The Indians wanted to come into the camp but were halted. They wanted to know what the white men would do to stop them. The trappers fired at some ducks swimming nearby, killing them. The Indians were astonished at the killings and so frightened by the noise, they fell to the ground.

A month later, on October 4, 1833, at the Humboldt Sink, the trappers fought the first large scale battle in Nevada between the Indians and the whites. After defeating the Indians, Walker crossed the desert to the Carson Sink, traveled up the Walker River, and crossed the Sierra Nevada. The party entered California in 1834, where they discovered Yosemite Valley and the Tuolumne grove of giant redwood trees. They returned that year over Walker Pass and recrossed Nevada by way of the Humboldt River.

Joseph Reddeford Walker (1798-1876). Walker led a fur-trapping expedition into Nevada in 1833-34 and fought the first battle in the state between whites and Indians. He discovered Yosemite Valley, California. He later guided emigrant wagon trains and scouted for Lt. John C. Fremont. Walker River, Walker Lake, and Walker Pass bear his name.
Courtesy of Nevada Historical Society

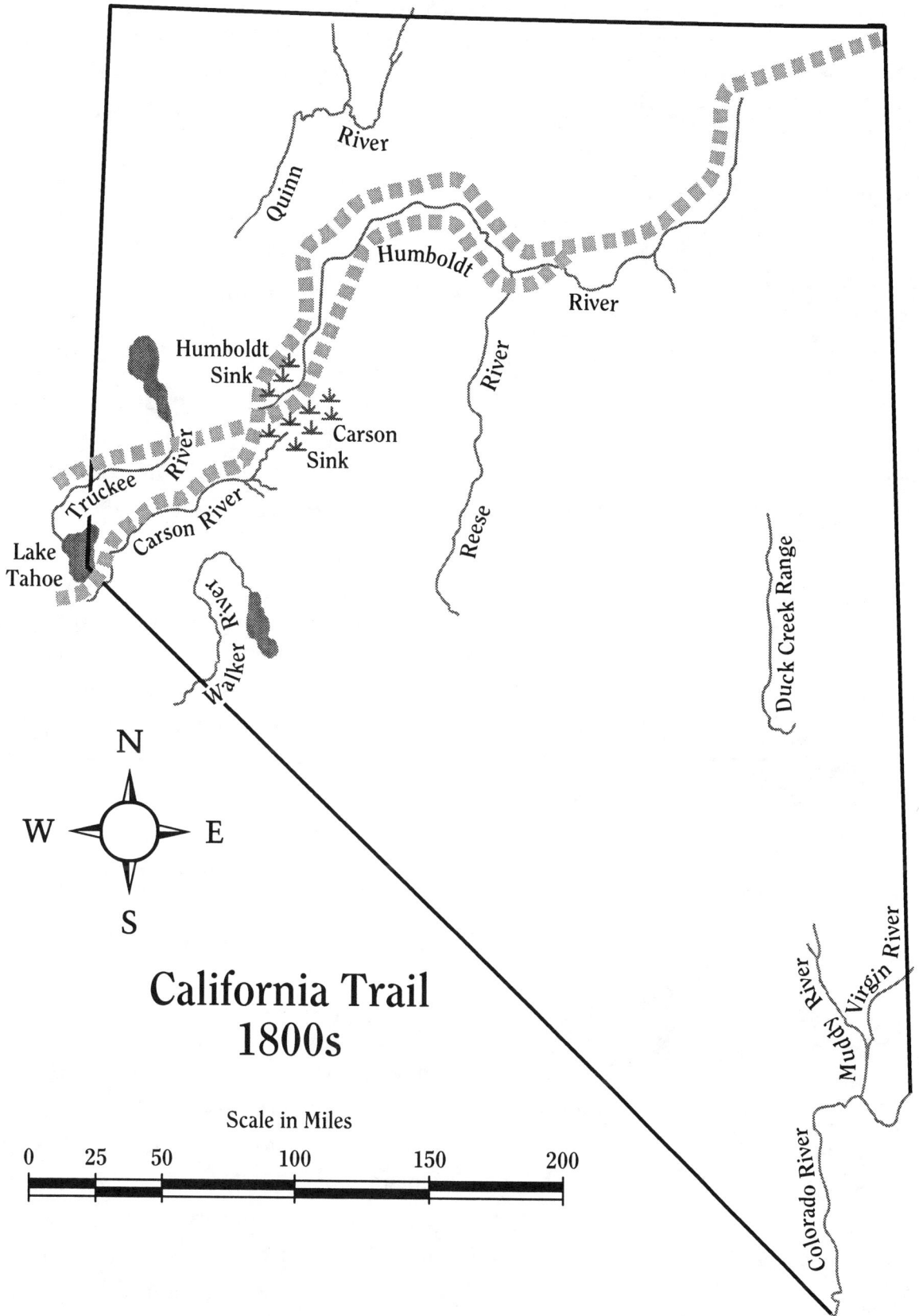

N

W   E

S

California Trail
1800s

Scale in Miles

0   25   50   100   150   200

John Bidwell (1819-1900).
*John Bidwell was a school
teacher from New York who, in
1841, helped lead the first party
of overland emigrants to
California, without a guide. He
became a prosperous rancher
in California and was later
elected to the U.S. House of
Representatives.*
Courtesy of Nevada Historical Society

Elisha Stevens (1804-1884).
*Stevens, a blacksmith, was the
leader of the first emigrant
wagon train to successfully
bring their wagons over the
snowy Sierra Nevada range
into California. The crossing
was in 1843, and it showed others
the way. Wagon trains made
the trip across the mountains
every year after that.*
Courtesy of Nevada Historical Society

In 1841, John Bidwell and John Bartleson formed an association of men and women to travel by wagon from Missouri to California. The party, which included the first white woman and child to enter the Great Basin, traveled down the Humboldt River and found its way across the Forty-Mile Desert to Walker River. After many hardships and adventures, which included having to abandon their wagons and most of their equipment, the Bidwell-Bartleson party crossed the mountains over Sonora Pass and entered California. Their success was astonishing because they had made the California Trail portion of the trip without any guide and only a general notion of where to go. These 34 people were the first of many thousands of emigrants who, in the next few years, traveled west by wagon train across the Great Basin.

Another expedition of emigrants, the Chiles-Walker party, crossed the Great Basin to California in 1843. Joseph Walker, the mountain man, guided them over the route he pioneered ten years earlier. Like the Bidwell-Bartleson Party, the 38 emigrants of the Chiles-Walker party failed to get their wagons over the mountains and had to abandon them. The mountain barrier to wagons was now the one remaining obstacle to emigrant travel to California.

The Movement West

Then the breakthrough came. In 1844, settlers found a way to get their wagons over the mountains. A Northern Paiute Indian, Chief Truckee, showed Caleb Greenwood and Elisha Stevens how they could get their wagons over the mountains and into California through Emigrant Gap. The movement west gained momentum. Later, in 1844, 53 persons traveled overland to California. In 1845, 260 people took their wagons west over Emigrant Gap.

Pyramid Lake as Drawn by Fremont's Artist
Courtesy of Nevada Historical Society

With all this interest in the West, the U.S. Government saw the need to develop the western regions. In 1843, Congress approved money for a U.S. Army exploring expedition into the West to map out a possible transcontinental wagon and railroad route. Lieutenant John Charles Fremont, accompanied by Christopher "Kit" Carson, led the exploration of the Truckee and Carson River basins. On January 10, 1844, Fremont discovered Pyramid Lake, which he described in his *Narratives of Exploration and Adventure:*

> *The hollow was several miles long, forming a good pass, the snow deepening to about a foot as we neared the summit. Beyond, a defile between the mountains descended rapidly about two thousand feet; and filling up the lower space was a sheet of green water, some twenty miles broad. It broke upon our eyes like the ocean....It was like a gem set in the mountains.*

John Charles Fremont (1813-1890) of Georgia. *Fremont was popularly known as "The Pathfinder." He was a soldier and explorer who led U.S. Army expeditions into Nevada in 1843-1844 and 1845-1846. Fremont was the presidential candidate of the newly-formed Republican Party in 1856. He later became a railroad promoter and governor of Arizona Territory.*
Courtesy of Nevada Historical Society

Fremont then made the first winter crossing of the Sierra Nevada in February, 1844, by way of Carson Pass. He was unable, however, to find a suitable crossing for wagons and had to abandon a small cannon on the eastern slope of the mountains.

It was on this crossing that Fremont first saw Lake Tahoe. On Valentine's Day, February 14, 1844, he climbed Red Lake Peak near Carson Pass. He wrote:

> *I ascended the highest peak to our right from which we had a wonderful view of a mountain lake at our feet.....so entirely surrounded by mountains that we could not discover an outlet.*

The great guide, Kit Carson, who made the trip with Fremont, described how they spent 15 days beating down the snow to make a road they could travel. Their animals got so hungry that they ate one another's tails and the leather off the pack saddles. Carson described the hardships in his autobiography:

> *Our course was through a barren, desolate, and unexplored country until we reached the Sierra Nevadas, which we found covered with snow from one end to the other. We were nearly out of provisions but we had to cross the mountains, let the consequences be what they may.*

Fremont and Carson went on, however, to make that first wintertime crossing of the Sierra Nevada.

Christopher Houston "Kit" Carson (1809-1868). *Carson, a native of Kentucky, was a mountain man, scout, soldier, and Indian agent. He first passed through Nevada on the Santa Fe Trail with Ewing Young in 1830. Carson guided Lt. Fremont during the Army explorations of 1843-1844 and 1845-1846. Carson River, Carson Sink, Carson Pass, and Carson City are all named after him.*
Courtesy of Nevada Historical Society

Map

N / W / E / S (compass)

OREGON TERRITORY

UNORGANIZED TERRITORY

MINNESOTA TERRITORY

UTAH TERRITORY

Nevada

Sierra Nevada

Sutter's Fort–Sacramento

San Francisco

Salt Lake City

Mormon Station–Genoa

Fort Bridger

Rocky Mountains

California Trail

IOWA

Council Bluffs

St. Joseph

Independence

MISSOURI

Mormon Trail

Spanish Trail

CALIFORNIA

Los Angeles

Sante Fe

Santa Fe Trail

NEW MEXICO TERRITORY

TEXAS

The West Prior to 1850

Scale in Miles

0   100   200   300   400   500

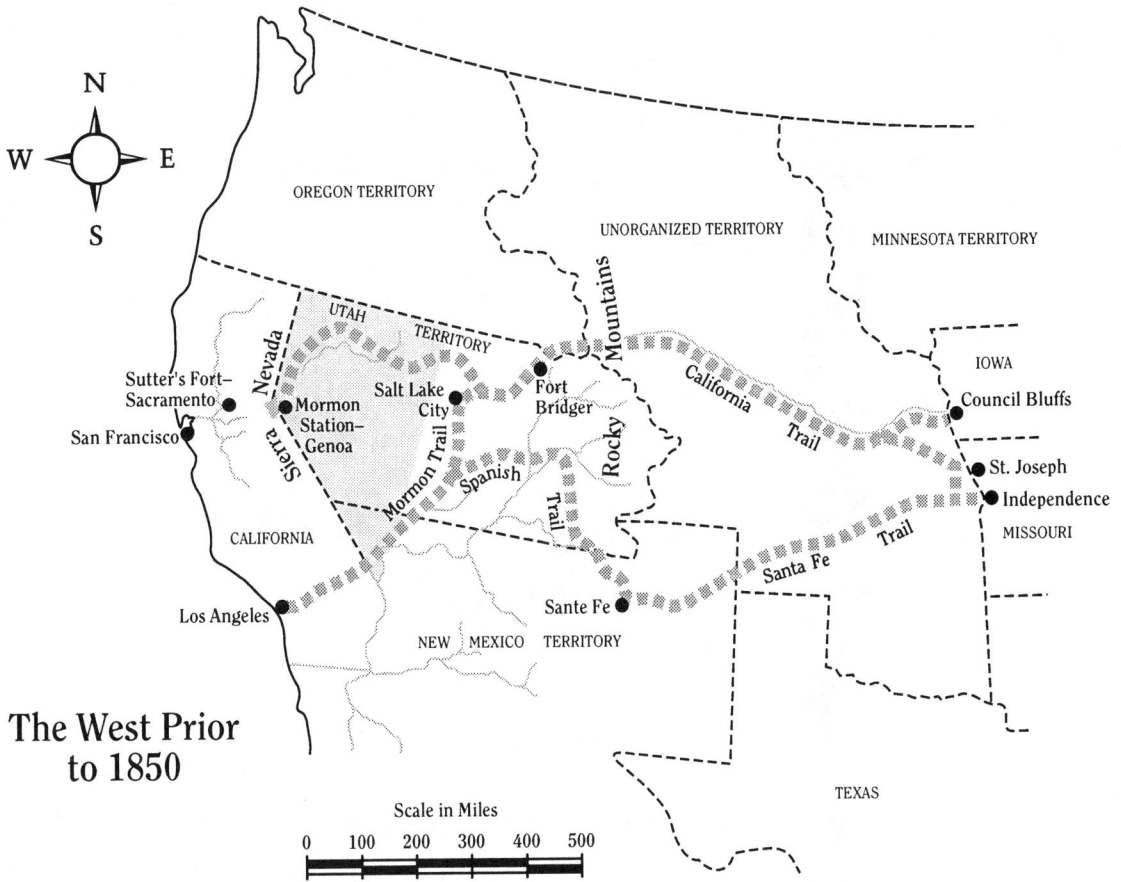

Congress authorized Fremont to make a second expedition into the Great Basin the next year to map the Humboldt, Carson, Truckee, and Walker River basins. In November and December of 1845, Fremont, with Chief Truckee as his guide, crossed the Sierra Nevada into California by way of Donner Pass. One party of emigrants who followed the new route pioneered by Truckee and Fremont endured a tragic fate. It was the Donner Party, for whom the pass and the lake were later named.

The party, led by George and Jacob Donner, met with misfortune all along the way. They got lost repeatedly, were attacked by Indians, fought among themselves, and finally reached the Truckee Meadows (near present-day Reno) late in October of 1846. It began to snow, but they were determined to cross the mountains. At the base of the highest part of the mountains, by the side of what now is Donner Lake,

**Travelers on
the California Trail**

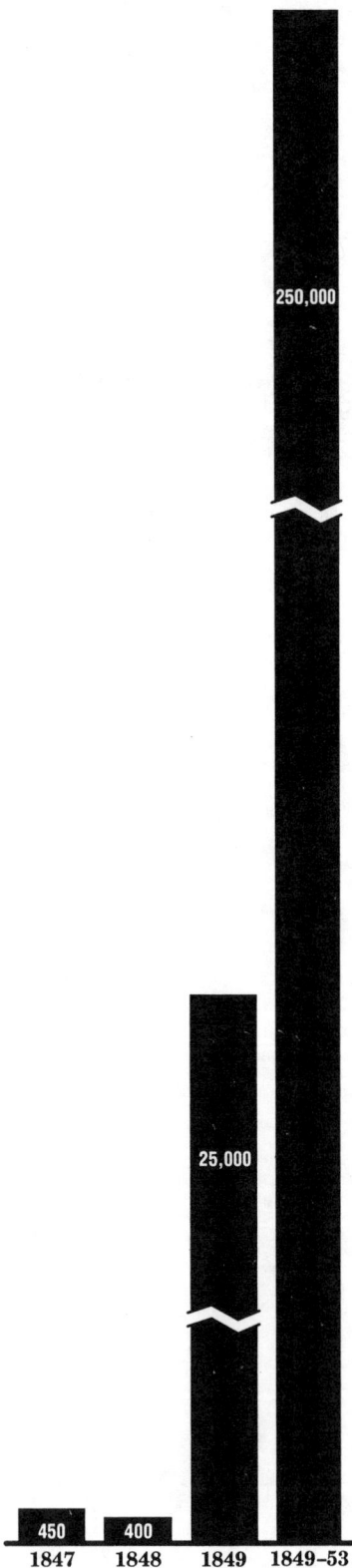

			250,000
		25,000	
450	400		
1847	1848	1849	1849–53

they became stranded. Even though they made shelters and hunted for animals to eat, they gradually starved. In desperation, they ate their dogs, livestock, and the leather from harness and shoes. Finally, in order to stay alive, some of them ate the flesh of their dead comrades. Late the next spring, they were rescued by a party that came over the mountains from California. Of the 89 persons who left Fort Bridger, Utah, only 45 were still alive.

War and the Rush to Gold

While the explorers and settlers were finding new routes to California, there was a war between the United States and Mexico. It was caused by a dispute over territory in southern Texas. In the treaty that ended the war, Mexico gave up its claims to Nevada and California. Now Nevada and California were an undisputed part of the United States.

Just nine days before that treaty was signed, gold was discovered in California. On January 24, 1848, workmen found gold in the American River at Sutter's Mill near Sacramento. This was the first major gold strike in the history of the United States up until that time. A "rush" to California began immediately. Prospectors, merchants, gamblers, and hangers-on hurried as fast as they could to get to the gold.

The discovery had a dramatic effect on travel across Nevada. In 1847, 450 persons traveled overland to California. The next year the number dropped to 400. In 1849, however, an estimated 25,000 emigrants, called "'49ers," traveled to California. They came on horseback, by wagon, buggy, and on foot. Most of them traveled across Nevada. In the four years between 1849 and 1853, at least a quarter of a million people journeyed across the continent to the gold fields of California.

Overland Emigrants. *This artist's sketch shows the massive western movement of the emigrants. In the four years after gold was discovered in California (from 1849 to 1853), at least a quarter of a million (250,000) people crossed the continent to California, and most of them crossed Nevada. Earlier, the trails had been pioneered by emigrant crossings that began in 1841.*
Courtesy of Culver Pictures

The emigrants damaged the environment, especially along the Humboldt River. This made it hard for the Indians to survive.

Soldiers of the "Mormon Battalion," returning from the Mexican-American War, started from Sutter's Fort and built a wagon road east over Carson Pass in 1848. This opened the Carson River section of the California Trail to emigrants traveling west to the mines of central California.

Finally, in 1851, a much easier way across the mountains was discovered by James Beckwourth, a black mountain man. Beckwourth Pass, at an elevation of only 5,218 feet, was so easy to cross that the oxen pulling the wagons scarcely breathed hard. That summer, Beckwourth persuaded a party of emigrants to leave the Truckee Route and journey north over his pass. He built a trading post to supply the traffic that soon developed.

James Pierson Beckwourth (1800-1866). *A black man from Virginia, Beckwourth discovered the pass named after him. In 1851, he formed a company which built a wagon road from Bidwell's Bar in California over the Sierra Nevada. Beckwourth was the son of Sir Jennings Beckwith and a mulatto slave woman.*
Courtesy of Nevada Historical Society

CALIFORNIA NEVADA

Sacramento River

Honey Lake Valley

Pyramid Lake

Humboldt River

Humboldt Sink

Carson Sink

S I E R R A

Oroville

Beckwourth's Pass Route

Donner Pass Route

Donner Pass

Donner Pass

Truckee River

Forty-Mile Desert

N E V A D A

Feather River

Emigrant Gap

Donner Lake

Lake Tahoe

Route

Carson River

Walker River

Sutter's Fort

American River

Johnson's Cut

Carson Pass

Genoa

Route

Walker Lake

Sacramento

Carson Pass

Ebbetts Pass

Sonora Pass

Route

Mokelumne River

Calaveras County

Stanislaus River

Sonora Pass

Tuolumne Yosemite Valley

N

W · E

S

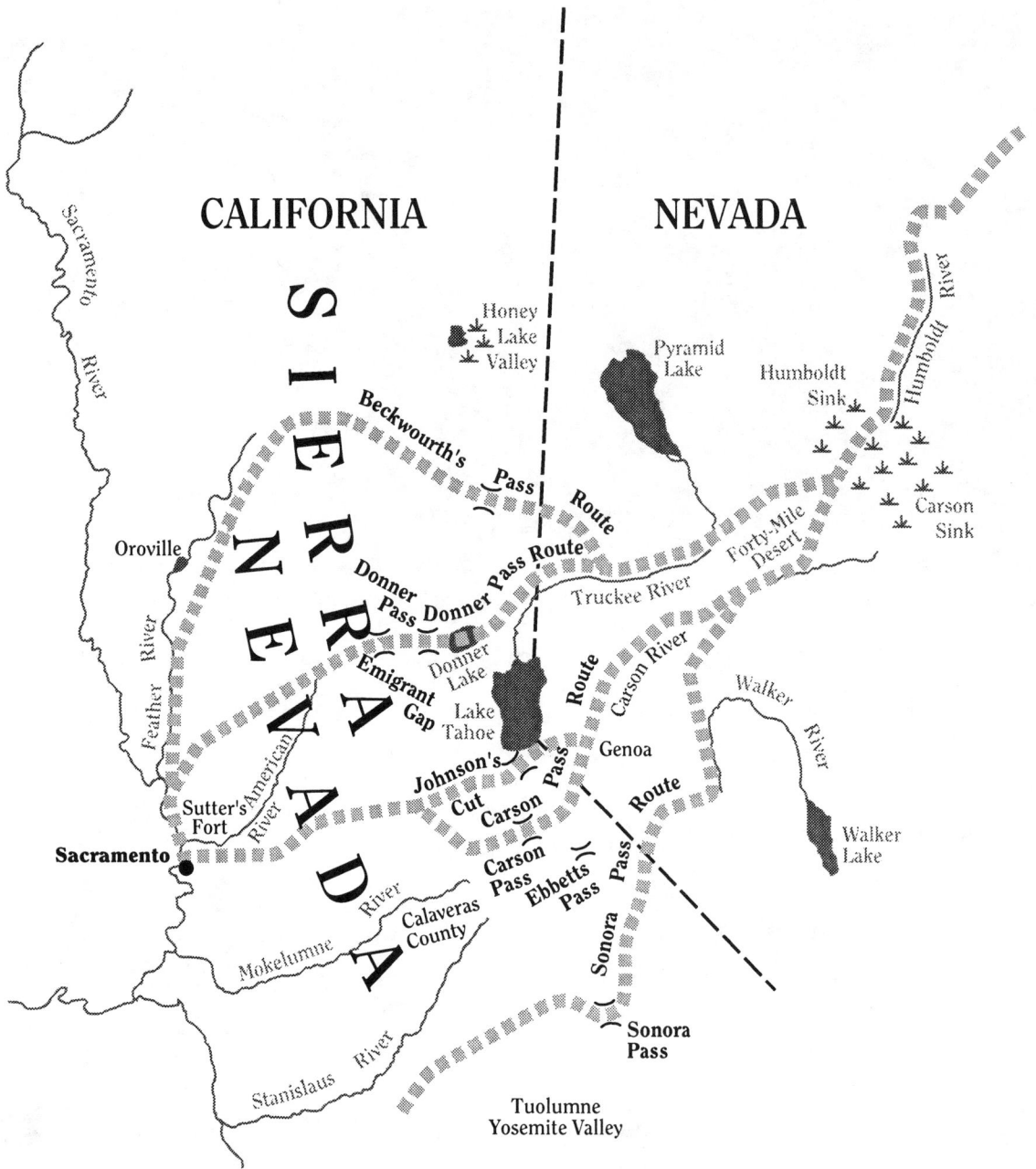

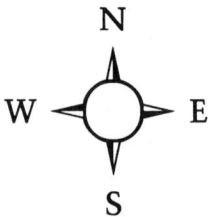

Routes and Passes Over the Sierra Nevada
1850s

Although a more distant route to the gold fields, Beckwourth Pass received use from that time on. As mining developed in Nevada, Beckwourth Pass became a much-traveled route from California into Nevada.

Even with some improvements, travel on the California Trail was still arduous. One of the worst stretches of the California Trail was the Forty-Mile Desert, which had to be crossed to either the Truckee or Carson River sections of the route. There was no water on the desert. What water the emigrants needed for themselves and their animals had to be carried. The trip across took almost two days. To avoid the scorching mid-summer heat on their trek across the shimmering sands, the wayfarers traveled by night. One '49er, Charles Tinker, almost died crossing the wasteland. He recalled:

>...when within 8 or 10 miles of the river I lay down several times to rest, it did not seam as though I could go any farther but it was death to stay their so I had to budge along as best I could thrugh the burning sand till I reached the water. water was all my wants I would have given all I possessed for a drink of cold water my tongue and lips was parched and fured over so it took one hour to soak it off.

After the gold rush began, roads were built from the California Trail up to the settlements. They were used by the wagon trains, pack trains, and stagecoaches. People could travel more, the mail got delivered on schedule, and settlers got the goods and supplies they needed. The growth of towns made possible by the road system is an important part of the history of Nevada.

The Forty-Mile Desert. *This waterless wasteland was the most feared part of the California Trail. Overland emigrants leaving the Humboldt had to cross this desert to reach either the Carson River or the Truckee River. Many emigrants and animals died here of thirst, hunger, heat, or fatigue. One emigrant reported counting more than 1,000 wagons that had been abandoned within a few miles.*
Courtesy of Nevada Historical Society

Mail Routes

The Congress of the United States wanted a national road system for the country. By granting contracts to carry the mail for the U.S. Post Office, Congress encouraged the construction of overland and local roads. Just such a contract, made in 1851 between the United States and the firm of Woodward & Chorpenning, established the first transcontinental mail service.

The first deliveries were made once a month by pack trains of mules traveling between Sacramento, California, and Salt Lake City, Utah, over the California Trail through Carson Valley and Placerville.

The first pack train carrying mail left Sacramento on May 1, 1851. Indian attacks on the pack trains began almost immediately. One of the contractors, Absalom Woodward, and his party were killed in an ambush on the Humboldt River later that year.

The Indian attacks and heavy winter snows made the first transcontinental postal service dangerous and uncertain. Early mail carriers, such as John "Snowshoe" Thompson, had to carry the winter mail over the mountains by snowshoe or ski. The mail station on the eastern slope of the Sierra Nevada range was Mormon Station (later Genoa) in the Carson Valley. It was the first permanent white settlement in Nevada.

Congress expanded the overland mail service to southern California in 1852. It authorized a mail route between Salt Lake City and Los Angeles along the Mormon Trail. The mail contractors established several way stations along the Route. One of these stations was at Las Vegas Springs in southern Nevada.

Congress entered into a new contract for a Sacramento-Salt Lake City mail route in 1853. The contract provided that the monthly mail was to be carried by wagons with a four-mule team. That same year, the U.S. Postmaster General designated Mormon Station as the first post office in Nevada. Two years later, in 1855, Orson Hyde, the new probate judge of the territory, officially named the station Genoa.

Stagecoach Mail

Road building efforts during 1856-1857 greatly improved the California Trail over the Sierra Nevada. This made it possible at last for stagecoaches to travel across the mountains. The first crossing took place in May, 1857, between Oroville,

John H. "Snowshoe" Thompson (1827-1876). In the early days of settlement in Nevada, "Snowshoe" Thompson of Carson Valley carried the mail and light freight over the mountains during the winter. Carrying 60 to 80-pound packs, the Norwegian-born "mountain expressman" covered the 90 miles between Placerville and Genoa in three to five days. Captain James H. Simpson, described Thompson's skis and techniques: "They are smooth pieces of board from six to eight feet long and six inches broad at forepart, four inches at the middle and less at ends, the forepart slightly turned up like a sleigh runner. A little in front of the middle portion a strap of thong is nailed across, in which he slips his toes. Then there is a cleat nailed across against which the heel of his shoe strikes or pushes. He then gently lifts the shoe, and at the same time pushes along with his foot, causing himself to slide first with one shoe and then with the other. He at the same time has a stick against which, as he goes down the hill, he supports himself, and which he also uses as a brake. He says he sometimes passes over precipices of 10 feet and would land at a distance of 20 feet and still stand upright." Courtesy of Nevada Historical Society

Mormon Station. *This log cabin was built in the summer of 1851 by John Reese and his merchant party from Salt Lake City on land purchased from the Indians. The trading post was the first permanent settlement in Nevada. By 1855, several homes and stores stood nearby, and the location took on the name of Genoa. It was Nevada's first town. A replica of the cabin stands on the original site at Genoa today. It is open to visitors and features a historical exhibit.*
Courtesy of Nevada Historical Society

California, and Honey Lake Valley, where California and Nevada border each other. Two more crossings followed within a few weeks. During June, 1857, a stagecoach traveled the Johnson's Cut-Off Route between Placerville and Genoa by way of Echo Summit. Another stagecoach made the trip over the Big Trees Road from Calaveras County, California, to Genoa. Regular local stagecoach operations began that same year over the three routes.

This early stagecoach travel encouraged Congress to approve a transcontinental weekly overland stagecoach mail contract in 1858, between Salt Lake City and Sacramento by way of Genoa and Placerville. The first of the stagecoaches carrying mail east left Placerville on June 5, 1858 for Carson Valley and on eastward.

Across the Mountains. *Stagecoaches serving Nevada carried passengers, overland mail, and the Wells Fargo & Company express from Sacramento to Virginia City. Passengers could see Lake Tahoe through the trees for 30 miles. Stagecoaches also provided transportation between the mining camps and the nearest railroad station, carrying passengers, mail, newspapers, and bullion.*
Courtesy of Nevada Historical Society

The experiment was quite successful. It followed the California Trail, or northern route, until 1862, when the overland stage began using the Central Overland Route.

The U.S. Government ended transcontinental mail by stagecoach in Nevada after the completion of the transcontinental railroad in 1869. Stagecoaches kept operating on the branch roads until the early twentieth century.

"Hands up! Throw down that box!" A double stage-coach robbery on a remote stretch of a Nevada road in 1866, as pictured in the *Police Gazette.* The artist shows some bandits breaking into the Wells-Fargo strongboxes, while others rob the passengers.

Henry M. "Hank" Monk (1829-1883). This famous stagecoach driver handled the Carson City-Lake Tahoe section of the overland mail stage route in 1859. He took the famous New York newspaper editor, Horace ("Go west, young man") Greeley on a ride to be remembered. Here is the way Mark Twain retold the story in **Roughing It**: "I can tell you a very laughable thing indeed, if you would like to listen to it. Horace Greeley went over this road once. When he was leaving Carson City he told the driver, Hank Monk, that he had an engagement to lecture at Placerville and was very anxious to get through quick. Hank Monk cracked his whip and started off at an awful pace. The coach bounced up and down in such a terrific way that it jolted the buttons all off of Horace's coat, and finally shot his head clean through the roof of the stage, and then he yelled at Hank Monk and begged him to go easier -- said he warn't in as much of a hurry as he was a while ago. But Hank Monk said, 'Keep your seat, Horace, and I'll get you there on time!' -- and you bet he did too, what was left of him!" Monk drove stages in Nevada for more than 20 years; when he died, his obituary in the Virginia City Enterprise stated, "In his prime he could turn a six horse coach in a street with a team at a full run with every line apparently loose."
Courtesy of Nevada Historical Society

The Pony Express

The Pony Express, though short-lived, is a famous subject in the history of the American West. It started in 1860, when the freighting company of Russell, Majors & Waddell began a trans-continental express service to carry important financial and government documents by fast horses between Sacramento and St. Joseph, Missouri -- a distance of nearly 2,000 miles. They named the new enterprise "The Pony Express." It employed eighty riders and used the newly-mapped Central Overland Route across Nevada. The first rider left Sacramento for Genoa, Carson City, and parts east on April 4, 1860. The first rider from Salt Lake City arrived at Sacramento on April 13. It cost $5 an ounce to have a letter carried by the Pony Express. It took about 17 or 18 days for the riders to cover the Sacramento-St. Joseph road.

At least two of Nevada's Pony Express riders performed legendary feats. "Pony Bob" Haslam was famous for long rides in a time of crisis. In May of 1860, during the Pyramid Lake Indian wars, Pony Bob rode 380 miles with 35 continuous hours in the saddle.

WANTED

YOUNG, SKINNY
Wiry fellows not over 18.
Must be expert riders,
willing to risk death daily.
Orphans preferred.

Wages
$25.00 per week

Time for Mail to Travel Coast to Coast

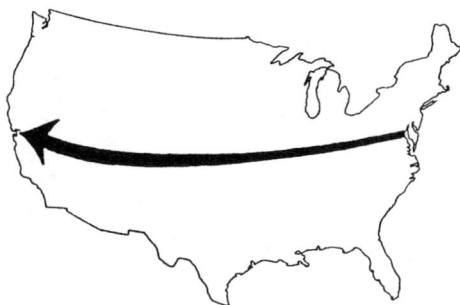

1850	**Train/Stage Coach**	**24 Days**
1860	**Train/Pony Express**	**17 Days**
1876	**Train**	**100 Hours** (or 4 2/3 Days)
1929	**Train**	**85 Hours** (or 3 1/2 Days)
1929	**Airplane**	**30 Hours** (or 1 1/4 Days)
1990	**Jet**	**5 Hours** (or 1/5 Day)

The Pony Express and the Talking Wires, 1861. A Pony Express rider races by a construction crew building the new overland telegraph line. In 1860, the U.S. government contracted to provide a transcontinental express mail service by horseback over the Central Overland Route. But, within a year and a half, the new overland telegraph service made the Pony Express unprofitable, and it went out of business in October of 1861.

The Overland Telegraph. This drawing shows the lines and poles of the Overland Telegraph Company between Placerville, California, and Carson City. The talking wires share the steep grade with fast-moving stage-coaches, overland emigrants, freight wagons, carts, and travelers on foot. The Placerville and Humboldt Telegraph Company built the line between Placerville and Genoa in 1858, extended the service to Carson City in 1859, and to Virginia City in 1860. In 1860, the U.S. Congress passed the Pacific Telegraph Act. As a result, all the Pacific coast telegraph companies merged to form the Overland Telegraph Company and completed the transcontinental connection between Salt Lake City and Carson City in 1861.

One of the youngest riders in Nevada was Billy Tate, only 14 years old. On his last run between Carson City and Camp Ruby, he was waylaid by a war party of about a dozen Bannock and Ute Indians. Billy turned loose his pony, with Indian arrows in its side, to run to the next station and give warning. Billy hid behind a huge boulder so he could fight the Indians and defend the mail. When the stationkeepers came to look for him, they found seven dead Indians and Billy's arrow-riddled body. One stationkeeper said, "The Indians respected Billy's courage. They didn't touch the mail and didn't even take Billy's scalp."

The Pony Express only operated for a year and a half. It stopped operating in October of 1861, when the transcontinental telegraph was completed.

The Silver Rush and Toll Road

Gold discovery was not limited to California. In 1850, emigrants found gold at the mouth of Gold Canyon on the Carson River, near Virginia City, Nevada. A colony of miners worked there for years. Then, in 1859, they discovered ore that was rich in silver. This brought a rush of thousands of people to what became the Comstock Lode at Virginia City, where the discovery was made.

Branch roads were built from the overland trails into the new mining communities. Supplying the mining camps with goods was profitable, and most of the supplies were packed into Nevada from California by mule trains. As freighting increased, new roads were built. In 1859, construction started on the first of these roads to the Comstock. It was called the Devil's Gate Toll road and ran between Dayton on the Carson River and Gold Hill, by way of Gold Canyon.

Devil's Gate Toll Road, 1863.
After the discovery of gold and silver on the Comstock Lode in 1859, traffic to and from the new mines increased greatly. Businessmen built toll roads and charged travelers a fee for using them. The Devil's Gate Toll Road, connecting Gold Hill with the California Trail by way of Dayton and Silver City, was one of the main routes linking the Comstock mines with the outside world.
Courtesy of Special Collections, University of Nevada Reno Library

In 1860, contractors built the Ophir Grade Toll road between Virginia City and the ore reduction mills on Washoe Lake. The last major road to the Comstock, completed in 1862, was the Geiger Grade Toll road between the Truckee River section of the California Trail and Virginia City.

Similar road building activities took place all over Nevada. Wherever the ore finds were rich enough to be worked for several years, businessmen built branch roads. The roads were based on the promise of the business the roads would provide. Most of the principal branch roads built during nineteenth-century Nevada were originally toll roads to mining communities constructed by merchants and businessmen. Many of these roads are a part of the modern road system.

The profit in toll road building was made from the number of travelers and freight wagons that had to pay a toll to use the road. In the early years of settlement, Nevada's legislature encouraged the construction of branch roads by granting franchises or licenses to the owners. These franchises gave the owners the right to charge a toll for the use of the roads.

Sometimes people didn't want to pay the tolls, and there were violent arguments. Some of the owners of heavily-traveled toll roads and bridges became very wealthy. The licenses were only granted for a limited period of time. The licenses of most of the toll roads expired during the 1870s and 1880s. The county governments then took the roads over and began to improve and maintain them at public expense.

Mule Trains and Freight Wagons

During the earliest days of an old-time mining boom, most of the supplies were carried into the mining camps by mule. Mules were sturdy but also stubborn! Packing by mule train over steep and rocky trails could be an exciting but exasperating experience. Prospectors also used mules and burros to get around in the desert and to carry supplies. They were very popular in the nineteenth and early twentieth centuries as a means of transportation.

Camels were also cargo carriers in Nevada in the 1860s and 1870s. They carried supplies to the ranches, salt to the mines, and firewood to the Comstock. They could travel farther, carry more than horses or mules, and were good for winter mountain travel. But horses ran away from them, cattle stampeded, and dogs barked hysterically.

"The Grade." In J. Ross Browne's drawing, a pack train descends the Sierra Nevada between Placerville and Genoa in the spring of 1860. The mules are packing a cargo of goods for sale to the miners of the Comstock Lode. Horses and their riders are bogged down, while sure-footed mules walk around them. In 1854, the first regular mule train service ran every week between Placerville and Carson Valley. The fare for passengers was $12 per trip.
Courtesy of Nevada Historical Society

Camels in Nevada. The Army imported camels in the 1850s to pack supplies across the deserts of the Southwest. They were practical but not liked. In Nevada, freighters used them to carry salt and cargo between Virginia City, Austin, and Eureka. Camels eventually went out of use and were turned out into the desert to fend for themselves. They were thought to have died out after 1910.
Courtesy of Nevada Historical Society

Freighting Wagons at Cave Rock. *In this late-afternoon Lake Tahoe scene, mule-drawn Conestoga wagons stop on the road for the photographer. Freighting wagons supplied outlying Nevada communities for two generations before they were replaced by trucks and tractor-trailers.*
Courtesy of Special Collections, University of Nevada Reno Library

The camels sprayed people with spittle and put out a foul stench. Despite their unusual value as cargo freight haulers, they were so disliked that they were only used a few years.

Once the roads to the mining camps were improved, freighting -- the business of hauling goods to market -- increased substantially. People going to and from the camps traveled by stagecoach. Goods hauled to the camps were carried by large freight wagons drawn by teams of mules or oxen. The men who drove the wagons were called freighters or teamsters. All this was a big improvement over the travel of emigrants who crossed Nevada by wagon train.

People Coming West

Here is an imaginary story about how it might have been for a family along the California Trail in 1848.

Joseph Davidson leaned against the dusty prairie schooner. He was tired but happy. The worst part of the trip is finally over, he thought.

"Isn't it absolutely beautiful here along the Truckee River?" his wife, Anna, said. "A whole river of fresh water and grass and trees. What a wonderful place for us to camp tonight. It almost seems worth the misery we've been through."

"Oh, mamma, you really don't mean that," 15-year-old Bessie said. "I was sure we were going to die of thirst out there on that horrible Forty-Mile Desert."

"I was scared, too, Bessie," Anna confessed. "All those animal carcasses and broken down wagons, and pieces of valuable household goods were just left in the desert. But it was the graves of so many children that really broke my heart."

Hearing his mother's confession of worry, 12-year-old Daniel said he was most worried about the animals. "I knew that we had enough water to stay alive ourselves. But what would we do if we lost the animals?"

The wagon master had planned well for the water, food, and other needs of the Davidsons' because he was their cousin. The Davidson family had left St. Joe, Missouri, in April as one of many families in the wagon train headed by their cousin, wagon master Thomas Kelly. Captain Kelly was a military officer and a scout, as well as being half Indian and half Irish. He could talk to the Indians they met on the trail.

With the end of the Mexican war and the discovery of gold at Sutter's Landing, the United States would need military men in California.

California was now a state, and good scouts like Captain Kelly were needed out west.

"Joseph, is the worst of it really over?" Anna asked her husband. "Coming down that dirty, muddy, crooked Mary's River and then having to cross that killing desert. It's like we've been in hell for a whole month. And now it's heaven here by this beautiful river. I wish we could just stay by this river. I'm worried to death over crossing those California mountains. We're crossing right where the Donner Party died aren't we?"

"Yes, we are," Joseph answered, "but that storm was at the end of October. It's just the first of September now, and we'll be across the Sierra within a week or ten days."

"I don't care. I won't rest easy until we're over that mountain," Anna responded. She wasn't put at ease by Joseph. "Why, oh, why did we leave our good farm in Missouri?" Bessie said. "I liked our sod house. Why did we have to sell the farm and come west?"

Her father laughed. "We can't help it. It's in our blood, Bessie. My folks came down the Ohio River to Missouri on a raft. And your mother's grandfather rode with Daniel Boone."

The Davidsons celebrated that night with a nice place to camp. Anna made biscuits over the campfire, and they ate the gooseberry jelly they had saved all the way from Missouri.

Just as they were eating dinner, a huge man with a red beard rode up. It was the wagon master.

"Hello, Thomas!" the children cried. "Eat dinner with us."

"Sorry, I can't," he said. "I have to meet an Indian scout. I just wanted to tell you about tomorrow. We go up the river through a narrow canyon to get to the big meadow. You'll have to ford the river from side to side. I took some men up the canyon yesterday and showed them where to ford the river. Young Thaddeus Miller went with us. He'll guide you through the canyon tomorrow."

At the mention of Tad, Mrs. Davidson saw a look of excitement cross Bessie's face. She said to herself, "I'll bet that girl stops complaining tomorrow."

Captain Kelly said, "When you come out of the canyon into the meadow, you'll face a slough. Don't try to cross it. Turn south and travel along the edge of the hills. You'll see a round butte about three miles south sticking out into the valley. There's a nice dry meadow at the foot of the butte. The whole wagon train will camp there and rest for a couple of days."

The second day of camping on the big meadow was Sunday. It was the first chance members of the wagon train had to hold a church service since leaving Fort Hall. They made a small half circle of the wagons at the foot of the butte. The Davidsons set out a table with a cover and the Millers placed a wooden cross on the table. The churchgoers sat on the ground facing out into the semi circle. Their outdoor church was like a small amphitheater.

It was a short service. Mrs. Davidson read the Twenty-third Psalm. Isaiah Nelson, who was a Baptist minister, spoke briefly praising the courage of the people in the wagon train and thanked God for the protection they had received along the trail. Mr. Davidson's strong, clear tenor led the voices singing "Amazing Grace." Mr. Miller was the group leader in reciting the Lord's Prayer, and Captain Kelly pronounced a benediction. That night, they gathered again at the same place. One of the scouts played his banjo and sang,

"Oh! Susanna, Oh! don't you cry for me,

I've gone to California,
With my banjo on my knee."

Then, while they watched the sun set over the rugged Sierra mountains which they would cross in the next few days, the group sang "Home Sweet Home."

Captain Kelly addressed the crowd before they broke up. "Tomorrow morning," he said, "we'll go straight west across the valley to the foothills and go back to the river along the edge of the hills. Several miles up the river we will ford it again. Then we stay on the north side. We won't try to go up the river. It's too narrow and rocky. We'll turn north into a beautiful little valley and camp there. The next day we'll go over a small mountain and down a very steep trail to get to the Truckee Lake. We'll camp there until we're ready to cross the mountain." After the meeting, Danny Davidson's curiosity got the best of him and he spoke to Captain Kelly.

"Thomas," he asked, "aren't you going to wrestle an Indian again? Everybody, especially the Indians, liked it when you wrestled with Black Eagle at Fort Hall."

"I hope so, Dan," the captain said. "The Paiutes are having a powwow at Truckee Lake this week. Chief Truckee sent word they want me to wrestle their warrior, Great Bear. I won't know till we get to Truckee Lake."

Three days later they were camped in the meadow east of Truckee Lake. The Indians were already there. They had camped down the valley by the bend in the river. The emigrants were out in the meadow between the river and Truckee Lake.

"I don't like it here," Bessie said. "This is where those Donner people died. And it was so cold this morning that it froze ice on our water buckets. I'll bet were going to get snowed in."

"Stop it, Bessie," her mother said impatiently. "It was cold last night because it was clear. There's no sign of a storm at all."

Tad Miller rode up on his horse. "Mr. Davidson," he said, "I rode with Captain Kelly up to Donner Pass this afternoon. I'd like to take Dan up there to see it tomorrow."

"I'd like for him to see it, too," Dan's father said. "Are you sure it's a safe ride?"

"Yes, Captain Kelly suggested it," Tad replied.

"Oh, could I go, too?" Bessie asked, sounding quite excited.

"Hmmm," Bessie's mother said to herself, "I'll bet that's what that Tad Miller had in mind all along."

The next day the three young people sat on their horses at the foot of a granite cliff. It was much too steep for oxen and wagons to climb.

"There it is," Tad Miller said. "That's where the first wagons were lifted over the mountains four years ago. Chief Truckee showed them this place and Caleb Greenwood was the guide."

"I don't see how," Bessie said. "That's too steep."

"Mr. Greenwood showed them how to take the wagons apart and hoist them up the granite rocks," Tad explained.

"Is that the way we have to take our wagons over?" Bessie asked.

"No," Tad said. "Since then, they've found a better route, south of Donner Peak, where the oxen can pull the wagons up the mountain."

That night, under the light of a full moon, the emigrants and the Indians formed a great circle out in the middle of the meadow. The Indians put on their feathered costumes and danced a peace dance, shuffling and stamping as they sang and shouted their chants.

Captain Kelly stripped to his jeans to take on Great Bear. The captain was the largest man the Indians had ever seen, but Great Bear was very sinewy and strong. The captain won the first fall, but Great Bear got him down to win the second fall. Then Chief Truckee stopped the contest saying, "We must smoke a peace pipe."

The Davidsons were up before sunrise the next morning. The pull up the mountain was rough and rocky. It was all the oxen could do to make it. At the end of the day, Tad, Bessie, and Dan stood in the saddle of the summit looking down across the beautiful foothills into the setting sun.

Danny broke the silence. "I sure wish I was old enough to hunt for gold," he said.

"Not me," Tad said. "I don't want to get rich quick. I just want to have the best farm in the world. And I think there's fertile land waiting for me somewhere down there."

Bessie didn't say anything. She just looked at Tad Miller with shining eyes.

Keith Fay

Historical Events

1861
Central Pacific, First Transcontinental Railroad, is Organized

1868
Townsites Auctioned to Establish Reno

1869
CP and UP Railroads Join

1869
V&T Railroad Started

1905
SP, LA, & SL Railroad

1905
Las Vegas Founded

1909
Western Pacific, Third Railroad to Cross Nevada

1912
NC&O Railroad Connects Southern Oregon with Reno

1917
Department of Highways Created

1920
First Airmail into Nevada

1926
Oregon Shortline Built in Nevada

Chapter Three

Railroads, Cities and Travel

Railroads, Cities and Travel

Keith Fay

The routes of the transcontinental railroads determined where the major cities in Nevada would be located in the future. The railroads served places which were centers of mining or ranching. At those places, branch lines were built to connect with the transcontinental lines. Major cities grew at these points of connection. Small cities grew along the branch lines wherever they served a center of business activity. So, the story of how Nevada grew in the last decades of the 1800s is very closely connected with the story of where the railroads were built. The pages that follow tell about the building of railroads in Nevada and the cities that were built along the railroads.

"Two Ways of Going West."
This illustration from an 1877 copy of Frank Leslie's Illustrated Weekly magazine shows the transition from wagon travel to train travel for emigrants going west. It was all by wagon or stagecoach until 1869, when the first transcontinental railroad was completed. Then, both wagons and trains were used for several years, until finally travel was mostly by train. The caption under this picture read, "An emigrant train is by no means a rare sight, even in these days of steam and Pullman coaches. We have passed several on our route .... There is the great wagon packed with bedding, household stuff, ancient trunks, iron-mongery and crockery, with a calico gown and a sunbonnet or two perched in front, and a guard of stalwart male emigrants on foot and in the saddle, each carrying his gun and pack."

The first transcontinental railroad built in Nevada was the Central Pacific. The Central Pacific was organized in the summer of 1861. Surveyors, starting in Sacramento, laid out a route across Nevada by the end of August. In Nevada, the route followed the Truckee River portion of the California Trail.

Before building the tracks across the Sierra Nevada range, the Central Pacific built the Dutch Flat Wagon Road in 1864. It crossed the Sierra Nevada range at Donner Pass. Then the tracks of the Central Pacific were built over the wagon road. Progress through the mountains was very slow. Many people predicted it couldn't be done. They were wrong. The rail line finally reached the summit of the mountain range in November of 1867. The next month, the first railroad locomotive to enter Nevada steamed into the state at Crystal Peak near Verdi. That was only 23 years after the Paiute Indian Chief Truckee had shown the Stevens party how to get wagons across the Sierra Nevada.

The First Transcontinental Railroad. *This woodcut from Frank Leslie's Illustrated Weekly shows Chinese workmen in the Sierra Nevada stacking wood, delivered down steep flumes to fuel the steam locomotives of the Central Pacific Railroad. The pioneer transcontinental rail line through California and Nevada was built with the help of hundreds of Chinese laborers between 1863 and 1869.*

As workmen built tracks eastward across Nevada, towns started in places where the railroad builders decided to locate railroad stations. Railroad promoters and local businessmen established Reno in the spring of 1868. The tracks reached Wadsworth and crossed the Forty-Mile Desert to Lovelock in the summer of 1868. The first trains arrived at Winnemucca in the fall. By early 1869, the tracks had reached Carlin and Elko. From there the tracks went on to connect with Union Pacific. The Union Pacific had been building to the west. The connection was completed with great fanfare and the driving of a golden spike at Promontory Point, Utah, on May 10, 1869.

This was a wonderful day for the West. The first transcontinental railroad was ready for use, and that really opened up the West. People no longer had to drive covered wagons or travel in stagecoaches to get from the Midwest to California. They could ride across the country in the comfort of a train.

The second transcontinental railroad to cross Nevada took even longer to build. In 1890, the San Pedro, Los Angeles, and Salt Lake Railroad decided to build a route westward across Nevada to connect Salt Lake City with Los Angeles. The route taken was approximately that of the old mail route of 1853 which followed the Spanish Trail through the southern part of Nevada. The tracks from Salt Lake City reached Caliente in 1903, Las Vegas in 1904, and Los Angeles on January 30, 1905. Caliente became a hub of railroad activity with a roundhouse and railroad shops.

The third and last transcontinental railroad to cross Nevada was built by Western Pacific Railroad Company. It connected Oakland, California, with Salt Lake City and was built between 1907 and 1909 -- in not quite three years. The route crossed the Black Rock and Smoke Creek deserts and then followed Beckwourth Pass over the mountains.

Branch Railroad Lines

Railroad branch lines in Nevada were either mining railroads or logging railroads. The mining railroads linked mines, ore mills, and mining communities with one of the three transcontinental railroads. The logging railroads joined logging camps and sawmills, then linked the mills with larger railroads so that the lumber could be transported to the market.

The first and most famous of the mining railroads was the Virginia & Truckee Railroad.

Steaming into Reno. *A brightly-polished V&TRR locomotive pulls into Reno across an iron bridge over the Truckee River. Sometimes called "the crookedest railroad in the world" because of its many turns, the V&T soon monopolized all transportation to and from the Comstock Lode mines. After the state of Nevada built a modern road system and trucks and buses began to compete with the V&T, the company's profits fell, and the railroad went out of business in 1950.*
Courtesy of Nevada State Railroad Museum

William Sharon and other businessmen, representing the Bank of California, built the Virginia & Truckee Railroad. It linked the mines of the Comstock Lode with the transcontinental railroad at Reno. The bank controlled many mines. It wanted to reduce the freight rates below those charged by the teamsters who hauled goods by wagon. Construction began in February of 1869, and trains were running between Carson City and the Comstock in December. The railroad was completed north to Reno in August of 1872, and a branch line was built to Minden in 1906. However, the railroad eventually became unprofitable. It went out of business in 1950. Some of the old engines, cars, and equipment may be seen in the State Railroad Museum at Carson City. Virginia City still has a short "sight-seeing" ride operating on the old railroad line. Other major mining railroads served Eureka, Tonopah, and Goldfield.

V&TRR Engine House. *This engine house stood in Carson City until it was dismantled in 1991. No less than ten sets of tracks converged on the turntable of this engine house. The V&T, built to connect the mines of the Comstock Lode with the transcontinental railroad at Reno, was constructed between 1869 and 1872.*
Courtesy of Special Collections, University of Nevada Reno Library

General Freight Lines

There were two large railroads that carried general loads of freight for long distance shipment. They were the Oregon Short Line and the Nevada, California & Oregon railroads. These railroads were not primarily dependent on the mining communities. They provided service over north-south routes that could not be served by the transcontinental railroads.

The Nevada, California & Oregon Railroad linked the ranching communities of southern Oregon and northeastern California with the transcontinental railroad in Reno. It took a long time to build the Nevada, California & Oregon Railroad. Construction began in 1888 in Reno and did not reach the end of the line at Lakeview, Oregon, until 1912 which was 24 years later.

RAILROADS

1   Central Pacific RR (Southern Pacific) 1868-
2   San Pedro, Los Angeles & Salt Lake RR (previously Union Pacific)
3   Western Pacific RR 1909-
4   Virginia & Truckee RR 1872-1950
5   Carson & Colorado RR (Southern Pacific) 1881-1960
6   Eureka & Palisade RR 1875-1938
7   Nevada Central RR 1880-1938
8   Nevada Northern RR 1906-
9   Las Vegas & Tonopah RR 1907-1918
10   Tonopah & Tidewater RR 1907-1918
11   Nevada, California & Oregon RR 1881-1926
12   Nevada Copper Belt RR 1926-
13   Oregon Short Line RR 1926-
14   Tonopah & Goldfield RR 1904-1946

The railroad is still in use today. Part of the line was sold to Western Pacific in 1926 and the remainder to Southern Pacific. Both companies still operate trains over sections of the track.

The Oregon Short Line, also known as the Idaho Central Railroad, was the last major railroad to be built in Nevada. The Oregon Short Line was a separate company owned by the Union Pacific Railroad. It connected southern Idaho's ranching communities with the transcontinental railroad at Wells, Nevada. Work on this railroad began in 1907, but it did not reach Wells until 1926.

Streetcars

The cities of Austin and Reno had their own railroads. They were municipal streetcar lines. They proved to be unprofitable and eventually went out of business. Austin's system operated from 1880 to 1889, and Reno's from 1884 to 1927.

Streetcars Over the Truckee. *A Reno municipal railroad car makes its way across the Virginia Street bridge over the Truckee River. The old Riverside Hotel and the Washoe County Courthouse are in the background.*
Courtesy of Nevada Historical Society

How Railroad Cities Started

Many of Nevada's first communities got started in the early and mid-1800s as stopping places along the old overland roads. These places were called way stations. The very first way stations were at Mormon Station (later called Genoa) and at Carson City. Both stations were started in 1851. Dayton started the next year. Fallon began in 1854 and Las Vegas in 1855. Fallon was first called Ragtown and was located a short distance to the west of today's Fallon. Elko was started the same year. Lovelock is made up of two way stations located near the Humboldt Sink and dating from 1855 and 1861. Winnemucca began as a way station in 1861, and Battle Mountain began after 1866. Other towns that got their start as roadside stopping places were Wellington and Glenbrook (1861), Yerington (1869), and Gardnerville (1878). All of these communities got started along the overland roads of travel before the railroads were built.

When the railroads came into Nevada, they caused more towns to be built. They also caused some existing towns to grow. The Central Pacific and the Carson & Colorado railroads were especially active in founding new communities. Central Pacific started the towns of Reno, Wadsworth, and Carlin in 1868 and Verdi, Elko, and Wells in 1869. Central Pacific set up another station at Palisade in 1870 and then established the city of Sparks in 1904. The Carson & Colorado Railroad founded the towns of Luning, Hawthorne, and Wabuska in 1881. The Virginia & Truckee Railroad started the communities of Mound House in 1869 and Minden in 1906.

All of these Nevada cities and towns have interesting histories. Here are the stories of some of them.

Battle Mountain

The mountain got its name from a battle that took place during the summer of 1857. The battle was a skirmish between Shoshone Indians and a band of overland emigrants. The town of Battle Mountain, which is located just off the California Trail near Copper Basin Spring, began as a mining camp in 1866. After the Central Pacific Railroad was built along the Humboldt River in 1868, Battle Mountain became a railroad station. The town became a shipping point for supplies to Austin and later to Tuscarora.

So much freight was being shipped to Austin that in 1880-1881 the Nevada Central Railroad was constructed to link Austin with Battle Mountain. The round house and machine shops for this new railroad were located in Battle Mountain. This increased the town's prosperity. The shipping became so active that, by 1881, Battle Mountain supplied the country for 40 miles each way north and south. Battle Mountain also shipped cattle to the market from ranches in the area.

A Mix of Trains at Battle Mountain, 1884. As a narrow-gauge locomotive of the Nevada Central Railroad pulls out of town headed for Austin, it passes a cattle car, a mail car, and a flat car. The NCRR connected the Austin mines with the transcontinental railroad at Battle Mountain, where the NCRR had its shops and engine house. The railroad, completed in 1880, operated until 1938.
Courtesy of Nevada Historical Society

Best small town?

Elko residents are delighted that an author has proclaimed their city the best small town in the nation, but doubt they even qualify for a spot on the list.

"We're shocked, surprised, delighted and overwhelmed," said Lorri Kocinski Puchlik, director of the Elko Chamber of Commerce.

She's also a little numerically skeptical.

Author Norman Crampton's survey included only cities with populations of 5,000 to 15,000. He estimated the number of people in Elko at 14,736 on the basis of a 1990 census.

But Elko is in the midst of a gold rush that has made it one of the fastest-growing spots in the nation.

Puchlik said the state Department of Taxation figured 18,360 people were living in Elko last year. The city put it closer to 19,000.

Crampton, who is a writer and researcher with the Indiana Institute of Recycling, went his own way in rating the nation's small towns in his book "The 100 Best Small Towns in America."

Courtesy of Nevada Appeal 1993

Battle Mountain became the center of county government in 1980, when the citizens of Lander County moved the county seat from Austin to Battle Mountain.

Elko

The city of Elko was planned by Central Pacific Railroad officials even before the railroad tracks reached the location. The railroad wanted a station for freight and passengers moving through northeastern Nevada. The location had been selected by a group of businessmen. They wanted to build a toll road to run out to the mines near the town of Hamilton, west of Ely, in White Pine County.

The railroad put the first lots up for sale in January of 1869, and a settlement grew up quickly around the station. In March, the State Legislature created Elko County and made Elko the county seat. By July, the town had a vigilance committee to maintain order in the streets. Elko's newspaper, *The Elko Independent,* noted that there was a tendency for some "gentlemen" to draw their pistols at the slightest provocation. They endangered the lives of peaceable citizens. The following notice was written in red ink and posted conspicuously around town:

Notice: Shooting has ceased to be a virtue and certain men are marked. They are requested to behave themselves or leave town; otherwise abide the consequences.
Signed: Citizens' Committee

The freighting business was very active, and the town prospered. Wagons freighted north to the mines of southern Idaho and southwest to Nevada mines.

The Town of Elko, on the Humboldt River. *This 1877 view from the Central Pacific Railroad station was made by an artist for* <u>Frank Leslie's Illustrated Weekly</u> *magazine.*

They hauled south to the mining towns of White Pine County. Elko became such an important city that the University of Nevada was founded there in 1874. The university added to the cultural life of the community.

Elko has served Nevada's livestock industry for more than a century. The construction of the Western Pacific Railroad through Elko in 1907 improved business. Much of Elko's growing prosperity today is due to the boom in gold mining. The Jarbidge Mountains to the north and the Ruby Mountains and Ruby Marshes to the south have made Elko County a major destination for hunting and fishing. While the area is noted for its outdoor recreation, a new convention center also brings many regional and state conventions to Elko.

Ruby Marshes
Courtesy of James Bean

Winnemucca

Winnemucca got a strong start as a busy location years before the railroad came to town. In 1858, Alex Chauvin built a station for the new stagecoach mail service between Sacramento and Salt Lake City. He located the station at a ford, a river crossing. It was on the California Trail at the big bend of the Humboldt River.

Bicyclists at Cherry Creek. *Men, women, and children lined up with their bicycles on the wooden sidewalks of the White Pine County mining camp of Cherry Creek, about 1908. Bicycles were first brought to Nevada in 1869 and were originally called velocipedes. The people who rode the bicycles were known as wheelmen. Riders formed social clubs to take weekend trips through the countryside for fun and relaxation, just as they do today.*
Courtesy of Nevada Historical Society

By 1861, the ford was owned by Joseph Ginaca. He established a ferry there during the floods of 1862. When one of Ginaca's competitors built a toll bridge over the Humboldt River in 1863, Ginaca responded by building a toll bridge of his own in 1865.

When the tracks of the Central Pacific reached Winnemucca in September of 1868, the community grew substantially in size. Freighting from the town increased with wagons hauling goods as far as Idaho, Reese River, and Unionville. The location of the Central Pacific's machine shops and railroad yards at Winnemucca also added to the local economy.

Freighting decreased at the end of the century as mines ceased production. Even so, the town kept its importance as a shipping point for livestock raised in the region. Freighting revived after the discovery of silver at Tonopah in 1900.

Winnemucca has the added advantage of being situated at a heavily traveled crossroads. Much traffic moves through the city north into Idaho. It is a busy center for tourism, shipping, electric power generation, and for serving mining and agriculture.

Historic Winnemucca Hotel. This hotel started out as adobe sleeping rooms in 1863 before the railroad was built. That is why the hotel is near the river where the bridge was, instead of near the railroad depot. The building was gradually expanded until it became this present hotel. Since pioneer days it has been a Basque hotel and still serves Basque meals, family style.
Courtesy of David Thompson

Winnemucca, about 1868. The Humboldt County seat as it looked in the early years of settlement, before the railroad came to town.
Courtesy of Nevada Historical Society

Hawthorne

In 1880, the Bank of California owned the wagon roads and was building a railroad to serve the mines at Candelaria, Aurora and Bodie. The railroad was the Carson & Colorado, and its superintendent was H.M. Yerington. The bank needed a location to connect the new railroad with its wagon roads. Yerington decided that the scenic area at the southern end of Walker Lake was the place to do this. He advertised lots for sale in the dry, bare desert area, and they were sold at auction on April 14, 1881.

The town was named after William Hawthorne who supervised construction of the railroad and the wagon roads. It got off to a lively start even though water had to be hauled by wagon four miles into town.

The area grew rapidly. It was the main division point for the railroad where the machine shops and roundhouse served the trains and workers. It became the county seat of Esmeralda County in 1883. Merchants did a brisk business for several years; but by 1900 the mines had stopped producing, and the freighting business decreased.

Hawthorne went into a period of decline. The county seat was moved to Goldfield in 1907. Later on, in 1911, Hawthorne became the county seat of the new Mineral County as it still is today. In 1926, the town was nearly destroyed by a disastrous fire, but its historic courthouse was saved.

At about the same time there was another fire in New Jersey where a federal ammunition depot exploded and burned. The U.S. Congress began looking for a more remote place to store shells and powder. United States Senator Tasker L. Oddie, from Nevada, used his influence to have the ammunition depot placed at Hawthorne. The base was built between 1928 and 1930.

The installation provided a new source of revenue and new residents. The population of Hawthorne, which had dropped down to 244 in 1920, rose to 13,000 as the area grew rapidly after the U.S. entered World War II in 1941.

Population declined again after the end of the war in 1945, but Hawthorne continued to be a major ammunition arsenal for the United States. It served the ammunition needs of the nation during the Korean War, the Vietnam War, and the Persian Gulf War. It now has the largest storage of ammunition in the world. As the United States reduces its military forces, the ammunition from bases that are closed is moved to Hawthorne for storage.

Las Vegas

Las Vegas Springs was originally a rest stop on the Spanish Trail. It was an oasis with several springs located in the middle of a large, arid region. Whether they were coming or going, travelers had to cross long distances over extremely dry land.

This was true in all directions, southwest to Los Angeles, northwest to Salt Lake City, and east to Santa Fe. Las Vegas is Spanish for "The Meadows." The Meadows was a wonderful place for those early travelers to stop and rest. The oasis, with its springs, provided life-saving water for themselves and their animals.

At first, Las Vegas Springs was an oasis for the Spanish traders, the fur trappers, and the U.S. Army explorers in the early years of the 1800s. By the middle of the century, the western part of the old Spanish Trail had become known as the Mormon Road. It was the main route for the Mormons to travel from Salt Lake City to Los Angeles. A mail route was started along this trail because it was the fastest and easiest way to get from Los Angeles to Salt Lake City. It was also the easiest way to get to other destinations east of Salt Lake City. Then, in 1854, the mail service was increased to provide permanent monthly mail delivery to southern California.

In 1855, the Mormon Church announced that Las Vegas would be settled by an agricultural colony. The first settlers arrived that summer. They planted corn and other produce around Las Vegas Springs. They built a fort and opened a post office in January of 1856. The settlement was named Bringhurst. Bringhurst was short-lived, however.

In February of 1857, the Church recalled the settlers to Salt Lake City. The Mormons feared that the United States Government was going to invade Utah Territory and destroy their religion. By the end of the summer of 1858, the last Mormon settlers had left the Las Vegas Valley. Las Vegas remained a station on the Mormon Road after the settlers had gone. Freight wagons moved along the road constantly between Los Angeles and Salt Lake City.

For the next few years, the meadows around the fort continued to be used as a resting place for weary travelers. Then, in 1867, Octavius Gass, a former prospector, bought the land and buildings at the fort. He established a supply ranch to serve the wagon trains and miners in the area. In 1882, the Gass ranch was acquired by Archibald Stewart, a miner and a freighter.

In 1902, William Clark, former U.S. Senator from Montana, bought most of the Stewart Ranch. He used it as a right-of-way and water supply for his San Pedro, Los Angeles, and Salt Lake Railroad.

The Old Mormon Fort at Las Vegas Springs. *This old fort, dating from 1855, was the first permanent building ever constructed in the place that was to become Las Vegas. The site was the Octavius D. Gass ranch, later owned by Archibald Stewart. Stewart's widow, Mrs. Helen Stewart, sold eighteen hundred acres to the San Pedro, Los Angeles and Salt Lake Railroad Company. The SP, LA&SL built its transcontinental rail line through the property. Almost in passing, they founded Nevada's largest city.*
Courtesy of Helen J. Stewart Collection, University of Nevada Las Vegas Library

William A. Clark.
A former state senator from Montana, Clark built and owned the SP, LA & SL Railroad. He selected the site for and founded the city of Las Vegas. Clark County is named for him.
Courtesy of Nevada Historical Society

Senator Clark won the right to build his SP, LA & SL Railroad into Las Vegas. In 1904 he began construction of the railroad and it was completed into Las Vegas on January 30, 1905.

The new railroad company quickly developed plans to build a townsite at Las Vegas. It advertised the sale of lots and the demand was so great that the company decided to hold an auction. On May 15, 1905, the city lots would be sold. The day of the land sale became the birthday of the city of Las Vegas.

A considerable hauling business started immediately, with wagon trains hauling supplies from Las Vegas to the mines in Bullfrog and Ryholite. As many as fifty freight wagons a day moved along the new road to the mines.

The city got electric power the next year. The railroad added to business in Las Vegas by building its engine yards and machines shops in the new city. The State Legislature created Clark County in 1909. This made Las Vegas the county seat of a new county in Nevada. The town was incorporated in 1911.

The building of the Boulder Dam on the Colorado River was another major benefit to business in Las Vegas. The dam was authorized by Congress in 1928 and built between 1931 and 1935. It was built by Six Companies, Inc., a team of six great construction companies working together. Massive amounts of material were required for the dam's construction. Most of it was hauled from Las Vegas on a railroad specifically built by the same companies for that purpose. The dam was dedicated by Franklin D. Roosevelt on February 29, 1936. It was then turned over to the Bureau of Reclamation for its operation.

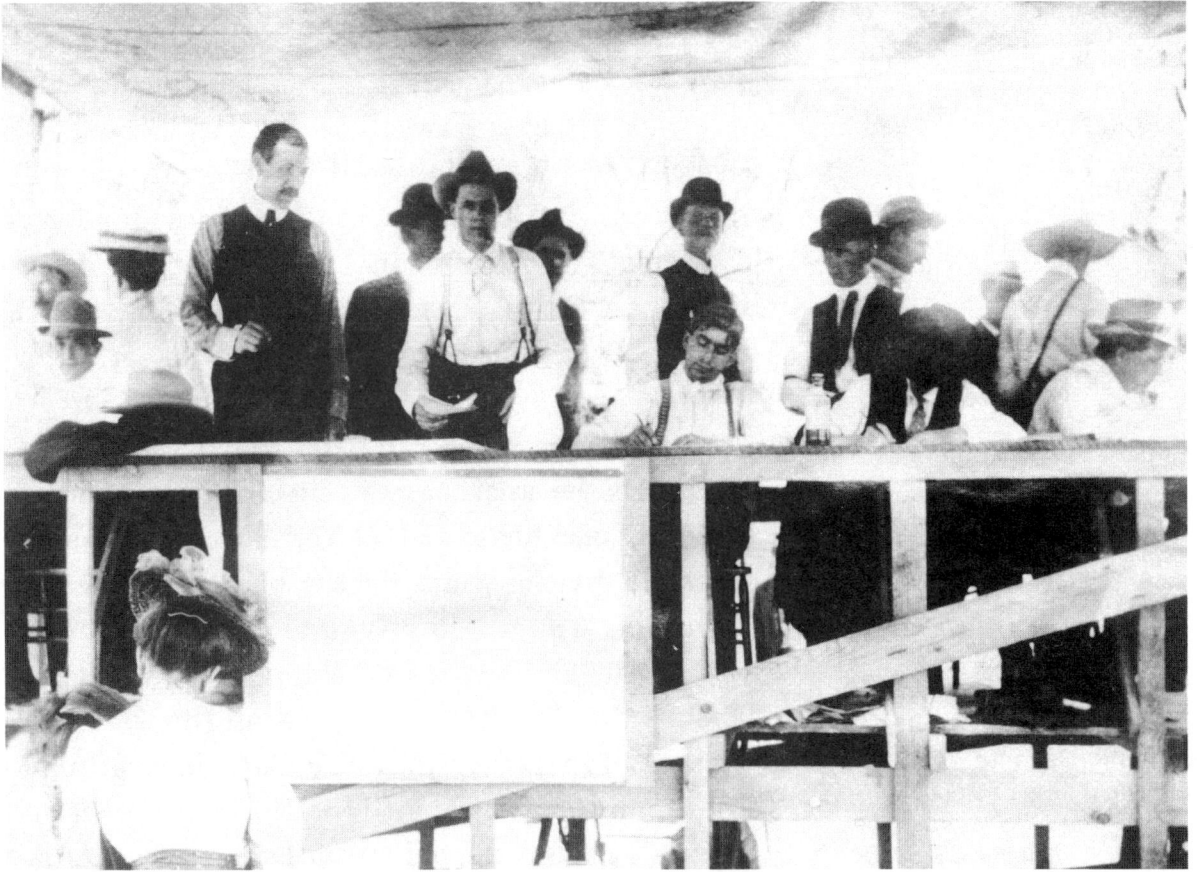

Las Vegas Townsite Auction. *On May 15, 1905, railroad and land company officials stood on a wooden platform under the shade of a large mesquite tree and sold lots for the new townsite of Las Vegas. The purchasers stood out in boiling hot sunlight. They were mainly local businessmen and investors from Los Angeles and Salt Lake City. The sale was introduced by C.O. Whittemore (in white suspenders), president of the Las Vegas Land and Water Company, which was owned by the SP, LA&SL Railroad. Ben E. Rhoades of Los Angeles was the auctioneer.*
Courtesy of Nevada Historical Society

After World War II ended, large hotel-casinos began to open in Las Vegas. The new hotels drew tourists who came in cars and buses from southern California. The new Boulder Dam provided inexpensive electricity. This made it easy for the casinos to use air conditioning to cool their buildings to make comfortable places for the tourists. Cheap electricity made it possible to light the desert city with neon signs. All this comfort and light made the city famous. Las Vegas became an exciting place to visit and not just a place to travel through to get someplace else.

Las Vegas prospered, and it continued to prosper year after year. Today it is the largest and richest city in Nevada. It owes its wealth to its location and the ease of travel to get there. It has been successful because of the ingenuity of its business leaders. They have been aggressive and enterprising in building their city.

Caliente

The same railroad company that founded Las Vegas created another new city, Caliente, about 150 miles northeast of Las Vegas. Caliente also became a division point for the new SP, LA & SL Railroad. A roundhouse and machine shops were built, and the trains changed crews there. This made Caliente the home of the railroad families. It became one of Nevada's busy railroad cities from about 1905 until the 1950s, when diesel engines replaced the old steam locomotives. After losing the railroad payroll, the town dwindled in population to its present 200.

Caliente Depot. *This beautiful mission-style railroad depot stands in Caliente today as a reminder of the opulence of railroads in the early years of the century. Originally, the depot contained hotel rooms and a restaurant. It is still used as the railroad depot by Amtrak. It also houses city offices, a library, and an art gallery.*
Courtesy of Nevada Historical Society

Caliente is dominated by the elegant, mission-style railroad depot which has been designated a historical landmark. Originally, it contained hotel rooms and a restaurant to fit the needs of the times. Today, it houses city offices, a library, and an art gallery. Amtrak trains stop there; and the waiting room still has its original, elaborate, wooden benches.

With a hospital and a medical clinic, Caliente is the medical center now for Lincoln County. It has the Caliente Youth Center, a state correctional facility for girls.

Reno

Like so many other Nevada cities, Reno owes its location to the railroad. It became a city when the Central Pacific Railroad auctioned off lots for a townsite on May 9, 1868. But, long before that date, the Truckee Meadows was an important area. For nearly twenty years before Reno became a town, thousands of travelers had been served by the way stations in the Truckee Meadows.

The first person to set up a way station was H.H. Jamieson, in 1852. Located at the east end of the meadows, it was just temporary. The next station was a trading post, also located at the east end of the meadows where the California Trail crossed the Truckee River. It became known as Glendale. The keeper built a free bridge over the river there in 1860. The first schoolhouse in Nevada was built there. The second permanent station was at the Huffaker Ranch south of Reno. It was a convenient place for miners to stop on their way to Virginia City.

The third stopping place eventually became the city of Reno. It was settled by Clarence William Fuller when the rush to Virginia City began in 1859. Fuller chose a ford over the Truckee River a little way north of the California Trail. This was an easier and shorter route to the mines than the road through Glendale. Fuller built a bridge over

The Glendale School in Sparks. Built in 1864 on the eastern edge of the Truckee Meadows near the Truckee River crossing, the Glendale schoolhouse is the oldest school building in Nevada. Children attended the school continuously for 94 years until 1958. In 1993, plans were made by the people of Sparks to move the old school from a historical display in Reno back to downtown Sparks where it becomes a part of the community's extensive heritage exhibit in Victorian Square.

Lake's Crossing of the Truckee. *Alongside Northern Paiute Chief Winnemucca, Myron C. Lake stands proudly in front of his hotel and toll bridge in June of 1862. The crossing, shown in this painting by Nevada artist C.B. McClellan, was originally settled by C.W. Fuller in 1859. It turned into a city nine years later, in 1868, when Lake donated a townsite to the CPRR. Lots were auctioned off immediately, creating the city of Reno.*
Courtesy of Special Collections, University of Nevada Reno Library

RENO!

VIRGINIA STATION,

—ON THE—

PACIFIC RAILROAD !

AUCTION SALE OF TOWN LOTS

—IN—

THIS NEWLY LOCATED TOWN

WILL·TAKE PLACE ON

SATURDAY, MAY 9, 1868.

THIS SALE WILL AFFORD A GRAND OPPOR-
tunity for favorable investments in town lots
suitable for all kinds of business and trades. The
depot being permanently located at this point will
give the town of RENO a commanding position of
vast importance to secure the trade of Nevada and
that portion of California lying east of the Sierras,
and will be the natural market for the produce of
the rich agricultural valleys north.

Situated on the Truckee River, affording water-
power unsurpassed in the United States, and where
the VIRGINIA AND TRUCKEE RAILROAD connects with the PACIFIC, it is unnecessary to enu-
merate the many advantages this town will pos-
sess as the center of immense milling and manufacturing operations.

The sale will take place on the ground, where,
prior thereto, a plot of the same can be seen and
information in relation to terms obtained, on applying to

D. H. HASKELL, Agent.
Reno, Lake's Bridge, Truckee River, April 30th.

Reno Lots for Sale. *The auction sale, on May 8, 1868, of lots that would become the city of Reno, was announced by this newspaper advertisement.*
Courtesy of Nevada Historical Society

the Truckee River. Then, the next year, he sold his station to Myron Lake. The territorial legislature granted Lake a toll road and a bridge franchise at the end of 1862. All the way stations did a lively business. The Central Pacific Railroad built its tracks into the valley in 1868. The railroad acquired 160 acres from Lake to use for the townsite of Reno. Lots were auctioned off in May. People built places to live. Business boomed.

Freight came by railroad to Reno and was shipped on freight wagons to the mines. The high cost of this shipping by freight wagons brought about the construction of the Virginia and Truckee Railroad through Reno. The new railroad linked the Comstock mines with the transcontinental railroad. Reno prospered. In 1871, the county seat was moved from Washoe City to Reno. Reno became the center for shipment to the mines and ranches. Reno also shipped livestock to San Francisco and Chicago.

Commercial Row, Reno, about the Turn of the Century. Passengers are crowded around the Southern Pacific Railroad depot as the Overland Limited, pulled by two coal-burning steam locomotives, prepares to travel west into the Sierra Nevada for a scenic sunset ride. At one time, four railroad lines operated to and from Reno, which was the biggest city in Nevada for some seventy years.
Courtesy of Nevada Historical Society

The Riverside Hotel at Lake's Crossing. The Riverside, shown here as it looked in about 1890, replaced the original Lake House after the property was taken over in 1885 by William Thompson, the son-in-law of the original owner, Myron C. Lake.
Courtesy of Nevada Historical Society

In 1885, the Legislature moved the University of Nevada from Elko to Reno. This enriched the cultural life of Reno.

For decades Reno led the state in improvements. It was the first city to have gas street lighting, electricity, and telephone service. The city became the center for tourism during the 1920s and grew with the prosperity from legalized gambling after World War II. Its central location made it a hub for the distribution of goods over a large region. Reno became the largest city in northern Nevada.

University of Nevada in Reno, early 1890s. Morrill Hall, the first structure built on the campus after the university was moved from Elko in 1885, is second from the right -- topped with its landmark cupola which still stands there today. It has been refurbished and houses alumni offices and the University Press. The other buildings contained classrooms and a dormitory and have since been replaced.
Courtesy of Nevada Historical Society

Sparks and Wadsworth, the "Rail Cities"

One city in Nevada is more a railroad city than any other. It is the city of Sparks, and it owes its rail-city origin to Wadsworth.

When the Central Pacific Railroad was built, the division point for Nevada was located at Wadsworth. That was where the roundhouse and the machine shops were built.

The Southern Pacific Railroad bought the Central Pacific Railroad in 1885. In 1901, Edward H. Harriman, the new owner of the Southern Pacific, decided to reroute the tracks in Nevada to eliminate dangerous curves and shorten the distance. Wadsworth was bypassed by the new route.

Southern Pacific had to build a new division point with a new roundhouse and new railroad machine shops. For its new location, the railroad bought farm land three miles east of Reno. At the same time, it bought enough land for its workers to live near the shops. Homesites for their houses were sold to the railroad families for $1 per lot. The Southern Pacific Railroad Company loaded the workers' homes onto flatcars and moved them to the new townsite. The new city was incorporated in 1905 and was named after John Sparks, the popular governor of Nevada at that time. Ever since that time, Sparks has been called Nevada's Rail City.

"Honest" John Sparks. John Sparks was the popular governor for whom the city of Sparks was named. A cattle rancher from Elko and Reno, he was elected governor in 1902 and died in office in 1908.
Courtesy of Nevada Historical Society

B Street in Sparks, 1904. These businesses on the north side of the street included a grocery store and the Lincoln Hotel. The south side of the street, called the "Reserve," was used only for the homes of railroad workers.
Courtesy of Nevada Historical Society

Moving Day. *The people of Wadsworth loaded their personal belongings into horse-drawn wagons for the move to Sparks. Their houses were moved on railroad flatcars.*
Courtesy of Nevada Historical Society

Southern Pacific's Sparks Roundhouse, 1912. *This photo was taken from the roof of the railroad machine shop, looking to the northwest. The Southern Pacific Clubhouse, an active social center in those days, can be seen outside the fence.*
Courtesy of Nevada Historical Society

Autos and Airplanes

Automobiles were used in Nevada in the very early years of the 1900s. Wherever roads were good enough, large touring cars replaced stage-coaches for carrying passengers. Huge autos, such as the ones you see today in auto museums, were used to carry passengers from the railroad cities out to the mining towns.

In 1903, autos first traveled all the way across the United States. More and more people began to own automobiles and wanted better roads. In 1913, the Nevada Legislature passed a law requiring car owners to license their vehicles.

Auto Stage for Buckhorn, 1913. By the time this photograph was taken, auto stages had replaced the stagecoach in most parts of the state. Passengers for the Buckhorn diggings got off the train at Palisade and then spent two hours in an open touring car, traveling forty miles over bad roads in heat, dust, and wind to reach their destination. The one-way fare was $10.00.
Courtesy of Nevada Historical Society

The resulting fees were set aside to help pay for the roads. The state began to improve the most heavily traveled roads. In 1917, the Legislature created the State Department of Highways to supervise the roads. In 1923, the state enacted a gasoline tax to raise money for road building and maintenance.

The federal government began to support the building of roads for autos. From 1916 to 1921, Congress passed several laws that helped the states build roads. These laws supported rural roads and state efforts to complete an interstate highway system. In 1928 and 1930, the federal government passed laws sponsored by U.S. Senator Tasker Oddie, the ex-governor of Nevada. These laws provided federal assistance to states in building roads across the public lands.

By 1920, trucks and buses were competitive with railroad lines, and within 20 years, most of the railroad branch lines went out of business. Nevada had entered the modern era of transportation. In 1956, Congress passed the National Defense Highway Act, and the present interstate road system was established. The freeways created by the new highway system have been a great benefit to business in Nevada.

The first airplane flight in Nevada occurred in 1910. Ivey Baldwin made a short flight at the Raycraft Ranch northwest of Carson City. Later that summer, several flights were made in Nevada by barnstorming pilots. The next year, C.P. Rogers made the first transcontinental airplane flight. Actually, it was a series of short flights from New York to California. Airplanes faced the same problem that wagon trains and railroads had faced: how to get over the mountains. The way was found on May 22, 1918, when the first flight over the Sierra Nevada arrived in Reno from Sacramento.

Regular Air Mail to Reno, September 11, 1926. *Pilot J.P. Woodward and a proud reception committee hold the mail from Salt Lake City, while two mechanics prepare the airplane's engine for take-off.* Courtesy of Nevada Historical Society

The federal government encouraged aviation by granting contracts for airmail service. The first flight into Reno was piloted by Bert Acosta and World War I flying ace Eddie Rickenbacker. It arrived in Reno in 1920. Regular airmail service began in 1926. An airplane flown by Leon Cuddeback for Varney Airlines carried 64 pounds of mail and landed at Elko. Varney Airlines was the start of today's United Airlines Company. Congress passed the Air Commerce Act in 1919, and today's air travel is closely controlled by the Federal Aeronautics Administration.

In Nevada, airplanes and helicopters serve the remote areas of the state. Ranchers use planes and helicopters to speed their private travel. Helicopters are used for rounding up livestock, and helicopters also make mercy flights to rescue people almost every day. Reno has become nationally known for recreation flying by private pilots. The National Air Races started in Reno in 1964 and have become a great event.

The air races bring the nation's top pilots and thousands of fans to Stead Airport near Reno every year. Championship soaring is also held every year at the Douglas County Airport south of Carson City.

Modern travel afforded by the airlines has been particularly important to business in Nevada. Each year from 1997, McCarran International Airport in Las Vegas had more than thirty million arrivals and departures. Reno Tahoe International Airport had more than seven million arrivals and departures each year. The numbers have been growing every year at both airports.

Reno Air. *A regional airline that began service in July of 1992, Reno Air is a Nevada-based corporation. It had an immediate impact, increasing tourist travel to Reno. Today, Reno Air is reorganizing for a better future.*
Courtesy of Reno Air

The Start of Las Vegas

Here is a factual account that might have been written by a very young reporter working for the Los Angeles Examiner. The time is the first of May, 1905.

The editor called me into his office and said, "Ike, I want you to go to Las Vegas and report on the land sale at that new townsite. I had to fire the guy we had up there. He didn't know anything about Nevada or boomtowns."

The editor knew I had come from Nevada. My hometown was Virginia City. So, I knew about towns built almost overnight. I took the new train to Las Vegas. Here are some of the stories I wrote.

Los Angeles Examiner

Las Vegas, Railroad Boomtown

LAS VEGAS, NEV. May 8, 1905. This is a great big railroad boomtown. But it is not yet officially a town. It is just a temporary tent city of more than 1,500 souls. These people are already served by stores and business houses of all descriptions.

The boom is here because Las Vegas is the division point for the new San Pedro, Los Angeles and Salt Lake Railroad (SPLA & SL Railroad). It is also the connecting point for freight to the mines. Wagon loads of machinery and supplies come in here by train. Then they are shipped out to the mines on freight wagons.

Right now Las Vegas consists of two townsites -- one where the 1,500 people live now and another undeveloped townsite. Everyone is excited about the undeveloped townsite because the lots there will soon be sold to the public.

The man behind this boomtown is a former Montana state senator named William A. Clark. Sen. Clark made a fortune in copper in Montana. He used his wealth to build the SPLA & SL Railroad. He needed to get right-of-way for his railroad. So, in 1902, he bought 1,800 acres of land and water rights from Mrs. Helen S. Stewart, who owned the Las Vegas Ranch. When he got through building the railroad, he had 900 acres left over. It was one piece of land on the east side of the tracks. He decided to use it to sell lots for a townsite.

In the meantime, a civil engineer named J.T. McWilliams could see that a boom was coming. He bought a different 80 acres from Mrs. Stewart on the west side of the tracks and started his own townsite. He called it the "Original Las Vegas townsite" and advertised it all across the country. His lots were sold for a small down payment and easy terms.

The McWilliams town became a "squatter" town. Early arrivals pitched their tents, and a few quickly erected small buildings. They provided shelter and food for the crews building the last of the railroad tracks and surveying the railroad land. They opened stores, bars, and barbershops. This new tent town quickly became an important location for serving the thriving freight wagon business that carried food, supplies, and machinery to the booming Bullfrog mining district about 120 miles northwest of Las Vegas.

The railroad announced that it would sell lots in its new townsite at fixed prices. The railroad began to take orders. The land sale was to have taken place today. But so far, no land has been sold

Auction of Lots Set for Monday

LAS VEGAS, NEV. May 12, 1905. We finally know when and how the lots for the new Clark's Las Vegas townsite will be sold. The railroad announced today that the city lots will be sold at auction on Monday, May 15. The auction method was chosen because there are many more applicants for lots than there are lots for sale. So the lots will go to the highest bidders. Most of the crowd waiting to buy made no objection. What they want is action.

While I wait for the sale I am staying at a very pleasant place. It is the Las Vegas Ranch Resort owned by the lady who sold the land to the railroad. The ranch has been converted into a resort hotel with comfortable guest rooms in adobe buildings and in new tent houses. Good meals are served here.

There also is a store and a meat market at this location and the Las Vegas Post Office where a Mr. Walter R. Bracken, who was the first employee of the SPLA & SL Railroad in Las Vegas, is now the new postmaster.

City Lot Sale A Huge Success

LAS VEGAS, NEV. May 15, 1905. The Clark townsite auction sale today was a huge success. A crowd of nearly 3,000 people watched the gavel bang down on the sale of 176 choice lots for a total of $79,566.

The sale was conducted from a wide wooden platform under the shade of a large mesquite tree. But the crowd had to stand out in the boiling hot sun.

Mr. C.O. Whitemore introduced the auction sale. He is a big man, six feet, six inches tall, and president of the Las Vegas Land and Water Company. This is the company that will provide city services to the new townsite. He said all the lots will be served with fresh water and that the streets to the lots will be graveled and oiled.

The man who wielded the gavel and actually sold the lots was Ben H. Rhoades, a well-known Los Angeles auctioneer. The sale started at 10 a.m. Los Angeles bidders were ac-

cused of running up the prices of lots for speculation. This made the prices high for the Las Vegas people, who need the land for immediate use for homesites and places of business.

The temperature went up to 110 degrees, wilting the carnations worn by some of the Los Angeles ladies. Finally, at 3 p.m., the auction was stopped because of the extreme heat. An announcement was made that selling would resume tomorrow.

People Moving To New City

LAS VEGAS, NEV. May 16, 1905. The lot sales continued, as announced, all day today. But there was a difference, there was no auction. The lots were sold for scheduled fixed prices. About half of the lots were sold. The two days of selling brought in about $265,000 of proceeds for the railroad.

Last night, after the auction sale closed, and even before the second day of selling, the new Clark townsite was accepted as the city of the future. Some people began that evening to drag their tents and small buildings over to the new townsite. Others began erecting temporary buildings on their new lots.

Fremont, New Business Street

LAS VEGAS, NEV. June 12, 1905. Right after the land sale, a business district was established along Fremont Street. The First State Bank built a two-story frame building, the first ever to be erected in Las Vegas.

The new bank is located right across the street from Block l6, which is the only block in town where liquor can be sold. Of course saloons opened up there immediately. It is an evening gathering place for teamsters, miners and railroad workers. They go there to relax.

I often go there in the evening. It is the best place in town for a reporter to find out what is going on in mining, freighting and railroading. Miners tell you about the new mineral strikes. Teamsters tell you about the new freight hauls and the bad roads to Bullfrog. Railroad workers gossip about what the SPLA & SL is going to do next.

The movement of residents and businesses from the old townsite of McWilliams to the new townsite has been going on rapidly. The Las Vegas Age newspaper building was moved on rollers to the new town. The Imperial Hotel was torn down and rebuilt at the new townsite. There are mercantile stores, lumber companies, grocery stores, temporary hotels, and barber shops that provide hot baths.

New City Serves Busy Mining Area

LAS VEGAS, NEV. August 25, 1905. I have spent the summer staying at the Las Vegas Ranch Resort and getting feature stories about Las Vegas for the Examiner.

This is a place where business men go to relax. There is a lot of shade and a nice swimming pool where the creek has been dammed. Bankers tell me about investments. Developers tell me what new buildings are planned. I find out what is going on in government by talking to public officials.

It is amazing to watch the procession of freight wagons pulled by teams of up to 20 horses and mules that pull out of here each day for the Bullfrog mining district. They are loaded with supplies, mining equipment, and machinery. They carry food and liquor to the miners and feed for their livestock. The corrals here are filled with horses, mules, and burros. They create an unbelievable fly problem in this hot weather. It is especially difficult for the wives and families of teamsters and railroad workers who have set up temporary homes in tent houses.

It is now late in the summer. My editor has called me back to Los Angeles. It already is apparent that Las Vegas will become an important city in the future. It serves the great mining regions of southern Nevada. It will be a halfway point in the commerce between Utah and New Mexico on one side and southern California on the other side. It also is obvious that Las Vegas will be a railroad city dominated by the policies of railroad officials.

Las Vegas, 1905.   Courtesy of Nevada Historical Society

Historical Events

Prehistoric Times
Indians Mined Salt

1700s
Spaniards Mined Near Las Vegas

1847
Silver and Gold Mined at Wahnomie

1850
Gold Discovered at Gold Canyon

1859
Discovery of Silver at Gold Hill

1860
Deidesheimer Invented "Square-Set Timbering"

1862
William Talcott Discovered Gold Ore in Central Nevada

1878
Sutro Built Tunnel to Drain Mines

1880
Ten Flumes Carried Logs to the Mines

1900
Burro Finds Gold at Tonopah

1907
Copper Boom at Ely

1980s
Revival of Mining in Nevada

Chapter Four

Mining

Mining

Mining is a very special part of Nevada. It is and has been a rich industry with an exciting past. The mining of silver made Virginia City the largest city in the West in the l860s and l870s. It was called "the richest place on earth." The silver from Virginia City also made San Francisco rich. In eastern Nevada, mines near Ely produced more than a billion dollars worth of copper for industry all over the world. Besides these two great mining areas, Nevada had many, many smaller mining communities that produced valuable minerals. Some of them still do. Others have become ghost towns where only a few people live. Mining got a new start in the 1980s, producing more than two billion dollars of income each year. Most of this is from gold.

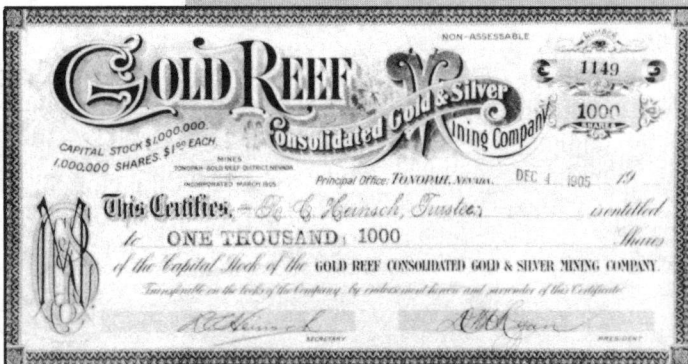

There was mining in Nevada even before the first white settlers came to the state. The prehistoric Indians in southern Nevada mined salt. In northern and western Nevada, the Indians mined flint and sinter to make arrowheads and points for spears.

The first white men to mine in Nevada may have been the Spaniards, mining along the Colorado River south of Las Vegas, in the 1700s. The Mormons operated the silver and gold camp at Wahnomie, north of Las Vegas, in 1847. But it was a discovery along the California Trail in northern Nevada that led to the spectacular development of the mining industry in Nevada.

Around 1850, some of the emigrants bound for California discovered gold. Later, others discovered silver. When this happened, many white people began to settle in Nevada.

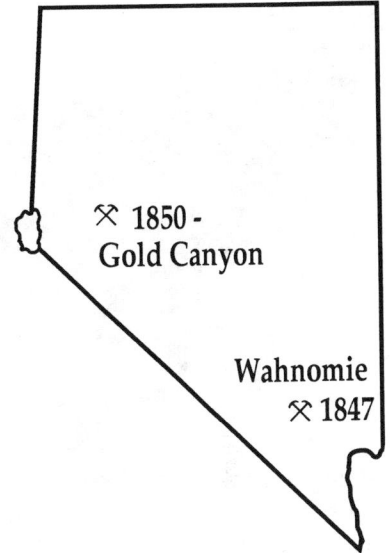

⚒ 1850 - Gold Canyon

Wahnomie
⚒ 1847

The Lore of Mining

Mining is different from any other business. It has its own language and depends on special knowledge and skills. Mining has always been important to Nevada because it produces so much wealth and so many jobs. Places to mine are found by people who travel over the countryside looking for indications of rich ore. Ore may be rock, sand, gravel, or dirt that contains valuable metals or minerals. The people who look for ore are called prospectors. When they discover ore, they have to get an assay made to find out if the ore is worth mining. An assay is a chemical test which tells the value of the ore.

Sometimes prospectors would "strike it rich" -- which means they found very valuable ore. They were then able to sell what they found for large sums of money. Often what they found was worth little or nothing.

Prospectors' Outfit, about 1905. Everything's ready to go as two shaggy "desert canaries" prepare to serve as beasts of burden, while determined prospectors survey the scene. The little cart carries their food, shelter, clothes, and tools. In the background, the tents of Goldfield adorn the surrounding plain.
Courtesy of Nevada Historical Society

Once the ore is located, the prospector measures the area he wants to mine and stakes it out. What he has found is called a "claim." As soon as he has "staked his claim," he has it recorded by the local government. This record protects him from having anyone steal his discovery. In mining language, stealing a discovery is called "jumping a claim." To keep ownership of the discovery, the ore must be mined.

There are three ways to do the mining: placer mining, strip or open pit mining, and tunnel mining. All three have been used in Nevada. Each of these different methods of mining is described in this chapter.

After the ore has been dug out of the earth, the valuable metal or minerals must be separated from the worthless dirt and rock. This separation is called milling, or refining, or reducing the ore. It is done in a reduction mill, a smelter, or a refinery.

At first, the mills in Nevada got their power to operate from water wheels or steam engines.

Today, the power is provided by electricity and using chemicals reduces the ore. Mining requires skilled workers and expensive equipment. This makes mining cost a great deal. Most mines are owned and operated by corporations. When people buy stock in a corporation, it provides money to do the mining.

Gold, silver, copper, lead and nonmetal minerals are the most important products of mining in Nevada. So much silver was found in Nevada that it was nicknamed "the Silver State". For a long time, gold, silver and copper were used to make coins for the United States Government. Today very little of these metals is used to make coins. Nevada's gold, silver and copper are now used to make jewelry and for manufacturing. Lead and nonmetallic minerals are used in industry for manufacturing and chemical processing.

Most Nevada mining communities had a similar history. After a rich discovery, people rushed to the mines. It was a rough life in the new mining camps. Claims were often threatened or stolen. This caused fights and lawsuits. Housing was temporary and living conditions were poor. Virginia City, at its heyday about 1860, had a population of 35,000. This was larger than San Francisco at that time.

As the deposits of ore became "mined out", people left the communities. Many of these communities then became ghost towns.

The Comstock Lode

The story of the discovery and mining of the Comstock Lode at Virginia City tells a lot about mining in early Nevada. The wealth from the mining of silver was the envy of the rest of the world.

The mine owners developed new mining technology never used before. From the discovery of silver in 1859, until the decline of mining in 1879, more than $500,000,000 (five hundred million dollars) was earned from the gold and silver. The story began a few miles away from Virginia City, in Gold Canyon.

Gold Canyon

In 1850, a party of Mormon emigrants discovered gold along the California Trail. They were camped at the mouth of a canyon along the Carson River. Some of the men found traces of gold and a small gold nugget in the canyon. John Orr, a member of the party, named the place Gold Canyon. The party went on to California, but miners heard of the discovery.

By autumn of 1851, more than 100 men worked the gravel in Gold Canyon. A trading post was started at the mouth of the canyon to serve the miners and the emigrants who passed by on their way to California. The town of Dayton is there now.

The miners of Gold Canyon used the placer method of mining. The gravel and sand in the canyon contained coarse lumps of gold. When the miners put the gravel in small pans and washed the dirt with water, the heavier gold stayed in the pan, while the lighter sand and rock spilled out. The miners collected the gold left in the pan, ounce by ounce. Soon the miners began to work the gravel on a larger scale. They sifted hundreds of pounds of dirt through screens or rockers to remove the large rocks. Then they washed the dirt that was left through a long narrow box called a "long tom." The box had small ridges along the bottom to catch the heavier particles of gold as the water washed through the box carrying the lighter dirt away.

How Placer Mining Was Done. *The miner in the left foreground is panning gravel and sand from the stream. Behind him, in the right foreground, workmen are "fielding" or dumping ore-bearing gravel into a "long tom." In the center, two burly miners are winching up rich ore from a shallow shaft or "coyote hole." In the background, the man on the left is washing ore in a "cradle," while miners tunnel into a hill. Other workmen are operating a flume and sluice in the distance.*

This new method of mining produced much more gold than the old method of panning.

By 1858, the miners were having hard times. Less and less gold was being found. The prospectors began to search for gold farther up the canyon. One of the miners wandering up the canyon toward Mount Davidson was "Old Virginia" Fennimore. On January 28, 1859, Fennimore, Henry T.P. "Old Pancake" Comstock, and several other miners discovered a rich vein of gold and silver-bearing quartz at the head of Gold Canyon. Since the place was not in Gold Canyon, but on a little hill, they decided to call it Gold Hill.

About five months later, in June of 1859, two other miners, Patrick McLaughlin and Peter O'Riley, moved up from Gold Canyon to work at another location about a mile away from Henry Comstock and Old Virginia. Their claim didn't have the water they needed to wash out the gold.

Henry Thomas Paige Comstock. *Henry Comstock was the man for whom the Comstock Lode was undeservedly named. He sold out early, drifted through Idaho and Montana looking for another Comstock Lode, and died a suicide.* Courtesy of Nevada Historical Society

Discovery of the Comstock Lode, June 1859. *This sedate painting by James Harrington, showing H.T.P. Comstock at left, does little to convey the dramatic excitement which gripped the Pacific Coast after Patrick McLaughlin and Peter O'Riley's find of fabulously rich silver and gold deposits in what is now Storey County.*
Courtesy of Nevada Historical Society

So, they began to dig a hole to store water. Their shovels turned up a blackish-colored sand, different from the yellow clay and gravel they had been digging.

They decided to wash a little of this new-looking sand. When the dirt was washed away, the bottom of their rocker was covered with gold dust. The dust looked different than usual, and the miners thought it might contain some other base metal. But it was unmistakably gold. They knew they had made a rich strike.

Comstock came by their claim at the end of the day. He saw the gold and claimed the land was his. It was a false claim, but O'Riley and McLaughlin wanted to avoid trouble. They gave a share in the mine to Comstock and his friend, Emanuel Penrod. They called the mine the Ophir. The lode they had discovered was named after Comstock who had no right at all to the discovery. Of course, they thought they had only found a rich gold strike.

They had no idea they had also discovered the richest silver strike in history.

In July of 1859, Augustus Harrison, a rancher living in the Truckee Meadows, visited the diggings at the Ophir mine. He took a piece of the ore to Grass Valley, California, to be assayed. The assay showed that it would yield several thousand dollars per ton in gold and silver.

It was agreed by those who knew in Grass Valley that the richness of the ore would be kept secret. But they told their friends, who told more friends. Within days, the hills around the Ophir Mine were covered with newcomers, hundreds of miners hoping to strike it rich.

Fame Came to Mark Twain While He Lived in Nevada

Samuel Langhorne Clemens (1835-1910) of Missouri, who wrote under the name of Mark Twain, is the most famous of American writers. He started as a river boat pilot on the Mississippi River, then came to Nevada in August of 1861. In the first territorial legislature, he served as an assistant to his brother, Orion, who was Secretary of State for the new territory. After the legislature ended, Twain tried prospecting, had bad luck, and thought it was too much work. Then, the Virginia City Enterprise hired him to write letters for the newspaper. Within a week he was made local editor. In his news stories, Mark Twain mixed up the facts with wild accounts from his own imagination. His stories got nationwide attention. Here in Nevada, he began to write the stories that would make him world-famous. One story, "Roughing It," was about his adventures in Nevada.

Courtesy of Nevada Historical Society

"Cave-in of the Mexican." *This 1863 J. Ross Browne drawing shows the kind of deadly incident that was common in the Comstock mines until the invention of square-set timbering.*
From *A Peep at Washoe* and *Washoe Revisited* by J. Ross Browne

Phillip Deidesheimer.
Deidesheimer was the mining engineer whose invention of square-set timbering in 1860 made it possible to mine the extraordinary ore deposits of the Comstock Lode.
Courtesy of Nevada Historical Society

The mines at Virginia City yielded the first silver ever discovered in the United States. They produced hundreds of millions of dollars worth of silver. But none of the discoverers got rich. Each of them sold out his interest for a few thousand dollars or even less. Once the rush was on, thousands of claims were located. There were violent fights over who owned the claims and many lawsuits over ownership.

The miners at Gold Hill and Virginia City began to have great difficulty getting their ore out of the ground. The gold and silver vein was very wide and deep. When the ore was dug out, great caverns were left under the ground. Miners were injured or killed by cave-ins. No one knew what to do about it.

A solution was devised by Phillip Deidesheimer, the superintendent of the Ophir Mine. He invented a system of "square set timbering" in 1860.

Digging the Tunnel. *In this view of the miners digging underground, the square-set method of timbering protects the crew. While workmen drive their picks into the ore, others sort the rocks and operate a hoist.*

It was like a pattern of hollow building blocks stacked under the ground. The blocks held up the earth, preventing cave-ins. The miners could work inside the blocks. This permitted mining on a much greater scale. The mining companies could hire more miners and dig out more areas under the ground.

While this solution made silver mining more profitable, it also required miners to spend more money to operate their mines. This turned out to be too expensive for individual miners. Soon, large corporations were formed to finance the mines. Stock brokers in San Francisco sold shares of stock in the mining companies to provide money for the Nevada mines. If the miners struck a rich deposit of gold or silver, it was called a "bonanza." If a mine was unsuccessful it was called a "borrasco."

A Little Difficulty with Disappointed Speculators, about 1875. *A San Francisco stock broker faces the wrath and revolvers of shareholders unhappy with their disastrous loss based on his advice. Many fortunes were won or lost in mining stock investments on the San Francisco Stock Exchange.*

As the mines dug deeper and deeper into the earth, they got extremely hot. The temperature of the rock 2,200 feet below the surface was 120 degrees Fahrenheit. In deeper mines, the temperature got up to 140 degrees. Huge blowers were used to ventilate the mines. Work shifts were cut to just a few minutes. Water was another threat to the mines. Underground pools of water flooded the mines. Pumping the flooded tunnels was extremely expensive. The solution was discovered by a man named Adolph Sutro.

Sutro got the idea of constructing a great drain tunnel. It ran for four miles, from deep in the mines through the mountain to the Carson River.

The Sutro Tunnel, about 1889. *This structure was one of the most spectacular engineering achievements of its day.*
Courtesy of Special Collections, University of Nevada Reno Library

The tunnel is 16 feet wide, 12 feet high, and it cost $4,500,000 (four million five hundred thousand dollars) to build. Work on it was started in 1869 and finished in 1878. It was regarded as one of the engineering marvels of the age. Sutro made a fortune and, for 20 years, was one of the most powerful men in San Francisco. He was mayor of San Francisco from 1894 to 1896.

Adolph Heinrich Sutro (1830-1898) of Prussia. *Sutro, the builder of the Sutro Tunnel, came to Nevada with the original "Rush to Washoe" and made a fantastic profit on his world-famous tunnel. His riches made him powerful and famous in San Francisco, where he became mayor.*
Courtesy of Nevada Historical Society

"Mining on the Comstock." *This 1876 illustration provides an education in mining technology. The square-set method of timbering, the size of the bonanza ore bodies, the system of shafts and tunnels, with elevators and ventillation shafts, as well as the tools of the miner are all clearly shown.*
Courtesy of Nevada Historical Society

"The 'Man at the Wheel' Operating the Shaft Elevator." *This 1877 drawing by an artist for Frank Leslie shows the huge machinery necessary to mine the Comstock Lode.*
From *Out West on the Overland Trail* by Richard Reinhardt

Drinking Water

Although the mines were flooded with water, there was very little on the surface for human consumption. As the Virginia City population reached the tens of thousands, there was a great need for water. To supply the water, the Virginia City and Gold Hill Water Company brought water from Marlette Lake across Washoe Valley. The company built 21 miles of pipe and 45 flumes to carry the water across the valley to Virginia City. Henry Schussler, the surveyor for the Sutro Tunnel, designed the system. It was built rapidly between June and August of 1873. The project was considered a major engineering achievement. In 1975 the American Society of Civil Engineers designated the system a national landmark.

Milling

Another problem was getting the gold and silver out of the ore after it was dug out of the ground. At first, the rocks were packed to San Francisco for refining. This was very expensive.

Then, mining engineers invented a better process for separating the gold and silver from other minerals. Large rocks were broken up into smaller pieces. They were crushed with power machinery called "stamps." The ore was then ground into a fine powder. Quicksilver, salt, and copper sulphate were added. The mixture was roasted, stirred, and poured into an elaborate separating system of basins which separated the gold and silver from the base rock. The rock left over was called "tailings."

The stamp mills which crushed the ore were driven by steam power. The wood to heat the steam boilers came from pine trees, fir trees, and cedars.

Deforestation at Summit Camp in the Sierra Nevada.
Logging locomotives brought the lumber from the sawmills of Lake Tahoe to Summit Camp. From there, flumes carried the wood to Carson City.
Courtesy of Special Collections, University of Nevada Reno Library

They were cut from the neighboring forests. The miners also used timber to shore up their tunnels and shafts. The railroads used wood to power their steam locomotives and for ties under the railroad tracks. People used wood for cooking and heating in their homes. Timber was being cut from the Nevada and California forests at a very rapid rate.

As the demand for wood increased on the Comstock, the forests on the eastern slope of the Sierra began to disappear. For a distance of 60 miles, the hills were virtually stripped of trees.

Getting the wood from the forests to the mines was a problem. It was solved in many ways. Some logs were floated down the Carson River and then moved by wagon to the mines. Some were moved by locomotive over logging railways. Some were floated down flumes to get them out of the forests. A flume is a chute built of wood with a small stream of water flowing through it. The water carried the logs down the mountain. By 1880, there were 10 flumes operating in Nevada. One of them was 20 miles long and cost $250,000 (two hundred fifty thousand dollars) to build.

Where Incline Got Its Name. The Incline tramway was an ingenious component in a system which provided lumber and cordwood for the Comstock. Trees felled in the woods around Lake Tahoe's south shore were trimmed into logs, roped into huge rafts, and towed north across the lake by steamboats to Sand Harbor. From there, the logs were hauled by a short rail line to the Sierra Nevada Wood and Lumber Company sawmill at Mill Creek, where they were sawed into lumber and cordwood. From the sawmill, the wood was then carried up the incline in six cars on rails, connected to a continuous cable driven by a steam engine. At the top of the incline, the wood was dumped automatically into a flume which whisked it away to Lakeview at the south end of Washoe Valley, where the wood was picked up by the Virginia & Truckee Railroad and taken to Virginia City.
Courtesy of Nevada Historical Society

"Everlasting Oblivion Lay Directly Ahead." A thrilling ride on the Sierra Nevada Wood & Lumber Company flume was just the thing to banish boredom in the woodcutting camps.
Courtesy of Nevada Historical Society

Well-stocked Lumberyard. *Wood piles tower over a V&TRR engine and its crew south of Carson City. Planks and beams stretch north to the horizon, all cut at the Glenbrook mills of Lake Tahoe. From there, the lumber was hauled to Spooner Summit and then sent down a flume, shown here.*
Courtesy of Nevada State Railroad Museum

The Verdi Lumber Company Sawmills on the Truckee River. *Cutting all those trees generated a lot of sawdust, and this created a problem -- pollution. Although lawsuits to stop sawdust pollution of Nevada waterways began as early as 1863, court action was largely ineffective throughout the nineteenth and early twentieth centuries. The sawdust blocked rivers, preventing trout and salmon spawning runs and killing the fish. The Truckee River had to be repeatedly re-stocked with fish after the 1870s.*
Courtesy of Nevada Historical Society

Seizing Control of the Comstock Lode

William Sharon (1818-1885). *Sharon was the United States Senator from Nevada between 1875 and 1881. He dominated Nevada's economic life for almost 20 years.*
Courtesy of Nevada Historical Society

John W. Mackay (1831-1902), of Ireland. *Mackay worked his way up from hard rock miner to millionaire and mining magnate in partnership with Fair, Flood, and O'Brien. He parlayed his Comstock fortune into even greater riches in the development of transoceanic submarine telegraph systems. His son, Clarence, and his wife left millions of dollars to the Univeristy of Nevada, donated in John W. Mackay's name.*

Silver mining was big money business. It made a lot of money, but it took hundreds of thousands of dollars, or more, to even operate a silver mine. This attracted investors who were able to invest large sums of money. Some of them founded the Bank of California and sent William Sharon to Nevada to open a branch of the bank. The bank loaned money to mine and mill owners who were having some hard times. When the mine owners could not repay the bank on time, the bank foreclosed on the mines and mills. Before long, Sharon and the Bank of California had control of the Comstock mines.

Another group called the "Silver Kings" got control of the Hale and Norcross mine away from Sharon. They struck a rich pocket of gold and silver. Then, in 1872, they acquired the Consolidated Virginia mine, which was considered worthless. Actually, it was the richest mine of the Comstock region. It had incredibly rich ore and was called the "Big Bonanza." John W. Mackay was one of the Silver Kings. Most of the money made from the Virginia City mines went to San Francisco. But Mackay and his family spent his riches in Nevada, giving generously to support the state's needs.

The Big Bonanza was the last major discovery of ore in the Comstock mining district. It was mined out by 1879. The value of the Comstock mines went into decline. Mining became less profitable. Mines shut down, and miners were put out of work. They left the Comstock for mining booms in other towns.

Some mines continued to operate on a limited scale until the 1920s. Virginia City survived to the present and is still famous as a fabulously rich mining town of the past. Now Virginia City is a destination for millions of tourists who come to see the historic ruins, museums, and the places where legends were born.

Nevada's Other Mining Communities

Nevada has had many other important mining communities. Many still serve the mining industry. Others, no longer mining centers, are thriving from other resources. Some are desolate places that have become ghost towns. Here are some of Nevada's important mining communities from the past.

Austin

On May 2, 1862, William M. Talcott discovered gold ore in central Nevada. Talcott had been a Pony Express rider and a station keeper for the overland mail in Reese River Valley. He was hauling wood over a cutoff of the Central Overland Route and stopped at Pony Valley, where he discovered an ore deposit. When it was assayed, the quartz rock was found to be rich in silver.

In a short period of time, a town had sprung up. In 1863, the town of Austin became the county seat of Lander County. The mines produced rich profits. In 1864, Austin was incorporated as a city.

Austin became the second largest city in Nevada. The Nevada Central Railroad was built to connect the Austin mines with the transcontinental railroad at Battle Mountain. The Manhattan Mine had produced more than $19 million in silver by 1887. It ceased production in 1890 and only operated off and on after that. The railroad was scrapped in 1938. The county seat was moved to Battle Mountain in 1980.

Today, Austin attracts visitors who are interested in the history of central Nevada and silver mines. Stokes Castle, a replica of a Roman tower, gets the attention of travelers because it is visible from Highway 50.

EMMA NEVADA

The world-famous concert singer, Emma Nevada, started out as a child in Austin. People in Austin knew she was a wonderful singer when she was just a little girl singing in the Methodist Episcopal Church choir. When her mother died, her father, Dr. William Wixom, sent her to attend Mills Seminary in Oakland. Her singing in the San Francisco area was so popular that she went with a choral group to sing in Europe. In Europe she was sponsored by Mrs. John W. Mackay, wife of the famous Nevada miner, who was living in Paris. When Emma was to sing for Queen Victoria, the London Times incorrectly reported her name as Emma Nevada. She liked the name and kept it for her stage name. Emma gave concerts for years in Rome, Paris, Berlin, and St. Petersburg. Then she returned to America to sing in New York, Boston, and San Francisco. Emma came back to Nevada and sang at Piper's Opera House in Virginia City, and at the old Methodist Church in Austin. She completed her career in Europe and retired in England.
Courtesy of Nevada Historical Society

The Stokes Castle. *A famous landmark at Austin, the Stokes Castle is visible in the distance to people who drive Highway 50. The three-story stone castle has a parapet which provides a marvelous view of the beautiful Reese River Valley. It was built for the Anson Stokes family of New York who financed the Nevada Central Railroad.*
Courtesy of Nevada Historical Society

Eureka

On September 19, 1864, a five-man prospecting party discovered an unusual rock not far from the Central Overland Route. The ore turned out to be a mixture of silver and lead, but there was no process for separating the two.

Five years later, in 1869, new owners bought up a substantial interest in the mines around Eureka. By the end of the year, they found that the ore could be reduced into silver, lead, and other metals by a smelting process. They built large smelting furnaces.

The new, profitable mines and mills started a boom in Eureka. People rushed to settle in the town.

The State Legislature created the county of Eureka on March 1, 1873, with the city of Eureka as its county seat. In 1875, a railroad was built to connect the mines at Eureka and nearby Ruby Hill with the transcontinental railroad at Palisade. This made Eureka the central shipping point for most of the mining camps in eastern Nevada. Mining peaked in Eureka in 1878, when the ore output was valued at more than $5,000,000 (five million dollars).

The smelters in Eureka used a lot of charcoal. They processed 750 tons of rock a day. It took 25 to 30 bushels of charcoal to process each ton. In 1879, the mining companies decided to reduce the price they were paying for charcoal from 30 cents a bushel to 27 1/2 cents a bushel. The Charcoal Burners' Association, with several thousand members, refused to accept the cut in price. This prevented any charcoal from being delivered to the smelters. The charcoal burners took over the town of Eureka on August 11, 1879.

Eureka. *The Eureka County seat had about 9,000 people living there during the height of the mining boom in 1878. They came from places as far away as Italy, England, and Mexico to earn a living here. The town had four churches, two militia units, an opera house, five fire companies, and nine cemeteries in its heyday.*
Courtesy of Nevada Historical Society

Charcoal Furnaces South of Ward. *These structures in White Pine County furnished the charcoal needed to superheat the ore smelters which refined silver and lead from rock that was hard to melt. It was the operators of charcoal furnaces like these who were killed in the "Charcoal Burners' War" at Eureka in 1879.*
Courtesy of Special Collections, University of Nevada Reno Library

Governor John H. Kinkead called out the state militia to deal with the disturbance, but it was over before the militia got there. On August 18, 1879, an over-zealous sheriff's posse of nine men attacked a group of about 100 striking charcoal burners at the Fish Creek charcoal camp. The posse killed six men and injured six others. That ended the "Charcoal Burners' War." The charcoal burners accepted the lower prices offered by the mining companies.

It wasn't long before the mines ran into trouble. In 1881, the miners struck water. It began to flood the tunnels and shafts of the main mines. The companies used pumps to keep the mines open, but this was expensive. The last bonanza ore was mined out in 1885. No new ore was found. In the early 1900s the main smelters closed, and mining operations were reduced to a small scale with uncertain success.

Today, Eureka serves a considerable revival of gold and lead mining in the area and also supplies the livestock ranches in east central Nevada. It is a beautiful, small city and still the county seat of Eureka County.

Ely and White Pine County

Although the Comstock is the most famous of Nevada's mining districts, the copper mines in the Ely region have produced more wealth than those of any other mining district in Nevada. The first major ore strike in White Pine County was not copper, and it was not at Ely. It was at Mt. Hamilton. There, in 1868, a rich deposit of silver was discovered high on the slope of the mountain, about 30 miles southeast of Eureka. There was a great rush of miners to the region. Mining companies were formed. Money was raised in San Francisco to finance the mining and milling.

Austin ✗   ✗ Eureka
✗ ✗ Ely
Hamilton

Hamilton. *Deserted in this photo taken about 1900, Hamilton was the first county seat of White Pine County. Located high on Mt. Hamilton, about 50 miles west of Ely, it served one of the richest ore deposits in Nevada history. However, it had one of the shortest mining booms, lasting only from 1868 to about 1874.*
Courtesy of Nevada Historical Society

A new city called Hamilton was built and was made the county seat of White Pine County. An estimated 15,000 people rushed to the district. Then the ore ran out and the mining at Hamilton was over by 1874.

Prospectors discovered gold and silver in the Ely area as early as 1867. But the mining of it was not very successful. The Ely settlement was just a stagecoach stop and a post office. It was also a supply center for prospectors and cattlemen. When the Hamilton ore deposits played out, the county seat of White Pine County was moved to Ely in 1887.

Copper deposits were known to exist in the Ely area in the 1870s. But the copper was not valuable enough to be worth mining. There was not much demand for copper. This changed dramatically when electricity came into use all over the country. Copper was used to make electric wires. This created a large and growing market for copper.

In 1900, David Bartley and Edwin F. Gray arrived in Ely. They got a lease to work several claims at a location not far from a place called Ruth. They also got an option to buy the mine, but they had no money. W.H. Graham, who ran the general store, provided them with supplies and food for two years. Bartley and Gray were able to find rich ore, but freighting the copper ore 150 miles to the nearest railroad station was very expensive.

In 1902, Mark Requa, a businessman from Virginia City, bought out the interest of Bartley and Gray for $150,000. Requa developed the property and bought additional properties. In 1905, he and others financed the construction of the Nevada Northern Railroad. This linked Ely with the transcontinental railroad at Cobre in Elko County. There was a rush to the copper mines. In 1907, the town of Ely was incorporated.

First Train to Ely. *This 1906 photograph shows crowds of people watching the arrival of the first Nevada Railway train ever to steam into the White Pine County seat.*
Courtesy of Nevada Historical Society

That same year, the mining companies started strip mining operations at Ruth. Strip mining removes the topsoil, and then the ore and then the underlying rock. It can level mountains or leave an immense pit. A huge smelter was built at McGill in 1908. Production of copper increased dramatically. The mines continued to operate until the early 1980s. The area had yielded more than a billion dollars in copper, gold and silver.

Copper mining started up again at Ruth and in 1996 when the mines closed, it was for business reasons, not for the lack of ore. Large deposits of copper still remain. Ely is a supply point for gold mining in the area and also for the oil wells in Railroad Valley. It is a service center for ranches, as it has been for more than half a century. A new maximum-security prison was opened at Ely in the 1980s. Ely has many tourist attractions, such as: the new Great Basin National Park, the restored railroad yards of the Nevada Northern Railway, the old "beehive" charcoal ovens and the huge open pits of the copper mines.

The Liberty Pit at Ruth From the Lower Levels. In this White Pine County scene, an immense self-propelled mechanical shovel dumps tons of copper-bearing rock into the ore car. A well-stoked steam engine stands ready to ascend the spiral grade to the surface and deliver the ore to waiting smelters. The workingmen, dwarfed by the machinery, show the huge scale of twentieth-century strip mining.
Courtesy of Nevada Historical Society

Aerial View of the Liberty Pit. This aerial photograph shows Kennecott Copper Corporation's open pit mine at Ruth during the late 1950s in White Pine County. These deposits provided ore for over 60 years, during which time the town of Ruth had to be relocated on several occasions to allow room for continued mining activity.
Courtesy of Nevada Historical Society

Million Dollar Mines 1859-1940

HUMBOLDT

National
Paradise Valley
Potosi-Getchell

ELKO

Mountain City
Jarbidge
Cornucopia
Gold Circle
Tuscarora

WASHOE

Gerlach

PERSHING

Mill City
Seven Troughs
Echo
Buena Vista
Unionville
Rochester

Battle Mountain
Lewis

LANDER

EUREKA

Safford
Buckhorn
Mineral Hill
Cortez
Eureka

WHITE PINE

Cherry Creek
White Pine
Ely
Taylor
Minerva

CHURCHILL

STOREY

Flowery
Virginia City-Gold Hill
Silver City

CARSON CITY

Wonder
Fairview
Reese River

DOUGLAS

Yerington

LYON

MINERAL

Hawthorne
Bruner
Union
Round Mountain

NYE

Sante Fe
Bell
Belmont
Garfield
Sodaville
Aurora
Candelaria
Manhattan
Tybo
Tonopah

ESMERALDA

Divide
Weepah
Silver Peak
Goldfield

LINCOLN

Bristol
Pioche

Delmar

Bullfrog

Ash Meadows

CLARK

Las Vegas
Arden
Sloan
Goodsprings
Eldorado
Searchlight

N
W   E
S

Million Dollar Mines 1859-1940

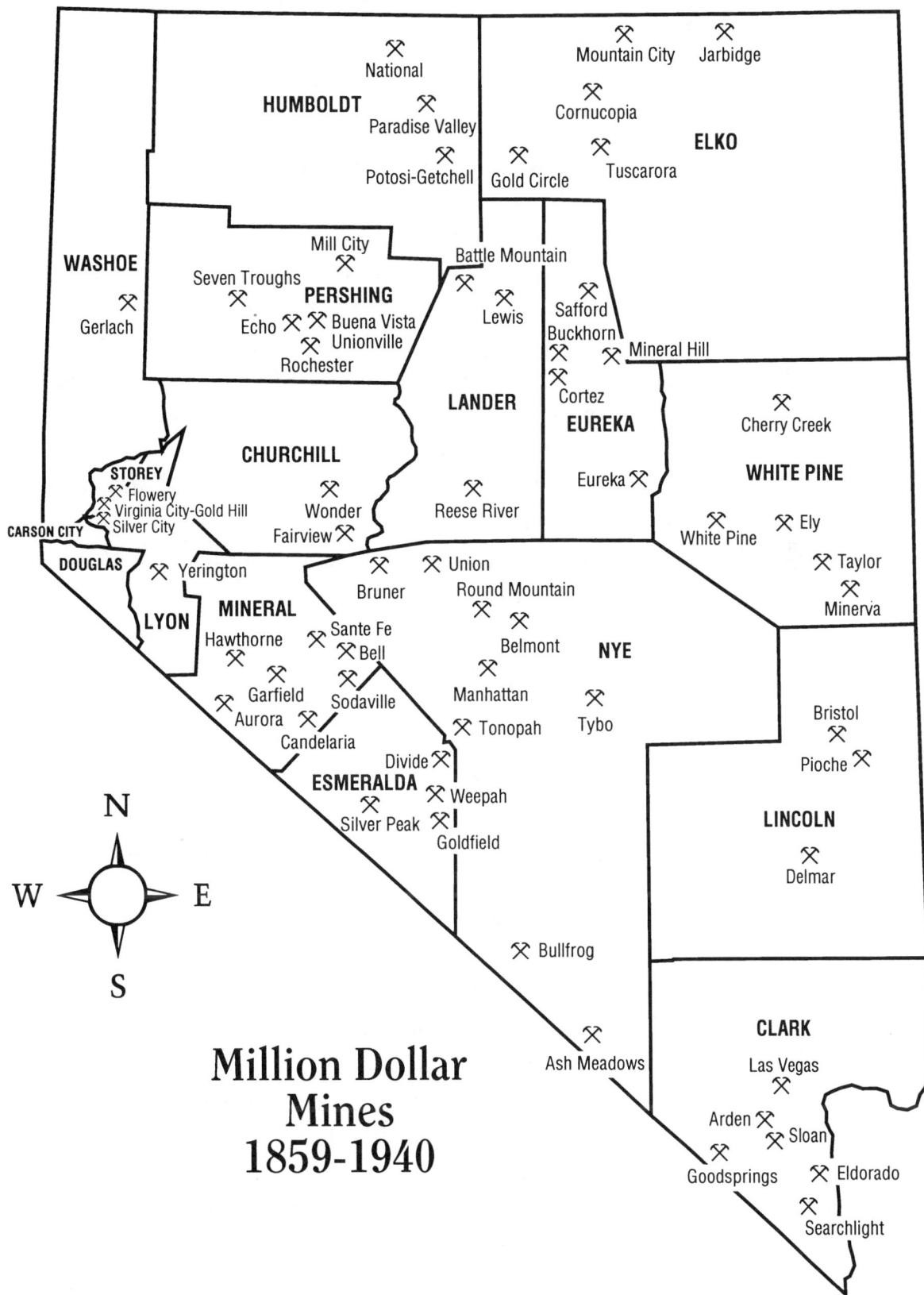

Locations of Million Dollar Mines of Nevada. Each of these locations produced a total yield of $1,000,000 or more prior to 1940.

The Mines in the South

In general, the mining enterprises in the southern part of the state developed later than those in the north. However, the silver deposit at Pioche was discovered in 1864.

Pioche

About 100 miles south of Ely, an Indian showed an outcropping of metallic ore to William Hamblin. Hamblin was a Mormon missionary at Meadow Valley. What the Indian had shown to Hamblin was the famous Panaca Ledge. Hamblin filed his claim to the ledge in March of 1864.

The developers encountered problems. The Indians were unfriendly. The miners had trouble separating the silver from the rock. An attempt to build a smelter failed. In 1869, the miners sold out to F.L.A. Pioche, a San Francisco businessman.

In 1870, a new technique showed the silver miners at Pioche how to get the silver out of the ore. A reduction mill was built and miners rushed to Pioche. The ore deposit was extensive and rich. Within five months, the population of Pioche was more than a thousand people. The mines were so rich that some miners tried to take claims away from the owners. The rival mining companies hired bullies and gunmen, called "roughs," to protect the mines they owned. Some of the companies also used roughs to try to take over claims they didn't own. Life in Pioche was so violent that 75 people were buried in the cemetery before one person was buried there who had died a natural death.

Within a few years, Pioche had a population of five or six thousand people. The ore production reached its peak in 1872, and the boom lasted only a few years. By 1878, the town was nearly deserted. The mines began to flood, and in 1880 they were closed down.

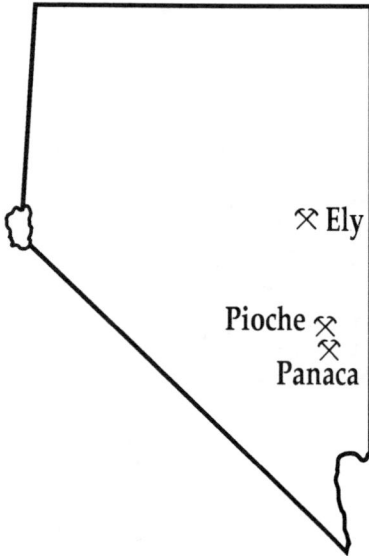

Pioche in 1881. The heyday of the early mining boom in this picturesque mining community was from 1870 to 1873. Then, cheap electricity from Boulder Dam became available in 1935 to use for the smelting of ore. There was a renewal of mining prosperity in this Lincoln County seat until 1959. Today, the area's mines intermittently produce manganese, tungsten, zinc, and lead.
Courtesy of Nevada Historical Society

The "Million Dollar Courthouse" at Pioche. This structure, which served as the courthouse in Pioche, is famous because of its amazing final cost. The contract to build it was for only $16,400. Lincoln County, booming in 1872, added so many expensive extras that the actual cost of construction was $75,000. The mining boom ended. The county couldn't pay its bills. Courthouse financing got mixed with other county finances. Bonds were issued. Payments on the bonds were missed for many years. Refinancing built up a large debt. When the county was finally solvent in 1938, 67 years after the courthouse was built, it was estimated to have cost $800,000.
Courtesy of Nevada Historical Society

About 50 years later, Pioche began a new era of prosperity. The Boulder dam was built in 1935, providing Pioche with inexpensive electricity. Cheap electricity made it economical to smelt the lead and zinc ore near Pioche. This created a long-lasting prosperity. Between 1935 and 1959, Pioche deposits produced $80 million worth of lead and zinc. This was more income than the silver mining had produced in the 1870s.

Today Pioche is a quiet town that remains the county seat of Lincoln County. Its famous "million dollar" courthouse has been refurbished and now contains a museum.

Tonopah

For many years prospectors walked over the ground where Tonopah is now located. They passed by rich ore that was virtually sticking out of the ground. They had given up the search for ore there by 1900.

In May of 1900, James Butler found one of his burros that had strayed away. The animal was under a rock cliff to get out of the wind. Butler broke off some of the rock and took it to Belmont to be assayed. The assayer threw away the sample saying he wouldn't give a dollar for a thousand tons of the stuff.

Butler then took a sample of the mineral to Tasker L. Oddie, an attorney at Belmont. He promised Oddie a quarter interest in his finding, if he could get it assayed. Oddie took the sample to Walter C. Gayhart in Austin. Gayhart was an assayer and also principal of the Austin school. Oddie promised Gayhart a half of his one-quarter interest, if the ore was valuable. None of these men had any money. Gayhart's assay showed the ore to be worth $300 to $400 per ton. James Butler and his burro had found the rich Mizpah vein of ore.

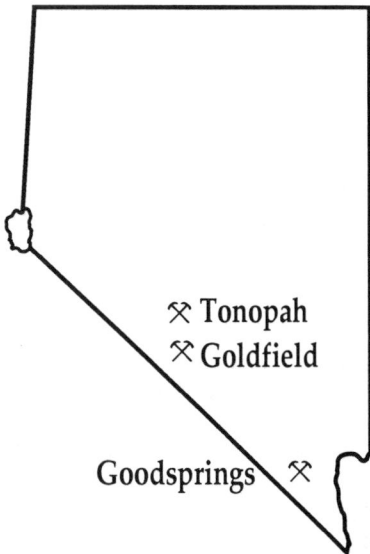

⚒ Tonopah
⚒ Goldfield

Goodsprings ⚒

The Pioneers of Tonopah. *This Nye County photograph shows (from left to right) the first tent in the town of Tonopah, Tasker Oddie, Wils Brogher, Mrs. Belle Butler, and James Butler.*
Courtesy of Nevada Historical Society

Oddie sent an Indian runner to Butler's ranch, 45 miles away, to tell Butler about the value of the discovery. But Butler did nothing for a while. He was described by a newspaper reporter as the "laziest man in the world." After about a month, Butler and his wife, Belle, established a number of claims. Miners who heard about the strike began to rush into the area. They wanted to find their own claims of the rich ore. Butler and Oddie didn't have enough money to develop their new claims. But they didn't want to end up like the men who had discovered the Comstock Lode, with little or nothing for themselves. So, they devised an ingenious plan. Instead of selling their claims, they leased them to miners who paid back a portion of the ore. The system was popular, and it worked. By the spring of 1901, more than a hundred leases for claims had been recorded. A town grew up rapidly. Butler named it Tonopah, after an Indian springs nearby.

Butler and Oddie did all of this on trust, simply by word of mouth. The miners trusted them, and they trusted the miners. There were no contracts or other written agreements. The ground was not surveyed. Everyone trusted everyone else. There were almost no resulting lawsuits. Butler may have been lazy, but he and Oddie were smart. Butler became a millionaire. Oddie went on to become governor of Nevada and a U.S. Senator from Nevada.

In 1902 and 1903, miners discovered more deposits of silver ore so rich that Tonopah continued to prosper for many years. The conveniences of civilization such as electric power and running water weren't long in coming to Tonopah. A power plant was built at the end of 1902, and a water supply followed soon afterward. The mills needed water for processing the ore, and the residents needed it for cooking and cleaning.

Tonopah, the Last of Nevada's Great Mining Boom Towns. *As seen in 1907 with Mount Butler in the background, Tonopah had the typical appearance of a mining town. Note the mounds of pilings, the jumble of dwellings and buildings, and the lack of vegetation.*
Courtesy of Nevada Historical Society

The needs of the mines and the town generated a large freighting business. Large wagons, with teams of up to 20 horses or mules, hauled freight between Tonopah and the railroad at Sodaville. Tonopah became an important distribution point for west-central Nevada. Transportation to other communities improved. Railroad lines were built in from Reno and Las Vegas. Prospectors working out of Tonopah discovered rich gold and silver ore at Goldfield, Bullfrog, Rhyolite, and other locations.

Tonopah was more orderly than earlier mining towns. Men did not have to wear guns. There weren't any hired roughs. New hotels, dance halls, theaters, churches, hospitals, stores, and homes were built. In 1905, Tonopah became the county seat of Nye County, replacing Belmont.

The silver mines of Tonopah reached peak production between 1910 and 1914. Then the ore production began to decline. The mines went out of business in about 1940. Not long afterward, the railroads serving the town ceased operations.

Its location as a crossroads and a supply point kept Tonopah alive after the mines closed. It became a World War II training base for the crews of B24 Bombers. During those busy years the population grew to 10,000. Since the early 1950s, Tonopah has thrived on providing services for the nearby Air Force testing range. In the 1980s, Tonopah was a city that served one of the nation's greatest military projects, the Stealth Bomber.

Goldfield

On December 4, 1902, Harry Stimler and William Marsh, who were prospecting about 30 miles south of Tonopah, found some black-looking quartz. The rock they had discovered was exceedingly rich in gold. Stimler and Marsh located several claims which they later sold to George Wingfield and George Nixon.

Goldfield's Beginnings, November 1903. *This early view shows the future Esmeralda County seat as a collection of sheds and tents set out in the sagebrush.* Courtesy of Nevada Historical Society

Other prospectors also found rich deposits of gold in the area. Within a month, 150 people lived in the camp. Then the rush began. Within two years of Stimler and Marsh's discovery, six or seven thousand people were living in Goldfield. Wingfield and Nixon continued to buy up claims. They were able to gain control of most of the productive mines by 1907. Their company, the Goldfield Consolidated Mining Company, produced tens of millions of dollars worth of gold in the next few years. Wingfield and Nixon became very wealthy.

Goldfield did not have the kind of roughneck violence that earlier mining boom towns had. It had a different kind of conflict. Instead of roughneck fighting, it had labor union strikes and labor disturbances. The trouble was related to the extreme richness of the ore. Some pieces were nearly solid gold. Some workers in the mines stole gold by hiding small pieces in their clothing and carrying them off when they left their day's work. This was called "high-grading." Some miners made so much money high-grading that they didn't care how little they were paid.

Company officials tried to stop the high-grading by making the men take off their work clothes in one room and then move to another room to change into other clothes before they left the job. This angered the mine workers.

Some of them had come to Goldfield from mines in Idaho, Colorado, and Alaska where they had belonged to labor unions. They organized a labor union in Goldfield and were represented by the Industrial Workers of the World, a radical labor union often referred to as the "Wobblies." Under the union influence, some of the miners went on strike against use of the "change rooms."

Wingfield and other mine owners persuaded Governor John Sparks to send a telegram to President Theodore Roosevelt asking for troops to protect Goldfield from violence. There had not been any violence as a result of the strike, and people in Goldfield were surprised when the soldiers arrived. The troops spent a few weeks in Goldfield and were withdrawn shortly afterward.

The presence of the troops did give the mine owners an opportunity to hire other miners, called "strike-breakers," who would work cheaper than the union miners. The strike failed. The union lost its influence.

It is hard to imagine a mineral deposit as rich as that at Goldfield. Almost all the town's ore production, amounting to more than $90 million, came from a zone less than a mile long and only a few hundred feet wide. The peak year of production was 1910.

George Wingfield (1876-1959). Born in Arkansas, Wingfield was a vaquero and gambler when he met Winnemucca banker George S. Nixon around the turn of the century. The two formed a team which dominated Nevada political and economic affairs after 1907, financed by their Goldfield Consolidated Mines Co. Almost wiped out in the Great Depression, Wingfield made a financial comeback through other mining ventures and remained influential until his death.
Courtesy of Nevada Historical Society

George S. Nixon (1860-1912) of California. Nixon was a worker in a box factory, a telegrapher, and bank clerk who later became a state legislator and then U.S. Senator from Nevada in 1905-1912. In partnership with George Wingfield, Nixon prospered with the rise of Goldfield and died a wealthy man.
Courtesy of Nevada Historical Society

Be It Ever So Humble. *During 1903-1904, dugouts like these were home to many Goldfield residents. Housing problems were characteristic of Nevada boom towns.*
Courtesy of Nevada Historical Society

Goldfield in 1907. *The town was already of imposing size in this photograph taken in its most troubled year. Labor strikes and violence gripped the town during a struggle for control of the region between the I.W.W. and the Goldfield Consolidated interests of Nixon and Wingfield.*
Courtesy of Nevada Historical Society

Goodsprings

At Goodsprings, about 30 miles southwest of Las Vegas, prospectors discovered silver and lead ore in 1868. But it wasn't mined because it contained very little silver. In 1892, the Keystone gold deposit was discovered and remained active until 1906. Lead ore was also being produced. It was discovered that the lead extraction contained high grade zinc. This brought a big increase in ore production. The Yellow Mining Company was formed. Goodsprings grew to a population of 800 in 1921. The total production of the Goodsprings district was $31 million. It had a major impact on the economy of southern Nevada. The Goodsprings mines produced about 40 percent of the total metallic mineral production in Clark County.

Candelaria

An ore deposit was discovered at Candelaria by mining prospectors in 1863, and the Northern Belle Mine began production in 1873. Freight costs were high, and wood was hard to find. Still, the Northern Belle built a stamp mill and paid dividends. Production averaged a million dollars a year for 10 years. There were other mines in the district. By 1881, Candelaria had a population of 1,500. In 1885, a fire destroyed part of the town. Silver dropped in price, and the bonanza was exhausted. There were brief revivals in 1890 and 1919. The district produced more than $20 million during its boom period. Once again, silver is being produced at Candelaria. Nerco Metals, Inc. began operating there in 1980 and has become a major contributor to silver production in Nevada.

Ore Mill at Belleville. *This ore mill served the Northern Belle Mine at Candelaria. The smoke-stacks of the Upper Mill belch steam and smoke, as well-dressed businessmen deal at arm's length. On a nearby trestle is a Carson & Colorado Railroad train.*
Courtesy of Special Collections, University of Nevada Reno Library

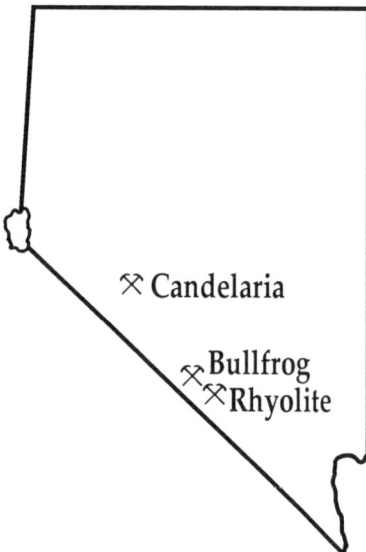

⚒ Candelaria

⚒Bullfrog
⚒Rhyolite

Rhyolite

The town of Rhyolite is named for the hard, volcanic rhyolite rock in the Bullfrog Mining District. Mining activity started there in 1904, when Eddie Cross and Frank "Shorty" Harris discovered gold in what became the Bullfrog mining district. Shorty Harris named his claim Bullfrog for the greenish copper-stained ore he found there. He then went into Goldfield to celebrate his good fortune and sold his claim for $500 and a "mean-faced mule."

The mining camp at Rhyolite started out as a "rag town" made up of rags, canvas, and adobe. A miner named Pete Busch dreamed of a town of stone and brick with smooth streets. He and his brother, Ed, staked out a town and got Rhyolite started. Within two years, in 1907, the town had 6,000 people with telephones, electric service, and hotels. A modern city built of stone and wood was in full swing before the mines ever began to operate. The mines in the Bullfrog district produced gold, silver, copper, and lead. Production in the years of 1905 to 1921 amounted to $2,792,930.

Boom and Bust at Rhyolite. *These Nye County photographs graphically illustrate the difference between bonanza and borrasco in a mining town. When the mines stopped producing, the inhabitants departed, leaving a ghost town. Rhyolite began in 1905; by 1920 it was abandoned, leaving only ruins. Around the decay, the lone and level sands stretch far away.*
Courtesy of Nevada Historical Society

Peak production was in 1908. By 1911, most of the mines had shut down. The population had reached 12,000, but it had dropped to 700 by 1910.

Today, Rhyolite has a train depot and the famous "Bottle House" built from 51,000 glass bottles. They stand among the ruins of the Busch brothers' dream city.

Nevada's Mining Revival of the 1980s

There was a great renewal of mining in Nevada in the 1980's. Nevada led the nation in precious metals production in 1996 and the 1990s. Mining now produces over 3 billion dollars of income each year for Nevada.

The greatest dollar value of mining in Nevada comes from the mining of gold. Nevada is the second largest producer of gold in the world exceeded only by South Africa. Nevada produces 7.8 million ounces of gold per year, worth about $2.2 billion dollars.

The mining of copper also produce millions of dollars each year for Nevada's income. Although gold and copper have accounted for the large dollar value of mining in Nevada, many other valuable minerals are produced.

Gypsum is mined in Elko, Clark, Washoe and Pershing counties. Gypsum is used in the making of wallboard for home and building construction. Wallboard plants are located near Lake Mead and at Empire, Nevada.

Since 1983, a million barrels of oil have been produced each year in Nevada. Oil wells are located in Railroad Valley in Nye County and in Eureka County.

The mining industry is also paying attention to protecting the environment. Although open pit mining continues, state and federal statutes and regulations have caused mines to restore the land.

Geothermal Plant at Beowawe. *This plant is one of 14 geothermal plants in Nevada providing electricity for more than 46 thousand households. A plant at Dixie Valley is the largest producer of electricity in Nevada. Another plant at Steamboat produces 11 percent of the electric power for Reno.*
Courtesy of Nevada Bureau of Mines

Mining provides its workers the highest average income of any industry in Nevada. The average pay is about $48,000 per year. This applies both to workers with college degrees and to workers without college degrees. Community college courses help to prepare workers, for the mining industry. Mining also provides work outside the mines, such as accounting, diesel mechanics and others that do require a college education.

Historical Play

The story of Virginia City is one of the most spectacular real-life events of the American West. This play "The Ghosts of the Comstock" features the famous characters that made up the history of Virginia City. The play may be acted out by students or performed as an oral reading.

GHOSTS OF THE COMSTOCK

by Craig Sodaro

Characters

Eilley Orrum

John Orr

Nick Kelly

Old Virginny

Miner One

Miner Two

Henry Thomas Paige Comstock

Woman One

Woman Two

Pete O'Reilly

Pat McLaughlin

Sandy Bowers

Phillip Deidesheimer

Julia Bulette

Dan DeQuille

Mark Twain

John Mackay

Voice One

Voice Two

Adolph Sutro

William Chapman Ralston

William Sharon

Augustus Harrison

Mr. Fair

Mr. Flood

Mr. O'Brien

President Ulysses S. Grant

Setting

The play takes place in and around Virginia City from 1850 to 1902. A rocking chair down left represents the last year. EILLEY ORRUM sits knitting in the chair at rise. A few crude benches and/or paper mache rocks can fill the playing area, along with a small table. A collage of Virginia City or Nevada history would make a good background or mountains representing the area around Virginia City.

At Rise

EILLEY ORRUM, now quite old, enters, sits, and begins knitting. After a moment she looks up towards audience and squints.

EILLEY: Why, isn't that just the way of it? My old eyes failing, and I didn't even see you come in! You'll have to excuse an old woman for not getting up, but my welcome to Virginia City and Eilley Orrum's boarding house is no less sincere. I suppose you're like most folks ... you've come lookin' for excitement. But I'm afraid that's all passed now. It's 1902, and there are just a few of us old-timers left. And I suspect before long we'll be joining the other ghosts of Virginia City. **(Thinking back)** Ghosts ... hmmm ... seems like the whole story of Virginia City is nothing but the story of ghosts now ... ghosts from as far back as 1850, when the area was called Washoe ... along with a few other words I wouldn't care to repeat in mixed company! In that year Millard Fillmore became president when Zach Taylor died ... "Old Folks at Home" was a popular song ... and people were reading "The California and Oregon Trails" by Francis Parkman. It was only two years after the discovery of gold in California, and John Orr and Nick Kelly were heading west to Sutter's Mill near Sacramento.

(JOHN ORR and NICK KELLY enter carrying backpacks and shovels.)

NICK: How much longer you reckon, John?

JOHN: I suppose another two, three days.

NICK: Ain't this just the worst spot in the world? Nothin' but dust, alkali, rocks ... and wind!

JOHN: They say you gotta get through hell to get to heaven!

NICK: Well then, after this California better be full of soft, white clouds, beautiful ladies, plates of oysters, and gold nuggets as big as boulders!

JOHN: I believe the sun's got to you, Nick! We're gonna camp here in this canyon. The water looks good.

NICK: I reckon. **(Looking downstage)** You suppose we'll find anything in this creek?

JOHN: If gold can wash down the west side of the Sierras, I don't see any reason why it can't wash down the east side. **(They crouch down and begin to pan for gold. They pick up rocks, examine them, and toss them back into the creek.)**

NICK: You know? Some folks think we're all just crazy.

JOHN: That so?

NICK: Well, it ain't exactly been a pleasure trip out here from the East. We could be back in Iowa or Kentucky right now, comfortable, warm, with money in our pockets.

JOHN: That might be fine for some, but then there's us, ain't there? We ain't content with warm, dry, and workin' for somebody else. There's more to be had than that, but it won't come take you by the arm, Kelly.

You gotta go lookin' for it. Only folks with enough fight and determination's gonna find it. Look here ... it might be inside this slate rock! **(He holds up rock.)**

NICK **(Laughing):** You are a dreamer, Orr! A real, true dream --

JOHN: **(Delighted, shocked)** Kelly! Kelly, you look here!

NICK: What'd you find?

JOHN: It's gold, Nick! This here's gold, wrapped up in a chunk of slate!

NICK: It's gold all right! And where there's one nugget, there's bound to be more!

JOHN: Why, this here's one big gold canyon! Let's try over there!

(JOHN and NICK exit with packs.)

EILLEY **(To audience):** Their enthusiasm was a bit premature. Sure, that nugget brought $8.35 ... but, during the summer, only bits of gold dust were found. They lost interest and headed on to California.

(OLD VIRGINNY enters with pan and his ever-present whiskey jug.)

VIRGINNY **(To audience):** 'Course there were some of us who still had this feeling about the canyon and the mountain behind us!

EILLEY: Why, if it isn't James Fennimore!

VIRGINNY: Now, please, Eilley ... call me Old Virginny. That's how I'm known ... named after my home state!

EILLEY: It's been quite a spell since you sat at my table gobblin' up my pork and beans.

VIRGINNY: And they were mighty good, too!

EILLEY: Tell me ... what's all this about you thinkin' the canyon and mountain were worth somethin'?

VIRGINNY: Us prospectors work by know-how and feel-how. And me and some of the other boys just had this feelin' about the area. No place could be just so plain ugly without hidin' something mighty important!

(MINER ONE enters carrying a pick.)

MINER ONE: Say, you the feller they call Old Virginia?

VIRGINNY: Sure am, stranger!

MINER ONE: I'm a mite green here. I've got my pick but not an inkling how to use it!

VIRGINNY: You *are* green! Now, son, the first thing you got to do is take that there pick and toss it into the nearest ravine, and then you'll be ready to work.

MINER ONE: What do I have to do?

VIRGINNY: We placer mine here. You see the gravel and sand bars there along the side of the creek? Well, that's where you'll find gold. Now, gold is a lot heavier than the rocks and gravel. So, what we do is shovel up some of the sand bar and dump it into a rocker. See, there's a screen on the bottom and we rock the box back and forth. Then the big rocks get caught and the fine stuff falls through. That's the stuff we wash down a "long tom." The heavier dust -- the gold -- gets caught in the small ridges at the bottom of the box. Nothin' to it!

MINER ONE: Why, neighbor, I sure appreciate the advice. Maybe I'll see you at the bank sometime, once we both strike it rich!

(MINER ONE exits.)

EILLEY: They always came with a lot of hope, didn't they?

VIRGINNY: And some of us held on to it!

EILLEY (Impressed): You sure did, didn't you?

VIRGINNY: 'Course we had cause. You see, word of mouth began to get around that two brothers, the Grosches, had found something mighty big ... bigger than anything in California ... somewhere around the hill. Nobody knew the truth, but some folks said the brothers had staked out claims and were headin' to San Francisco to make it all legal.

EILLEY: But they never made it, did they? One brother died of fever, and the other perished in a blizzard on his way.

VIRGINNY: Yup ... so we all wondered even more!

(COMSTOCK enters.)

COMSTOCK: Say, Virginny ... I heard you've been poking around the hill ... right near the head of the canyon.

VIRGINNY: Why Henry Thomas Paige Comstock! It's been a month of Sundays.

EILLEY: Old Pancake himself!

COMSTOCK: Howdy, Eilley. Sure have missed your pork and beans.

EILLEY: C'mon, now, Pancake. You didn't get your nickname for nothin'. If I saw you once a month it was too much. You lived on pancakes for breakfast, lunch, and dinner!

COMSTOCK: Couldn't be too careful about my money. And I can't be too careful about my claims.

VIRGINNY: What claims?

COMSTOCK: Oh ... well ... you know the poor Grosch brothers are gone now ... but they left me with a bit of information!

VIRGINNY: I hear it's all just a rumor. There's no big strike around here ... is there?

COMSTOCK: Then why don't you head back down the canyon?

VIRGINNY: The ore pockets are almost all played out. You know that.

COMSTOCK (Slyly): Well, there ain't nothin' around here. You can take my word for it. (COMSTOCK **struts off.**)

VIRGINNY (**Looking after him, shaking his head**): I don't trust that feller somehow. He knows somethin' he ain't tellin'! (**VIRGINNY exits.**)

EILLEY (**To audience**): Those boys were like two kids fightin' over a present that was all wrapped up ... and they didn't even know what was inside. And so it went ... them boys pickin' and pokin' all over the hill until January 28, 1859.

(**VIRGINNY, MINER ONE, and MINER TWO enter and look for gold.**)

MINER ONE: See there, fellers? The willows?

MINER TWO: Looks like an Indian spring.

VIRGINNY: So it does! Let's try it!

(**COMSTOCK enters and sneaks around them unseen.**)

MINER ONE: Say, look here! (**He holds up handful of dust.**)

MINER TWO: Well, I'll be! It's gold!

VIRGINNY: Gold! And fine stuff, too! Finest gold dust I ever saw!

MINER ONE: I'm gonna buy a big house and put it right here!

MINER TWO: I'm gonna head to San Francisco and have a fine time!

COMSTOCK (**Appearing angrily**): Get off my claim, boys!

VIRGINNY (**Friendly**): Why, Henry T.!

MINER ONE (**Angrily**): *Your* claim?!

MINER TWO: This find is ours! All ours!

COMSTOCK: We'll see about that.

(COMSTOCK and VIRGINNY, MINER ONE, MINER TWO **exit in opposite directions.**)

EILLEY (To audience): Comstock finagled his way into a share of the discovery, but that didn't stop others from coming to Washoe to try their luck. Before that discovery, there was a town a bit aways from what the boys now began calling Gold Hill. Soon all the miners moved up to Gold Hill and was hangin' onto the mountain for dear life!

WOMAN ONE (Entering): And so were you, Eilley. How you ever got those miners to build your cabin at Gold Hill, I'll never know!

EILLEY: It pays to know the secrets of good home cookin'!

WOMAN ONE: Don't tell me ... your pork and beans!

EILLEY: Not to mention my biscuits! They'd melt in your mouth!

WOMAN ONE: 'Course, the men about these parts would just about do anything for us women folk.

EILLEY: That's right! You know, since I was just a small twig of a thing in Scotland, I knew I was destined for something great. As I saw that town beginning to carve out a spot for itself on Gold Hill, I felt like it was getting closer and closer!

WOMAN ONE: That must have been the way Pete O'Reilly and Pat McLaughlin felt in June, 1859, when they were digging by a spring near the head of Six Mile Creek looking for some water to rinse some strange-looking yellow sand from their pans.

EILLEY: Wouldn't you know, it was two Irishmen!

(PETE **and** PAT **enter with pans and other equipment. They crouch down as if beside a stream.**)

PETE: If this isn't the durndest looking stuff, Pat!

PAT: Aye, but wait a minute, Pete. Look there, how it shines!

PETE: I'll be Paddy's pig! It's gold, Pat! Gold dust right out of a leprechaun's pot!

(COMSTOCK **enters.**)

COMSTOCK: Well, if it isn't Mr. O'Reilly and Mr. McLaughlin hard at it! Any luck?

PETE: A wee bit, Mr. Comstock! Look here!

PAT: It's gold spun from an angel's hair!

COMSTOCK: Why, so it is. Let me be the first to congratulate you! And now, perhaps, you'll want to talk business.

PETE: What kind of business?

PAT: This is our claim, Comstock. We won't fall for the shenanigans you pulled on Old Virginny!

COMSTOCK: Did I say this isn't your claim?

PETE: Then it seems the only business we got is pullin' the gold out of this mountain!

COMSTOCK (**Craftily**): But, boys ... you need water. Lots of it!

PAT: So? Look at it! We got plenty!

COMSTOCK: That's right. For a price. See, boys, I own the water rights. Bought it from a feller named Caldwell.

PETE (**Angrily**): But ... but!

COMSTOCK: I'll be happy to allow you all the water you like.

PAT: In exchange for what?

COMSTOCK: A share in whatever you got here.

PETE (**Furiously**): That's robbery!

COMSTOCK: That's business! Either sign over a share or you'll have to haul your water by the bucket!

(**Angrily, PETE and PAT follow COMSTOCK off.**)

EILLEY (**To audience**): Needless to say, the boys signed over a share to Comstock.

(**MINER ONE enters**)

MINER ONE: They named the place Ophir. Ain't that just the stupidest name you ever heard of?

(**WOMAN ONE enters from the opposite side.**)

WOMAN ONE: Shows what you know! If your eyes ever saw a page of the Bible you'd know that they named the mine after an African country from which gold and silver were taken as gifts for Solomon.

MINER ONE: Then it was a good name because O'Reilly and McLaughlin were soon washing $50 to $75 a day from a single tub of crushed ore! 'Course everybody began to call it Comstock's Lode, seein' as how he was the partner with the biggest mouth!

WOMAN ONE: And that's just about the time you met Mr. Bowers, wasn't it, Eilley?

EILLEY: Sure was! (**Dreamily**) He walked right into my boarding house one day ... tall, thin, and shy!

(**MINER ONE and WOMAN ONE exit as SANDY BOWERS enters.**)

SANDY (**Shyly**): Why, Ma'am ... I believe you've got a sign in the window ...

EILLEY (**Rising, businesslike**): That's right. I got a bed upstairs ... you have to share it with two other fellers. And I serve the best pork and beans this side of the Pacific.

SANDY: Sounds fair to me.

EILLEY: I s'pose you're into prospecting?

SANDY: Got a couple of claims, and I've been working steady.

EILLEY: Don't sell out. Be patient. I've been trying to tell the boys not to sell too quick, but they just don't want to listen. Some of 'em pay me in claims when they're low on cash. See here? (**Pulls claims from her apron.**)

SANDY: I'm too smart for that, Ma'am. I won't let nobody cheat me out of my share to a mine. No, sir. I aim to hang onto my claims. See here? (**He pulls out his claims. EILLEY notices one.**)

EILLEY: I'll be! You know we got claims right next to each other, Mr... Mr...

SANDY (**Embarrassed**): Bowers, Ma'am. Lemuel Sanford Bowers. But my friends call me Sandy. I'll just go take my things upstairs, if you don't mind. (**SANDY exits.**)

EILLEY (**Dreamily**): Mind? Why should I mind? (**Businesslike to the audience**) As you can see, I was quite taken with Mr. Bowers.

(**WOMAN TWO enters.**)

WOMAN TWO: And in due time -- two months -- you and Sandy got yourselves hitched!

EILLEY: A wedding was something Gold Hill didn't see often!

WOMAN TWO: It lasted from morning to night!

(**WOMAN TWO exits.**)

EILLEY (**To audience**): At the same time, a new discovery surfaced -- literally!

(**MINER ONE enters holding a black rock. He studies it.**)

MINER ONE: I never seen so much black rock. Makes it mighty tough to get the gold out!

(HARRISON **enters wearing cowboy hat.**)

HARRISON: Augustus Harrison's the name, sir. You just mentioned black rock. I know something about your black rock.

MINER ONE (**Handing** HARRISON **the rock**): Got any suggestion as to how we can get rid of the stuff? We'd be mighty obliged!

HARRISON (**Holding the piece of rock**): Sir, this is something you don't want to get rid of! I took some of your black rock over to Grass Valley and got it assayed. What I hold in my hand is pure silver!

MINER ONE (**With a laugh**): Are you all right, Mr. Harrison!

HARRISON: This is silver, I tell you!

MINER ONE (**Nervously**): But ... but there's tons of this stuff already pulled out of the Ophir Mine! It's piled up into a mountain!

HARRISON: A mountain of silver!

MINER ONE: And the walls inside the mine shaft are thick with it!

HARRISON (**Shouting right and left**): Silver! Silver by the ton!

MINER ONE (**Shouting the same**): Silver! Silver by the ton! Washoe or bust! Rush to Washoe! Your dreams will come true!

(MINER ONE **and** HARRISON **exit, while** WOMEN ONE **and** TWO **cross from the opposite way.**)

WOMAN ONE: Silver! Imagine that!

WOMAN TWO: I'm gonna find *me* a rich husband!

(OLD VIRGINNY **crosses from opposite direction as** COMSTOCK **enters opposite.**)

VIRGINNY: Nothin' like it ever before ... no, siree!

COMSTOCK (**Proudly**): Head to the Comstock Lode!

(As COMSTOCK **passes in front of** OLD VIRGINNY, **the prospector sticks his tongue out.**)

EILLEY (**To audience**): And come they did ... by the thousands. They threw up their tents, carved caves into the side of Gold Hill, or slept under the stars. They were as rough and tough a gang of men as ever congregated in one spot. And they called the town Silver City.

VIRGINNY (**Enters with a whiskey bottle**): Silver City ... HA!

EILLEY: Evenin', Virginny. Looks like you've been drinking again!

VIRGINNY (Sadly, carrying a whiskey bottle): It's all I got left, Eilley. I came out here with such high hopes ... and you know I'm the best placer miner around here! I had two good claims ... includin' a share in the Ophir. But I got cheated! I got nothin' left now ... but you know? I ain't gonna leave this place without leaving my mark! **(Throws his whiskey bottle on the ground.)**

EILLEY: What're you doin'?!

VIRGINNY: I'm baptizing this place Virginia! Dear old Virginia, my home. And you tell 'em all, Eilley! Nobody can cheat me out of that! This place is Virginia from now on! **(VIRGINNY rises proudly and exits.)**

EILLEY (To audience): And so it was. Silver City became Virginia City overnight.

(SANDY races on.)

SANDY (Excitedly): Eilley! Eilley! There's a feller from San Francisco who says he wants to give us $400,000 for our twenty feet of claim in the new silver mine!

EILLEY: $400,000! My, Sandy ... but that's a powerful lot of money.

SANDY: We could buy the mansion you're always dreamin' about ... and maybe a trip to Europe!

EILLEY: The answer's no, Sandy.

SANDY (Dumbfounded): But, Eilley! You want me to say no to almost half a million dollars?

EILLEY: I said no, and I meant it!

SANDY (To audience): Well, now ... Eilley always knew best, and this time it was no different. We hung onto our claim ... and soon it was yielding a million dollars a year! We had enough money to throw at birds.

EILLEY (Dreamily): So we did, Sandy. We built our mansion and headed off to Europe to have tea with the Queen.

SANDY: We never *did* catch up to her ...

EILLEY: But what a grand time we had!

(SANDY exits as WOMAN ONE enters.)

WOMAN ONE (To audience): But most folks took more simple pleasures in Virginia City!

(MINER ONE enters.)

MINER ONE: No time for pleasure, Ma'am. We're working in the mines day and night ... workin' to find that big bonanza! That big strike!

WOMAN ONE: Bigger than the Ophir and the other strikes?

MINER ONE: It's down there ... we all know it!

(WOMAN TWO enters.)

WOMAN TWO: But there were problems in pulling all that gold and silver out of the mountain.

WOMAN ONE: Pulling so much out left a big hole inside the mountain!

MINER ONE: Giant caves honeycombed Gold Hill. Soon the houses and buildings on top began to sag as the weight of Virginia City grew.

MINER TWO (Entering): Cave-ins occurred, miners were killed ... and many were injured.

WOMAN TWO: Couldn't you shore up the shafts with timbers?

MINER ONE: We tried, but the caves were so big and the weight was so great, the timbers just couldn't take it ... they split like match sticks.

WOMAN ONE: But something had to be done! My husband was down there day in and day out. I couldn't live with that terrible fear! That one day --

(A whistle blows.)

MINER ONE: Another cave in !

MINER TWO: Quick! Bring picks and shovels!

(PHILLIP DEIDESHEIMER enters with blueprints and pencil as MINERS ONE and TWO exit.)

WOMAN ONE (Desperately): Mr. Deidesheimer! You're the superintendent of the Ophir ... you must *do* something!

WOMAN TWO: The entire mountain will collapse one day! **(WOMAN ONE and TWO exit.)**

PHILLIP (To himself, calculating): It would seem that if we could ... hmm ... yes!

EILLEY (To audience): Mr. Deidesheimer was a very smart man and understood things like physics and engineering -- things the rest of us couldn't even spell!

PHILLIP: But it's so simple, Eilley! We build boxes of timbers ... each box like a separate, powerful unit. We build the box eight feet high by eight feet deep. Then we put another box the same size on top and so on. Each box is strong, and many strong timber boxes will create a structure inside the mountain that will hold it up. Not only that ... we can build safe tunnels, install pulleys so we can raise and lower supplies easily ... and guarantee the safety of the miners!

(PHILLIP **exits making calculations.**)

EILLEY (**To audience**): See what I mean about smart? Soon the entire inside of Gold Hill was being square-set timbered. And that made profits that jingled in the pockets of mine owners and workers alike,. 'Course there was always somebody willing to take a little of that cash off your hands!

(WOMAN ONE **entering with laundry basket.**)

WOMAN ONE: Wash! I'll take in your dirty duds, miner, and have 'em clean for you tomorrow morning!

(**She exits crossed by** MINER ONE.)

MINER ONE: Buy your shovels, picks, and pans right here. There's more gold and silver out there to be had if you can dig it out!

(MINER ONE **exits as** WOMAN TWO **enters.**)

WOMAN TWO: Fresh baked chicken dinner, just like your wife used to make! C'mon in and try our apple pie ... only two bits a slice!

(WOMAN TWO **exits as** MINER TWO **enters.**)

MINER TWO: Step right up, men! I've got the finest cotton work shirts for only five dollars apiece! (MINER TWO **exits.**)

(JULIA BULETTE **enters wearing a lavish dress and feather boa.**)

JULIA: C'mon in, boys! Drinks are on the house!

EILLEY (**To audience**): And, of course, there was Julia Bulette, Virginia City's famous hostess who entertained the miners.

JULIA: Why, evenin', Miss Eilley. It certainly is a beautiful sunset tonight, isn't it?

EILLEY: Aside from me, you're the one person around here who appreciates the beauty.

JULIA: Oh, I do! I'm from New Orleans where the buildings are so high and the streets are dark ... and there's a foul smell drifting in from the riverfront. I do love these open spaces and the view from my porch.

EILLEY: I see your flowers are doing nicely.

JULIA: Aren't they, though? I like to think I've got the nicest garden in Virginia City.

EILLEY: You've got the only garden, Julia. And you've got crystal chandeliers in your parlor, I hear tell ... and champagne that's even chilled.

JULIA: Champagne isn't good unless it's chilled, Eilley. Anyway, the boys who stop by for a drink are tired after their long day in the mine. They want a bit of refinement ... a bit of civilization.

EILLEY: You are an angel, Julia. Especially after the way you nursed the sick during the last epidemic.

JULIA: There were so many sick men, and no one else to care for them.

EILLEY: Well, you've got the respect of all Virginia City.

JULIA: That's all I ever wanted, Eilley. The jewels and furs I've got ... well, they aren't nearly as precious as being made an honorary of Fire Company #1.

EILLEY: That honor ain't bestowed on too many women.

JULIA: I'm the only one, Eilley.

(MINERS ONE and TWO enter and sheepishly approach JULIA.)

MINER ONE: Evenin', Miss Julia ... on behalf of Fire Company #1, we got something we'd like to ask you.

JULIA: Go right ahead, boys!

MINER TWO: How'd you like to be Queen of the Fourth of July parade this year?

JULIA: Why, gentlemen ... I'd be honored. Come into my parlor and give me the particulars ...

(With a MINER on each arm, JULIA exits.)

WOMAN ONE (Entering opposite side): Unfortunately, that would be Julia's last parade.

WOMAN TWO (Entering): A stranger in town strangled her that winter and stole her jewels and furs.

EILLEY: Oh, there were bad fellers aplenty! 'Course, all these stories were duly reported in the most famous of all western newspapers, the *Territorial Enterprise*.

WOMAN ONE: Mr. Jernegan and Mr. Janes founded the paper in 1858 and moved it to Virginia City in 1860.

WOMAN TWO: Joe Goodman and Dennis McCarthy bought the paper and promptly made it a success.

WOMAN ONE: Not only did they print the news ...

WOMAN TWO: They printed rumors, speculation, and downright lies!

WOMAN ONE: On days when there was real news, you could trust what the *Territorial Enterprise* had to say.

WOMAN TWO: But on days when there wasn't any news, Goodman and McCarthy let their reporters make up stories of interest to the rough and tumble mining crowd.

WOMAN ONE: Two reporters became world-famous. One was a feller named William Wright ... otherwise known as Dan Dequille.

(WOMEN ONE and TWO cross DAN DEQUILLE as he enters opposite. He tips his hat as they exit.)

DAN (To audience): My specialty was mining, pure and simple. I knew just about everything there was to know about the Comstock Lode and the business of running the mining operations. But that wasn't what the folks wanted to read about. So, like other good reporters of the day, I took a little poetic license and made up a few stories.

(MINER ONE enters with newspaper.)

MINER ONE: Say! You see here where this feller found the Traveling Stones of Pahranagat Valley?!

(MINER TWO enters with newspaper.)

MINER TWO: Says the stones actually move around by themselves!

MINER ONE: Maybe it's some kind of curse!

MINER TWO: Or maybe it's done by ghosts!

MINER ONE: Either way ... if the *Enterprise* says it's so ... it's so!

(MINERS ONE and TWO exit.)

DAN (Proudly): P.T. Barnum, the fellow who started up the big circus, actually offered me the astounding sum of $10,000 for the traveling stones. But, being an upstanding member of the newspaper profession, I declined. After all, my traveling stones were nothing more than the product of an active magnetic field and an overly active imagination!

(MARK TWAIN enters with a newspaper.)

MARK TWAIN: Don't go being so free with the secrets of the trade, Dan.

DAN: Why, Sam! Sam Clemens!

MARK TWAIN: Better call me by my "nom de plume," Dan ... I wouldn't want anybody knowing my true identity!

DAN: You're absolutely right, Mr. Twain ... Mark Twain.

MARK TWAIN (To audience): It was rough around here in those early years. Editors and reporters were prime bait for being beat, robbed, or strung up, if somebody didn't like what they wrote. So, we all adopted pen names. I got mine from my river boat days.

DAN: You never intended to be a reporter, did you, Mark?

MARK TWAIN: Shucks, no! I was a prospector like every other self-respecting bum out here! But, as luck would have it, I didn't have any luck! So I wrote an editorial lambasting a judge in these here parts. Joe Goodman liked what I had to say and hired me.

DAN: We learned reporting by doing!

MARK TWAIN: I recall my first day I got told to find some news. I roamed Virginia City from one end to another, but not a thing happened. A squirrel didn't even cross my path.

DAN: So, Joe told you to go out and make some news!

MARK TWAIN: He said go write about the arrival of the freight wagons from San Francisco. But only one broken down buggy arrived that day.

DAN: So, what'd you do?

MARK TWAIN: Did what any self-respecting *Enterprise* reporter would do. I wrote how sixteen wagons rolled into town laden with the treasures of an Arabian prince! I tell you, Dan ... I learned how to write fiction while working at the *Territorial Enterprise*!

(JOHN MACKAY enters.)

MACKAY: Say, feller ... I'll take a copy of that paper. (TWAIN **hands MACKAY the newspaper.**)

DAN: Don't I recognize you from the Kentuck Mine?

MACKAY: Mackay's the name. John Mackay. I work the mine, sure as you're standing there.

MARK TWAIN: A pity it isn't a going concern at present.

MACKAY: Well, now, sir ... they've been payin' us in shares in the mine, so I can't say we're going entirely without.

DAN: That's pretty risky.

MACKAY: Life's pretty risky, sir. Good day to you! (MACKAY **exits.**)

MARK TWAIN: Odd fellow. Doesn't seem to have the drive most of the men around here do ... or the fear.

DAN: Maybe he'll have some luck. Well, Eilley ... it's time we headed over to the hangin'.

MARK TWAIN: Evenin', Eilley! (DAN **and MARK TWAIN exit.**)

EILLEY (**Calling to them**): And try and get the facts straight this time, boys!

VOICE (From offstage): Fire!

ANOTHER VOICE (From offstage): Fire!

MINER ONE (Enters excited): Man the hoses! **(Runs off stage.)**

MINER TWO (Enters excited): I'll get the pumps! **(Runs off stage.)**

WOMAN ONE (Enters excited): Fire! Hurry! Man the buckets! **(Runs off stage.)**

EILLEY: Virginia City burned down three times during her exciting history. And no wonder! Buildings made of wood, tar paper, and canvas lighted by kerosene made a wonderful kindling ... and when those Washoe Zephyrs roared down the mountain, well, there was no stopping the flames ... no matter how much water we poured onto them. 'Course, each time the town burned up, it rose from the ashes like a phoenix ... bigger and more beautiful -- and I use the term loosely -- than before! You know ... flames caused a lot of problems and heartache ... but water caused even more!

(MINER ONE and MINER TWO enter with picks.)

MINER ONE: We've gone as deep as we can.

MINER TWO: You've struck water again?

MINER ONE: It's rushing through our last tunnel. The men just got out in time.

MINER TWO: Hard to believe, in a land so dry, there's so much water underground. So much we can't even get the silver and gold out!

MINER ONE: We've tried pumps!

MINER TWO: But even the new 120 horsepower steam pump they put in at the Ophir isn't powerful enough to do much good.

MINER ONE: You mean there's no way to get all that silver and gold out?

MINER TWO: We're just going to have to close up.

MINER ONE: But this could mean the end of Virginia City! The Comstock Lode might be bust!

(ADOLPH SUTRO enters holding a map.)

SUTRO: Now just a moment, gentlemen!

MINER TWO: Mr. Sutro ... you've got an idea?

SUTRO: But, of course! I'm not a genius for nothing! It stands to reason that we can drain the water out of the mountain and into the Carson River. That's due east of Virginia City and the Comstock Lode. This will allow us to dig 1,600 feet deeper into the mountain without having to pump!

MINER ONE: But, Mr. Sutro ... how do we drain the water out of a mountain?

SUTRO: Poke a hole in it ... just like a blister.

MINER TWO: How do you ... poke a hole in a mountain?

SUTRO (Proudly): You dig a tunnel, my boy! A tunnel!

MINER ONE: But it will have to be almost four miles long!

SUTRO: 20,145 feet to be exact!

MINER TWO: And it'll cost a fortune!

SUTRO: $4,500,000!

MINER ONE: It's ridiculous!

MINER TWO: It's foolhardy!

SUTRO: Are you with me?

MINER ONE: Why not?!

SUTRO: Now all we have to do is find somebody with $4,500,000!

(MINERS ONE and TWO exit with SUTRO.)

EILLEY: While Adolph Sutro, the engineer, tried to raise funds for his tunnel, Virginia City fell on hard times. You see, as the men worked, they pulled out what gold and silver was hidden in the mountain. And one by one the mines were played out ... that means they became empty.

SANDY (Entering, sadly): Even we found that out, didn't we, Eilley? Our mine lost its vein.

EILLEY: And you, you poor feller ... you had to dig and dig day and night to try and find enough gold or silver to keep us going.

SANDY: But a body can only work so long.

EILLEY: You got that cough ... and then one day ... well, Sandy Bowers ... you left me with a terrible mess!

SANDY: I'm right sorry for that, Eilley. I didn't think we'd ever spend *all* our money.

EILLEY: I made do. I always could. I guess I never really did run out of luck.

SANDY: How so?

EILLEY: You know our beautiful mansion out on Lake Washoe? The bankers decided nobody'd buy it, so they thought to raffle it off to pay our bills. Well, I took the last of my cash and bought a thousand tickets, and I won the place fair and square!

SANDY: Now, don't that beat all!

EILLEY: I turned the place into a resort and did right fine.

SANDY: I always knew you'd fare well, Eilley. And my, but didn't we have a fine time while it lasted! A fine time!

(SANDY exits as RALSTON and SHARON enter.)

EILLEY: I guess we all win some and lose some. But there are folks that believe you just gotta win all the time and not necessarily fair and square. They want to win no matter what!

RALSTON (Haughtily): I want control of the Comstock, Mr. Sharon.

SHARON: They say it's bust.

RALSTON: Nonsense! The biggest bonanza of all still lies somewhere in that mountain!

SHARON: You already own the Bank of California ...

RALSTON: But we're nothing without the Comstock. And there must be a way of grabbing up every claim we can!

SHARON (Slyly): Well, perhaps there *is* a way. You realize, now that it's 1864, nobody's got much money in Virginia City. Perhaps I could go and set up a branch of the bank in Virginia City, and then here's what I'll do -- **(SHARON whispers to RALSTON.)**

EILLEY: Meet Mr. William Chapman Ralston, a Californian who thought Comstock cash ought to build San Francisco into the Paris of the Pacific ... and his sly, conniving partner, William Sharon.

RALSTON: Perhaps, Mr. Sharon, your scheme might just work!

(RALSTON exists as SHARON sets up table with two chairs. MINER ONE enters nervously.)

MINER ONE: Mr. Sharon?

SHARON (Sitting down): Welcome to the new branch of the Bank of California. How can we help you? **(Indicates to MINER ONE to sit and he does.)**

MINER ONE: It's this bust that's going on ...

SHARON: Merely temporary, I'm sure.

MINER ONE: Our mine is operating, but we're not pulling out enough gold or silver to pay the men. Our geologists say we're about to strike a new bonanza, if we can just hang on a little longer.

SHARON: How much do you need to keep going?

MINER ONE: Why, Mr. Sharon, I came all ready to ...

SHARON: Beg? No ... the Bank of California is behind you and will see you through this crisis.

MINER ONE: Thank you, Mr. Sharon! It's good doing business with you!

(MINER ONE **signs a paper, shakes hands with** SHARON, **and then exits.**)

MINER TWO (**Entering**): Only five percent, Mr. Sharon? How can you loan money for that?

SHARON: This is the Bank of California. We can do as we please!

MINER TWO: Well, I thank you, and my men thank you! You've seen to it we can stay open until our next bonanza. Good day, sir.

(**They shake hands. MINER TWO exits.**)

EILLEY: Soon Sharon had almost every mining company working the Comstock in his debt. The next step of his plan was easy.

(MINER ONE **enters.** SHARON **moves to him.**)

SHARON: I'm certainly glad you stopped by, sir.

MINER ONE: Your message sounded urgent.

SHARON: I'm afraid you're behind in your payments.

MINER ONE: But, Mr. Sharon ... we've been paying what you required.

SHARON: The directors of the bank, however, have told me that we are going to have to extract a higher figure of repayment from you -- effective immediately!

MINER ONE: But, Mr. Sharon! We're paying everything we can!

SHARON: It's out of my hands. Either pay the bank what you owe, or we shall be forced to foreclose.

MINER ONE: We'll be ruined! We trusted you, Mr. Sharon! We trusted you with our fortunes!

SHARON: This is business, sir. I'm sorry.

(MINER ONE **exits while** SHARON **exits the opposite way.**)

EILLEY: It wasn't long before William Sharon had control of most of the mining in the area except for a chunk of the Kentuck Mine which was being bought up by a group of men who wouldn't give in to Sharon or Ralston.

(FLOOD, MACKAY, O'BRIEN, **and** FAIR **enter and group around the table on which they put a lantern.**)

FAIR: I say we sell out!

MACKAY: I know it's down there, Fair!

FAIR: But how much longer? It's hard holding onto nothing!

FLOOD: I say we listen to John here. He knows mining. He knows the Comstock.

FAIR: And what do you know? You two are nothing but lunch saloon owners from San Francisco.

MACKAY: Fair! Enough of this! We're partners.

FAIR (Thoughtfully): That we are.

O'BRIEN: We can trust John, here.

MACKAY: It's a waiting game. The Comstock's not played out yet. There's plenty for all of us if we're patient.

(The men exit.)

EILLEY (To audience): Soon John Mackay was the superintendent of the Kentuck Mine, but everyone still held his breath waiting for the big bonanza that everybody figured was down there somewhere. Slowly but surely, Mackay and Fair took over control from Ralston by buying stocks in Ralston's mines.)

(RALSTON and SHARON enter.)

SHARON: My information is that the Con Virginia and California Mines are virtually worthless. If we offer them for sale, we can make up for some of your recent losses, Mr. Ralston.

RALSTON: Then sell! Sell as quick as you can!

(RALSTON moves upstage as FLOOD and O'BRIEN enter.)

FLOOD: Stock in the Con Virginia? I'll take a thousand shares.

SHARON: I'm sure it will show promise, sir! (SHARON snickers.)

FLOOD: That's what I hear tell. Thank you, sir!

(FLOOD exits and O'BRIEN steps up to SHARON.)

SHARON: And how can I help you, sir?

O'BRIEN: I went to a fortune teller the other day, sir. She said to put two thousand dollars into the California Mine.

SHARON (Pleased): She did, eh? Well, I'm sure we can oblige her!

O'BRIEN (Handing SHARON money): Here you are!

SHARON: A pleasure doing business with you. (FLOOD **and O'BRIEN exit as SHARON moves up to RALSTON**) You see, Mr. Ralston, how stupid some of these people are? It almost makes me feel like I'm taking advantage of them! (**They laugh as they exit.**)

EILLEY (**To Audience**): But, in the late fall of 1873, Mackay and Fair invited Dan DeQuille down into a section of the Con Virginia Mine.

(**MACKAY and FAIR enter holding lanterns. DAN follows with FLOOD and O'BRIEN.**)

DAN: Can't imagine what you boys wanted to show me down here at the bottom of this mine shaft!

MACKAY: We figured you'd know best, Dan. Just have a look around!

(**MACKAY and FAIR hold up lanterns.**)

DAN (**Looking around, shocked**): Well, I'll be, boys! I'll be! This is it! This is the big one!

O'BRIEN: You ever seen so much silver?

DAN: That corridor ... it's what? A hundred and twenty --

MACKAY: Hundred and forty feet long.

FAIR: And solid silver!

DAN: And the ceiling ... it's eighteen --

MACKAY: Twenty feet high.

DAN: It's solid silver, too?

FLOOD (**Proudly**): Like my Aunt Margaret's teapot!

MACKAY: Assayed at $632 per ton!

DAN: You're the new kings, boys! The Bonanza Kings!

(**All the men exit.**)

EILLEY: Within two years, William Sharon had managed to get himself elected Senator from Nevada, then proceeded to destroy his old partner -- who lost everything when his bank failed. In August, 1875, the body of William Chapman Ralston, once the richest man in California, was found floating near Alcatraz Island. Meanwhile, the Bonanza Kings went on to make a fortune, as over a billion dollars worth of silver was pulled from their mines.

WOMAN ONE (**Entering**): That's the way it's always been, Eilley ... boom or bust.

WOMAN TWO (**Entering**): Champagne and caviar one day ...

WOMAN ONE: Beans and bacon the next.

EILLEY: Eventually modern mining methods stripped out every last silver and gold nugget from the Comstock Lode.

(PRESIDENT GRANT and ADOLPH SUTRO enter. The women clap.)

SUTRO (Proudly): Well, Mr. President, you have walked the entire length of the tunnel, and we can now consider it dedicated.

PRESIDENT GRANT: It is a remarkable structure, Mr. Sutro ... one you can be proud of, as indeed the entire state of Nevada can be proud! I am sure it will aid the future of mining in the area and will help the many mining companies find still untold riches beneath Mount Davidson.

(The women clap and follow GRANT and SUTRO off as they continue to examine the tunnel.)

EILLEY: That was in 1878. Even though the opening of the Sutro Tunnel was greeted with bands playing, champagne flowing, and parades -- a dark secret brewed within the mines ...

(MACKAY, O'BRIEN, FLOOD, and FAIR enter dejectedly and look around.)

FAIR: It's finished?

O'BRIEN: So soon?

FLOOD: We've used the best methods possible to strip it.

MACKAY: We knew it wouldn't last forever. The silver's gone, boys.

FAIR (Dreamily): It was great while it lasted.

O'BRIEN: For us? Sure!

FAIR: No, I mean for everybody.

MACKAY (Nodding): Who would have suspected one little dried-up hill next to nowhere would have attracted so many thousands and given so much to the world?

FAIR: It was the richest place on earth, wasn't it?

(The men back away during EILLEY'S last speech.)

EILLEY: That it was. The Comstock Lode was the greatest find of gold and silver in the history of the world. It built businesses, cities, ways of life, and created an important chapter in the history of America. But, like all things ... it passed quietly like an old man in his sleep. All that's left now are the ghosts ... still wandering the forgotten streets ... still looking for the next big bonanza!

(The lights dim.)

Historical Events

1851
First Farming at Genoa

1854
First Irrigation Ditch

1855
First Crop in Las Vegas Area

1860
Mormons Settled Muddy Valley

1863
First Alfalfa Grown in Nevada

1869
Livestock Could Be Shipped by Railroad

1870
Pedro Altube Began Ranching Using Basque Sheepherders

1874
Barbed Wire Patented by Joseph Glidden

1905
Newlands Irrigation Project Began Operation

1914
Lahontan Dam Completed

1915
Branding Law

1918
TCID Started

Chapter Five

Agriculture

Agriculture

In many ways, how the land was used tells the history of Nevada. From the summer in 1849 or '50, when some unknown rancher first planted a garden on the eastern slopes of the Sierra, to the last shipment of cattle last week from Elko, ranchers and farmers have grown crops and livestock to feed Nevada and the world. Through times of boom and bust in other industries, ranching and farming have always produced a living.

The growing of crops and the raising of livestock in Nevada depend on two things -- where the water is and where the people are. Nevada is the driest state in the nation. This means that ranchers and farmers can only grow crops and livestock in the unusual places where there is water.

Besides water, ranchers and farmers need to have people who will buy what they raise. In Nevada, agriculture developed wherever water was located -- close enough to people so that the ranchers had buyers for their products.

The first growing of food in Nevada was done by the Indians in the Colorado River Basin. The first of these Indian farmers were the prehistoric Anasazi Indians who lived there thousands of years ago. Later, the Southern Paiute Indians also grew crops along the rivers that drained into the Colorado River Basin.

When the first white settlers came to Nevada, the earliest ranching was done by cattlemen who were driving their cattle across Nevada into California for fattening. Some of them found such good grass on the eastern slopes of the Sierra Nevada that they decided to stay there, and they began ranching in Nevada.

Just a few years later, beginning in about 1850, the way station keepers along the emigrant trails started the next phase of agriculture in Nevada. They opened up their stations to sell equipment and supplies to travelers. At first, the food they sold was limited to bulk dry foods such as flour, salt and sugar. Some of these way stations were located where there was water. In these locations, the station operators also began to raise crops and livestock to meet the demand of the emigrants for fresh meat and produce.

Within a few more years, in the early 1850s, the Mormon settlers came to Nevada to establish colonies. They grew crops and livestock to feed their own communities. In some locations their settlements happened to be along the emigrant trails. In these places, the settlers also set up way stations to serve the needs of the California-bound travelers.

Then, in 1859, the mining boom began in Virginia City. The population of Nevada doubled in one year and multiplied nine times in the next 20 years. Wherever there was water, for raising crops and livestock, ranches were established to provide food for the miners.

Mining slowed down in 1880. But in the meantime, in 1869, the transcontinental railroad had come to Nevada. Now agriculture changed and expanded again because the railroads provided transportation. Using the railroads, it was possible for ranchers to ship their crops and livestock to markets outside the state. Nevada became a livestock producer for markets in other states.

How Water Was Used

From the very beginning of agriculture in Nevada, irrigation was developed at individual ranches. Farmers and ranchers used canals and diversion dams to draw water from the rivers. The final stage of agriculture came between 1902 and 1915, when federal funds financed the great irrigation projects on the Truckee and Carson rivers.

There is a great need for water because Nevada is the driest state in the nation. Nevada requires a dependable supply of water from rain, rivers and springs.

Average Annual Rainfall

CLIMATOLOGICAL DATA: Selected Stations,

1995-96

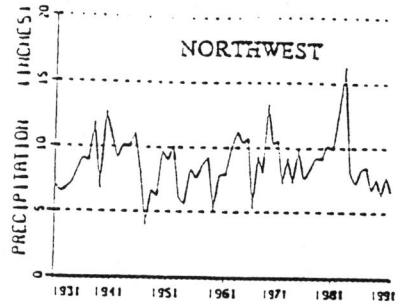

NORTHWEST

Northwest
Carson City   Lovelock
Fallon   McDermitt
Reno   Winnemucca
Yerington

	Annual Precipitation		
Station	1995	1996	Normal
	- - - - - - - Inches - - - - - - -		
Northwest			
Fallon	8.00	4.89	5.32
Lovelock	8.13	6.67	5.33
McDermitt	12.12	10.10	9.74
Reno	12.56	12.21	7.53
Winnemucca	9.82	10.70	8.23
Yerington	9.42	5.39	NA
Northeast			
Battle Mountain	10.05	12.20	8.23
Elko	11.46	15.24	9.93
Ely	12.10	7.31	NA
Mountain City	13.22	15.13	13.22
South Central			
Hawthorne	5.71	4.94	NA
Tonopah	6.75	3.93	5.69
Extreme South			
Las Vegas	3.69	2.76	4.13
Pahrump	9.24	2.24	4.76

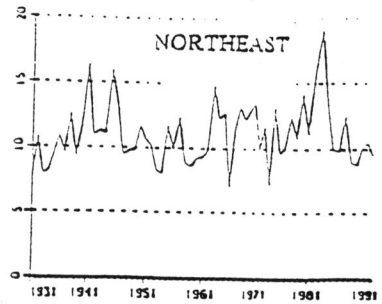

NORTHEAST

Northeast
Austin   Mountain City
Battle Mountain
Elko
Ely

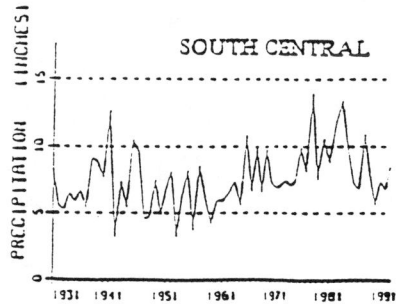

SOUTH CENTRAL

South Central
Hawthorne
Tonopah
Caliente

The Anasazi Indians learned how to use the water from the Virgin and Muddy rivers in southern Nevada to raise corn, beans, squash and cotton. The remains of ditches and canals that exist today show how they had developed an irrigation system. Because they could grow crops and store food, Anasazi Indians were able to develop their civilization. They built

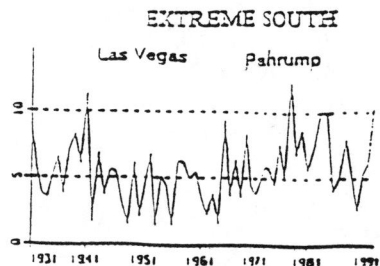

EXTREME SOUTH

Las Vegas   Pahrump

AGRICULTURE 181

adobe houses and villages, where they lived continuously in one area for several centuries.

The Anasazi Indians disappeared from southern Nevada and were replaced by the Southern Paiute Indians. The first white emigrants found that the Paiutes there were also using irrigation. They were able to make vegetables grow in the same fertile valleys where the Anasazis had lived. But the Paiute practice of agriculture was much less extensive than that of the Anasazis.

There is some evidence that the Northern Paiutes in the Mason Valley area also diverted water from the Walker River to increase the growth of their own native plants.

Earliest Agriculture of Settlers

The earliest use of agriculture by white settlers in Nevada was done by the ranchers. They were the first settlers who made homes in Nevada. The ranches of these first settlers were located at the edge of valleys where water flowed from the mountain ranges. In areas where there was sufficient water, farming and ranching replaced the natural vegetation.

Dugouts in Nevada. Very simple shelters characterized life for the earliest settlers in Nevada; but hard work, good weather, and high prices for ranch produce paid for good homes within a few years. This 1877 print is from *Frank Leslie's Illustrated Weekly* magazine.

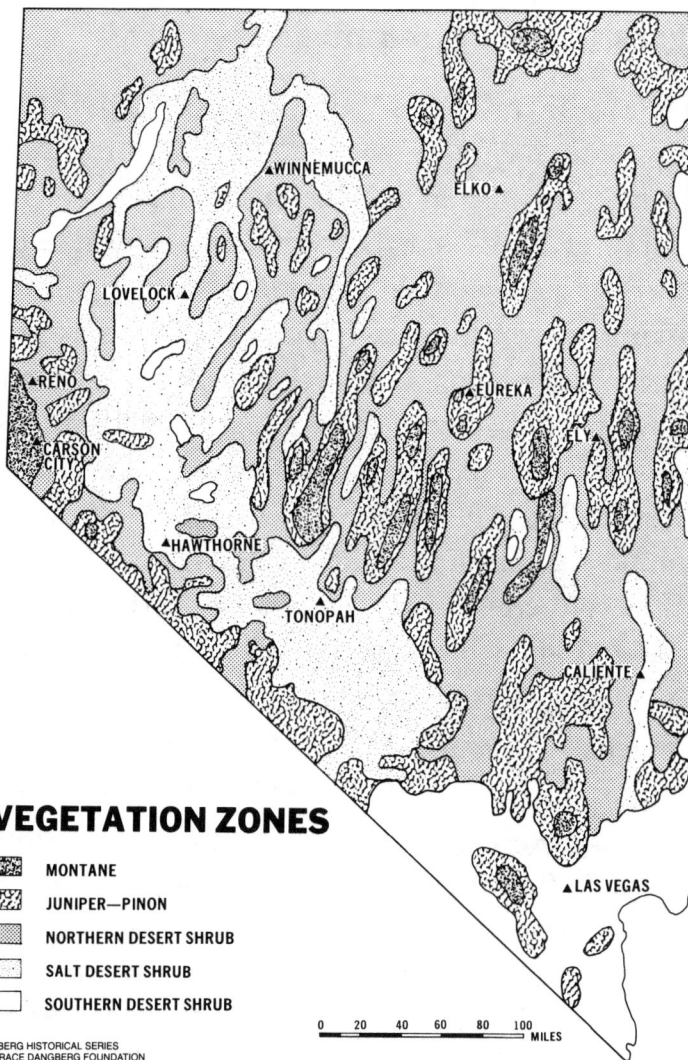

VEGETATION ZONES

- MONTANE
- JUNIPER—PINON
- NORTHERN DESERT SHRUB
- SALT DESERT SHRUB
- SOUTHERN DESERT SHRUB

DANGBERG HISTORICAL SERIES
THE GRACE DANGBERG FOUNDATION

0 20 40 60 80 100
MILES

Other ranchers settled at springs or meadows that provided water. The ranchers cut the native grasses from the meadows and along the river channels to make hay. They sold the hay to feed the livestock of the emigrant wagon trains. Some of the hay was also used to fatten cattle to provide meat for the emigrants or to be sold in California.

These livestock ranches were located where there was water -- water for their cattle and water for their homes. They all used water to irrigate vegetable gardens, berry patches, and fruit trees to provide food for themselves. This was the first real agriculture in Nevada.

First Ranch Communities

It was in Carson Valley in 1851, right after the first ranches were settled, that farming to grow crops really began in Nevada. John Reese, with his party of Salt Lake City traders, moved into the Carson Valley. They planted grain and vegetables using water diverted from nearby streams to irrigate the land. At his settlement (where Genoa is now located), Reese built a log cabin that was the first permanent building in Nevada. The settlement was called Mormon Station. The Reese party found the soil in the Carson Valley very fertile, and they sold crops to the emigrants in the summer of 1851. This is how Reese described his first year:

I had some 17 men with me and all in my employ. A good many of them worked with me for quite a while, in chopping timber and building log houses. &c. I paid them about $75.00 a month, and they worked well. We got pine there that made good shingles. That year I fenced a field of some 30 acres and plowed it up ready for the next year. I put in Wheat, Barley, Corn and Water Melons in one side, and mixed things all round.

Reese's example was quickly copied. By the end of 1851, more than 100 other farmers had settled on the land around Mormon Station. A somewhat different use of Carson Valley was made by Captain H.S. Parker, a wagon master. He wintered his stock, including milk cows, in the valley. A band of sheep also was driven from California into Carson Valley in 1851. In 1852, Reese cultivated 35 acres of vegetables and opened up 1,000 acres for growing wheat. Settlers also took up land in adjacent Eagle and Washoe Valleys. This was at the same time that the placer miners were working the ore deposits in nearby Gold Canyon. They provided a market for produce grown on the new farms.

Emigrant parties, who were crossing Nevada in great numbers, bought the rest of the crops and livestock.

Then, in 1855, the Church of Jesus Christ of Latter Day Saints (the Mormon Church) sent Probate Judge Orson Hyde to Carson Valley. Judge Hyde was ordered to create a large settlement and establish a local government. Sixty or seventy Mormon families came into the valleys in 1855 and 1856. Judge Hyde renamed the settlement Genoa. The *Stockton Argus* reported, in August of 1856, that, "Two hundred Mormon families have settled in the Carson Valley, and about 350 in the Washoe Valley the present year."

Unfortunately, this highly successful Mormon colony was short lived. It only lasted for two years. A conflict developed between the Church of Jesus Christ of the Latter Day Saints and the United States government. The Mormon governor of Utah Territory (and head of the church), Brigham Young, was afraid that the United States government would take action against his Utah government. He called the Mormon colonists home to Salt Lake City. On September 22, 1857, a train of 130 wagons left Carson Valley carrying the Mormon settlers back to Salt Lake City.

Brigham Young of Vermont (1801-1877). Prophet and revelator of the Church of Jesus Christ of Latter Day Saints, Young led the Mormon people westward to Utah across the mountains and prairies in 1846-47. The first governor of Utah Territory, Young sent exploring and colonizing missions to southern, eastern, and western Nevada, hastening settlement of these remote regions. This photograph was taken in 1853.
Courtesy of Nevada Historical Society

In Las Vegas Valley

In 1855, at about the same time that the Mormon Church sent Orson Hyde to colonize the Carson Valley, the church also sent out a party of 30 men to settle the Las Vegas Valley. Under the leadership of William Bringhurst, the settlers grew melons, corn, potatoes, vegetables, and cotton. Another 29 men and their families came the next year. They encountered endless problems.

William Bringhurst. President of the LDS mission to Las Vegas, Bringhurst was responsible for setting up a ranching community there in 1855-1858. The town's first post office bore his name.
Courtesy of Nevada Historical Society

Emigrant cattle broke into their fields and ate some of the corn. Then the corn crop was damaged by frost. Indians stole their vegetables. There was conflict over manpower between the Las Vegas settlement and a Mormon lead-mining project at Potosi Mountain. Both projects were sponsored by the church. The Las Vegas colony never really became self-sufficient, and the colonists were released from their mission in 1857. They were permitted to return to Salt Lake City at the same time that the northern colonists were recalled from the Carson Valley. A few tried to remain but, finally, they all abandoned the Las Vegas project.

Other Northern Valleys

At the same time, back in northern Nevada, other valleys near Carson Valley began to be settled. H.N.A. Mason, a California cattleman, had seen the grass-rich Nevada valleys. In 1859, he drove his cattle from California into Nevada and began ranching in the valley that is now Mason Valley. In the very early 1850s, Fred Dangberg, who settled about five miles east of Genoa, began a farming and ranching operation that eventually grew to more than 50,000 acres. In 1859, two cattle ranchers named Smith, R.B. Smith and T.B. Smith, drove their herds into the area west of Mason Valley and decided to stay.

This is how Timothy Smith described the valley which is now named Smith Valley, after them:

The grass on Walker River when we reached our destination was a fine sight. In the meadows it was standing practically undisturbed except where the Indians had made trails through it on the way to the river. The spot chosen for the camp was on the edge of a fine large meadow ....

Residence and Dairy Ranch of T.B. Smith, Smith Valley, 1881.

Corrals for the stock were constructed and a house was erected. As there was no sawmill within forty miles of the valley, the only building material for the house was tules. This house served very well for the first winter, and, there being very little we could do with the cattle, we spent most of our time within its walls.

That same year, in June of 1859, everything in Nevada changed almost overnight. The famous Comstock Lode of silver was discovered at Gold Hill and Virginia City. By the end of the year, thousands of miners and adventurers had come to Nevada. Virginia City became the largest city in the West, even larger than San Francisco.

Suddenly, there was an unlimited demand for all the crops and livestock that could be grown in Nevada. All the ranchers and farmers in the valleys along the Truckee, Carson and Walker rivers prospered as never before. Paradise Valley, north of Winnemucca along the Little Humboldt River, was settled. By 1864 they had irrigated fields of barley, corn, potatoes and garden vegetables, along with the growing of hay and wheat. Another major beginning of agriculture occurred at Big Meadows, where Lovelock is now located. There, water was taken from the Humboldt River for irrigation.

During these years, many of the ranchers continued to do a lively business at way stations serving the passing emigrants and teamsters. The travelers were looking for places to graze their livestock and spend the night -- something like an agricultural gas station and motel operation. Andrew J. Newman, who was just a boy when his parents set up a way station on the Carson River below Dayton during the 1860s and 1870s, recalled:

> *Most of them in those days had their own blankets; we accommodated them with beds. It was a story and a half high house, and we had a large upstairs there with single beds; then the balance of the house was used for the families to live in; and there was a great deal of our customers that had their beds with them, and slept in the wagons, and outside and teamsters, you know.*

Right at this same time, ranchers in Nevada and other western states benefitted from the policies of the U.S. Congress. In 1862, the famous Homestead Act became law. It allowed persons who settled up to 160 acres of surveyed public land to buy it for a very low price. All they had to do to qualify was to build a house on the land.

Agriculture in Southern Nevada

After the disappointments of the early 1850s, the Mormon Church decided to try again to colonize southern Nevada. In the early 1860s, the church established a seaport at Callville on the Colorado River and a farming colony in Muddy Valley. The plan was to grow cotton there and ship it to San Francisco, to provide cash income for the church. About 5,000 pounds of cotton were produced in 1865. Some food crops were also grown and sold to the mining camps at Meadow Valley and El Dorado Canyon. Intensely hot weather and small profit on the crops made extreme hardships.

Then a new problem occurred. This region was transferred in 1866 from the Arizona and Utah territories to the new Nevada Territory. Nevada tried to collect taxes where previous taxes had already been paid to the other territories. The colonists refused to pay taxes a second time. Finally, Nevada sued for the back taxes in 1870. The colonists were released from their obligations to the church. Some 600 Mormons left Muddy Valley in 1871, leaving behind 150 homes, 500 acres of cleared land, 8,000 acres of wheat ready to harvest and an irrigation system valued at $100,000.

Another Mormon settlement started in Meadow Valley in southeastern Nevada in 1864. Finally, this one became permanent. The town of Panaca was established with homes, public buildings, and a school. Fields were laid out with irrigation systems. Vegetables, fruit, nuts, meat, and forage crops were grown and sold to nearby mining communities. There were hardships in Meadow Valley, but the success of the settlers prevailed. Today Panaca is the oldest Mormon community in Nevada.

In 1877, another agricultural community was established on the south bank of the Virgin River. It was about thirty miles northeast of the former Muddy Valley colony. Mormon Bishop Edward Bunker settled there with his family, relatives, and a few friends. They built a dam and a canal to provide irrigation. Grapevines, vegetables, cotton, and sorghum were grown. A flash flood washed out the dam in August, but it was rebuilt in time to save the crops. Agriculture flourished in the valley. Now Bunkerville is the oldest permanent community in Clark County. Success brought other families. Some of them resettled the Muddy Valley. Other settlers established the towns of Overton, St. Joseph, Mesquite, and also St. Thomas, which later was covered by the waters of Lake Mead.

Irrigation

When the number of emigrants crossing Nevada increased, so did the demand for hay. The wild grass that ranchers cut from along the river bottoms wasn't enough. The emigrants were willing to pay large sums of money for more hay. Nevada ranchers met this demand by using irrigation. This allowed them to grow grass over larger areas. The first step in irrigation was to build ditches and divert the water to low-lying ground that had fertile soil.

The pioneer irrigating ditch in western Nevada was built by ranchers on the Carson River in 1854. It was described by Benjamin Palmer, Nevada's first black settler. Palmer came into the Carson Valley in 1853 and owned his own ranch there for more than forty years. In 1894, Palmer told about this ditch while testifying in a water rights case in court. He described the ditch as "a cut four feet wide and 16 or 18 feet long, to let the water out from the river into an old slough."

High prices for hay and garden crops encouraged ranchers to dig many more ditches in the Carson, Humboldt, Truckee, and Walker River valleys. Between 1860 and 1880, ranchers built large private irrigation systems that carried water to thousands of acres of land. Ranchers paid for them with the money they made from selling hay or cattle.

Ben Palmer's Barn. *Built near Sheridan in 1868, this barn still stands in Carson Valley. Palmer, who was Nevada's first black settler, began farming there in 1853. He was a leader in the first group of ranchers who built a ditch to take water from the Carson River for irrigation.*
Courtesy of Carson Valley Historical Society

Desolate Farm. *This scene shows the bone-dry soil of farm land in Nevada. The irrigation ditch in the foreground carried water to make the land produce, as shown by the haystack, corral, and good house belonging to the hardy couple, apparently at work in their garden.* Courtesy of Special Collections, University of Nevada Reno Library

A number of these ditches are still in use today, after more than a hundred years.

The irrigation ditches were a novelty. They were a change from the old way of doing things. But they worked so well and were so profitable that they soon became an accepted way of ranching. Sometimes, when the rivers were low, the ditches would not divert enough water into the fields. Ranchers solved this problem by building diversion dams made from dirt and brush. The dams backed the water into the ditches and forced the water out onto their fields. These dams also made it possible to cultivate even more acreage. But the new cropland had to be cleared and broken first. The ranchers hired local Indians and others to grub up the sagebrush to make the land fit to grow hay. This allowed ranchers to harvest a bigger crop than ever before.

New Crops

In 1863, two Washoe County ranchers, Peleg Brown and Ervin Crane, began growing alfalfa rather than the natural wild grasses of the region.

ERVIN CRANE

The Crane Ranch. *Ervin Crane, a native of Vermont and Nevada pioneer, was the first to grow alfalfa in Nevada on his farm in Washoe County. This agricultural innovation was a great benefit to the livestock business because it allowed ranchers to harvest several cuttings of hay each season, instead of the single crop of wild hay that they used to reap. Crane has also been given credit for being the first person in Nevada to successfully grow shade trees on sagebrush land.* From Angel's *History of Nevada*

They were the first to raise alfalfa in Nevada. Alfalfa soon became a very important crop. It was the most important source of food for livestock in the state.

The amount of hay grown by ranchers increased so much that it became impossible to harvest it with the old hand-held scythes. They were replaced first by horse-drawn mowing machines and then by steam-powered machinery. Later, in the twentieth century, gasoline-powered tractors came into use. By using irrigation and mechanical harvesters, and by planting alfalfa, the ranchers could raise much more hay. They could get as much as three cuttings, or harvests, each year, instead of just one crop of wild grass.

The ranchers who made the most money were the ones closest to the market. They could haul their products over good roads to the mining camps.

Steam-powered Threshing Machine. *This threshing machine, owned by the Dangberg Brockliss Company, is at work in the Carson Valley during 1906. The grain was cut by a mower, then hauled to the machine and stacked. Men pitched the loose material into the threshing machine which beat the grain out. Grain flowed out of a funnel, where it was sacked as it came out. This was a primitive way of threshing, which required a lot of manpower.*
Courtesy of Special Collections, University of Nevada Reno Library

Combines Replaced Threshing Machines. *This was one of the first combines. It cut and threshed the grain as it traveled through the field. The combine was pulled through the standing grain by an early farm tractor that ran on tracks instead of wheels. The man standing under the shade sacked the grain as it came out. He put the sacks on the chute in the foreground. The sacks fell from the chute into the field to be picked up from the ground.*
Courtesy of Nevada Historical Society

The prosperous mining camps needed fresh fruits and vegetables; otherwise, the townsfolk had to pay high prices to buy canned produce hauled in from California or Utah. Nevada ranchers were able to get good prices for grain, potatoes, onions and other garden vegetables, as well as for milk and butter. The ranchers either drove their crops to market themselves or sold them to businessmen for shipment by railroad.

Floods, Storms and Rainfall

Water, so necessary for agriculture in Nevada, sometimes caused terrible disasters, not only for ranchers and farmers, but also for cities, mines and industries. Floods, such as the one that washed out the first dam at Bunkerville, are a common occurrence in Nevada. Flash floods have wiped out whole towns. Floods on the Carson River have cut new channels several times in the past 140 years. In recent times, Las Vegas and Reno have suffered costly floods. They have caused great property damage and suffering. Storage dams built on the Truckee River have reduced the flood danger considerably in Reno.

The winter moisture that comes as snow sometimes caused great hardship to all of Northern Nevada. A winter storm trapped the Donner party in the Sierras in 1846. A heavy snow in November of 1861 brought snow five or six feet deep to Virginia City. The snowmelt caused such a flood on the Carson River that it washed out quartz mills belonging to William Stewart that were valued at $500,000. Extreme floods are especially destructive to farming and to ranching. Farmland is damaged and animals drown.

Nevada's most severe winter followed two years of drought. It was called "The White Winter of Death" and occurred in 1889-90. It killed an estimated 134,000 cattle and 120,000 sheep in northern Nevada.

The Carson River Flood in 1997. *This picture shows the flood of 1997 in approximately the same vicinity on the Carson River as that shown below, ninety years earlier, in the flood of 1907.*
Courtesy of Marilyn Newton

The Carson River Flood in 1907. *A cameraman stood on floating debris to get a picture. These two floods did great damage to the rich farm lands along the Carson River. They are both called "Hundred Year Floods". Such extreme floods generally occur only about every hundred years.*
Courtesy of Nevada Historical Society Davis Collection

Despite the floods and storms, the benefits from rainfall in the last half of the 1880s were the greatest in the history of Nevada agriculture. During a seventy-year period from 1847 to 1917, there were 19 floods. Grass for livestock feed grew rich on Nevada's rangelands and in its meadows. This rainfall was of great benefit to the livestock industry, especially in the very prosperous period just before the great drought and snowstorm of 1888-1891. In those years, Nevada livestock men ran an estimated 800,000 cattle and more than a million head of sheep.

The Livestock Industry

The mainstay of agriculture in Nevada has always been the raising of livestock, especially cattle and sheep. At first, the chief market for Nevada cattle was in the mining camps of California, but the discovery of gold and silver in Nevada changed that.

The grazing industry developed very rapidly as settlers moved into Nevada and started ranching. Nearly every productive valley in the state was occupied within 20 years after John Reese first came to Genoa in 1851. The ranchers fattened their cattle on the lush, thick grasslands of the Carson, Humboldt, Truckee and Walker River valleys. The fattened cattle were driven to the slaughterhouses in the mining camps to feed the hungry miners. The milk, cheese, cream, butter and other foodstuffs from the ranches increased in the valleys nearest the mines, resulting in small ranching communities all across western Nevada. Ore discoveries in eastern Nevada brought the same results in the valleys.

Most of Nevada's ranching output reached the market as beef. Looking closer to the current time, the 1994 cash income from cattle was 54.8% of all agricultural activity. By 1996, the cash income had dropped to 28.3%.

By 1873 all the suitable grazing land in Nevada was occupied, and it produced a major part of California's meat supply.

When the Nevada mining towns went into decline in the late 1870s, the livestock industry had other markets. By 1880, Nevada ranchers enjoyed a valuable combination of conditions. They had nearly free food for their animals on the open ranges. They had control of the state's water resources. They had access to a national railroad system to haul their livestock to market, and the markets for their livestock were growing in California and the Middle West. By the early 1880s, Nevada's livestock growers were shipping their animals by rail to Omaha and San Francisco. Freight rates were high, but the ranchers could still make a profit because they had almost free feed for their herds on the Nevada rangelands.

"Shipping Cattle on Board a Train From a Corral at Halleck," 1877. *Frank Leslie's Illustrated Weekly's* artist sketched this scene of seeming pandemonium at the loading pens of the Central Pacific Railroad Company's freight station at Halleck, west of Wells, while drovers loaded the train's cattle cars with beef.

Inventory of Cattle and Calves, 1900-1993

THOUSAND HEAD

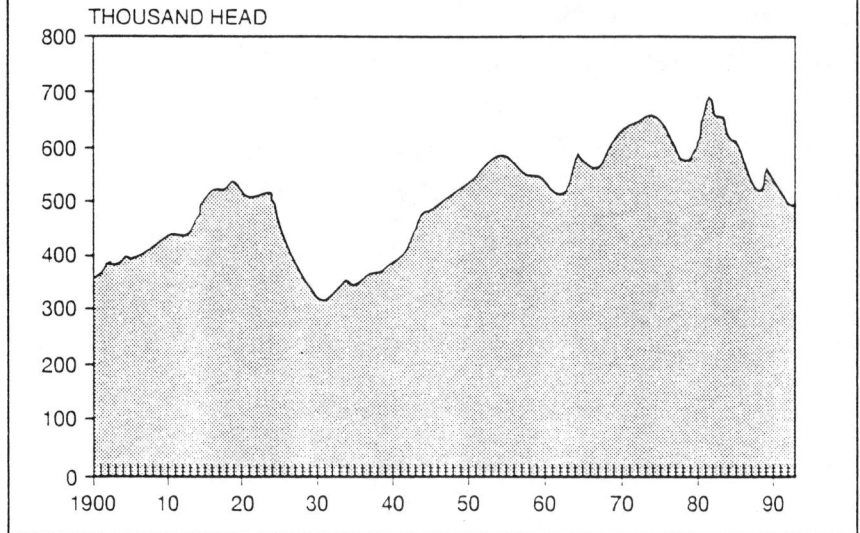

Courtesy of Nevada Agricultural Statistics Service

CATTLE AND CALVES:

Inventory, Supply

Nevada, 1987-97

Year	Cattle Jan. 1	All Calves Born	Inshipments
1987	580	235	10
1988	530	235	10
1989	520	245	20
1990	530	245	40
1991	520	250	30
1992	520	240	25
1993	500	225	35
1994	490	220	47
1995	500	220	39
1996	500	220	47
1997	520	.1	.1

/1 Data has not been released.

The transcontinental railroad and its branch lines caused some changes in the ranching business. Livestock could be transported rapidly by rail across great distances at relatively low cost. This made ranching profitable in valleys that formerly were too far from any market. The livestock could then be driven to the closest freight depot. From there, they could be shipped to distant cities such as Chicago or San Francisco.

In northeastern Nevada, the ranching business began to flourish after California had a prolonged drought. In 1871, the dry conditions in California forced cattlemen to look to other places for rangeland. Many of them moved to the valleys of Elko and Humboldt counties.

The most successful cattle ranches were large operations. By 1880, three quarters of the cattle ranging north of the Humboldt River were owned by perhaps only a dozen stockmen. The owners of these large cattle operations were called cattle kings or cattle barons. They had large ranches, but they owned only a fraction of the land where their cattle grazed. Much of the grassland was open public land owned by the government.

Cattle ranching is an exciting way of life. Activities on a ranch are repeated in the same pattern each year with the passing seasons. Ranch life was different in the nineteenth and early twentieth centuries, before the Bureau of Land Management began to supervise the ranges. Ira H. Kent, a Churchill County rancher, described the early system when he testified in a court case:

In the summer they took these cattle out in the various pastures that were available near the water, and in the winter they fed them hay. In the fall they brought the cattle back on the grass land that had been mowed for hay, and then when the snow or storms came on and the weather got cold, they fed the hay to the stock cattle.

In order to keep their own cattle from straying, and to keep stray cattle out of their own fields, ranchers fenced their property. Until barbed wire was patented by Joseph Glidden in 1874, ranchers used whatever materials were handy to build their fences, such as rocks, logs, planks, and smooth wire.

"Settlers Building a Corral Near Wells." This drawing from *Frank Leslie's Illustrated Weekly* magazine shows some of the early fencework in the days before barbed wire became available. The Elko County rangeland proved ideal for ranching, and the transcontinental railroad connections at Wells and elsewhere made shipping live or butchered beef and mutton a simple matter.

William Bailey of Churchill County used cables out of the Virginia City mines. The ranchers fenced their own fields, and some even fenced federal lands. But the government put a stop to fencing public land. Today, most ranchers lease grazing land from the federal government.

In the springtime, the first work on a cattle ranch was the roundup, or rodeo. Stockmen rode out all over the deserts and brushlands looking for the cattle they had turned out to feed the winter before. Where there were several cattle ranches in the same vicinity, ranchers would generally cooperate to have one big roundup. The cows belonging to various ranchers could be sorted out by brand. Then the new calves, belonging to those cows, were branded by their owners. Today, cattle must be branded, and the brands are recorded. The law requiring branding was passed by the State Legislature in 1915. In the early days, some cattle were branded or were given earmarks by having their ears clipped. When there was a lot of cattle around, it was wise to brand those you owned so they wouldn't become part of someone else's herd. Elizabeth Magee Murphy described how her father started to brand cattle in Churchill County in 1868 for just that reason:

> It was the year that Mr. Bailey got possession of the Big Dobe and the Big Island, and brought his cattle down there by the thousands, and everybody that had from ten to a hundred head gathered their cattle and branded them, because the big cattleman was entitled to all the unbranded cattle when the roundup came, and everybody branded cattle, and my father got a branding iron and branded our cattle; it was an iron with a ring around it; and we were very angry, because we didn't want to see the cattle branded. I believe there was a law of

the range, when the rodeo was over, all the unbranded cattle went to the cattleman that had the rodeo. So all the men branded their cattle.

There had been brands on some of the first cattle to enter Nevada. But the first brand wasn't recorded in the state until 1871. That year, E. Burner of Elko County registered his mark. Livestock brands have a very interesting history and figure prominently in the stories about cattle rustlers, how ranches got started, and in the personal stories about the ranchers themselves.

After the roundup and branding, some of the cattle would be driven to market. A true story at the end of this chapter, about a teen-age buckaroo named John H. Sheehan, tells a lot about cattle ranching in Nevada at this time.

Cattle Branding. *As the long shadows show, the day is almost over for this tired crew of buckaroos, while spare branding irons smolder in the fire.*
Courtesy of Special Collections, University of Nevada Reno Library

The First Cattle

The first tame cattle entered Nevada with the Bidwell-Bartleson party in 1841. Other emigrants brought cattle with them; and many head were lost, stolen, or strayed as they traveled across Nevada. Cattle rustling in the state dates from this period. Some white men conspired with Indians to attack the overland travelers and steal their cattle. Cattle rustling was a chronic problem throughout the late nineteenth century.

The first cattle driven into Nevada were longhorns. In the early days, purebred cattle were unknown. The first imported stock came into the state in the 1870s. Shorthorns were introduced in 1874, Durhams soon afterward, and Herefords in 1878. The hard winter of 1889-90 killed off many of the old longhorn cattle. The ranchers replaced them with better stock. The new breeds made up the basis for almost all of Nevada's herds of cattle today. The state's ranches are well known as the producers of fancy stock. Cattle ranching has never been an easy way to make money. It has frequently faced harsh winters, long dry spells, and poor market conditions. Cattle have had to share the range with wild horses. But cattle ranching has survived, and Nevada is still one of the West's major cattle ranching states.

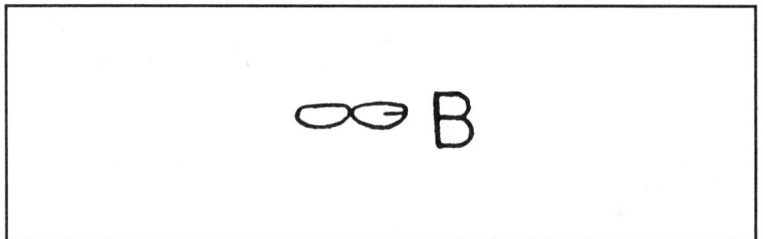

Nevada's First Official Earmark and Brand, 1871.

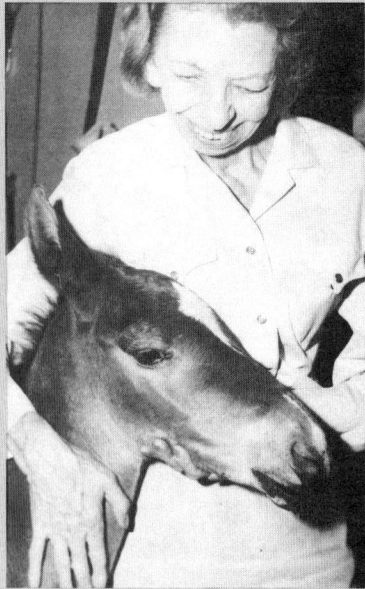

WILD HORSE ANNIE

Wild Horse Annie, whose real name was Velma Johnson, spent her whole life helping and protecting wild horses. When she was very young, she was shocked at the brutal way some wild horses were rounded up and sold for pet food. She tried to get laws passed to protect the horses. Some people laughed at her because she wanted to help the horses. They nick-named her "Wild Horse Annie." She liked the colorful nickname and used it to get school children to write to congressmen asking for their support to protect the horses. As a result, the Free-roaming Wild Horse and Burro Act was passed by Congress and became law in 1971. Since then wild horses have multiplied. Now they compete with livestock for rangeland grass. The Bureau of Land Management rounds up the excess horses, and they are put out for adoption. Wild Horse Annie was a living example of how much one completely dedicated person can accomplish.

Courtesy of Reno Gazette Journal

Earmarks. *Cutting the ears of cattle is another way of marking the stock, and these earmarks must be recorded along with the brand. In Nevada, over 30 different types of earmarks have been recorded.*

R L
crop
upperbit of peak
underbit
round underbit, half-noose
swallowfork
slit
uppercut
undercut
overslope
underslope
upper half crop
under half crop
fingermark, fingerprint
slit and downfall
sawtooth, or saw
"M" punch
punch (a hole through the ear)
"L" slit
kitchen slit
cloverleaf, swallowtail or fantail
figure seven
lop
double figure seven, paddle
earrings
stovepipe
reef or hatchet
keyhole
jingle or jinglebob
square swallowfork
shoestring
pennant
stair or step

changed to
changed to
changed to
changed to
changed to
changed to

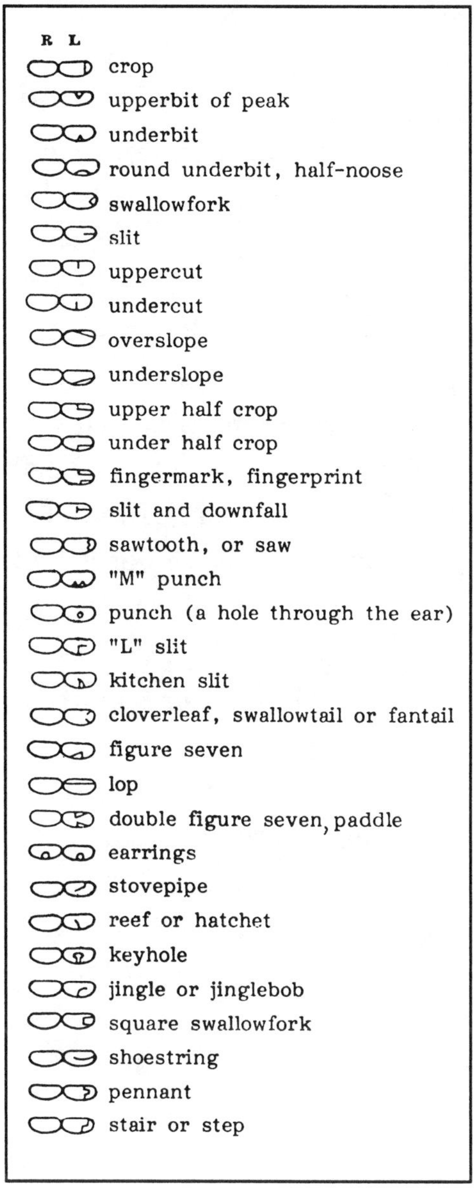

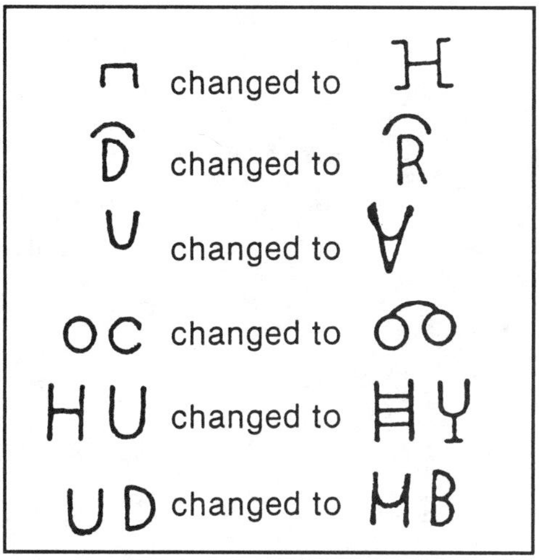

Altered Brands. *Cattle rustlers could skillfully alter a brand. Skinning the animal was sometimes the only way to prove a changed brand. When the inside of a hide is revealed, the old brand can be traced on the underside, the new one cannot. Here are some examples of rustlers' work, adapted from Velma Truett's* *<u>On the Hoof in Nevada</u>*.

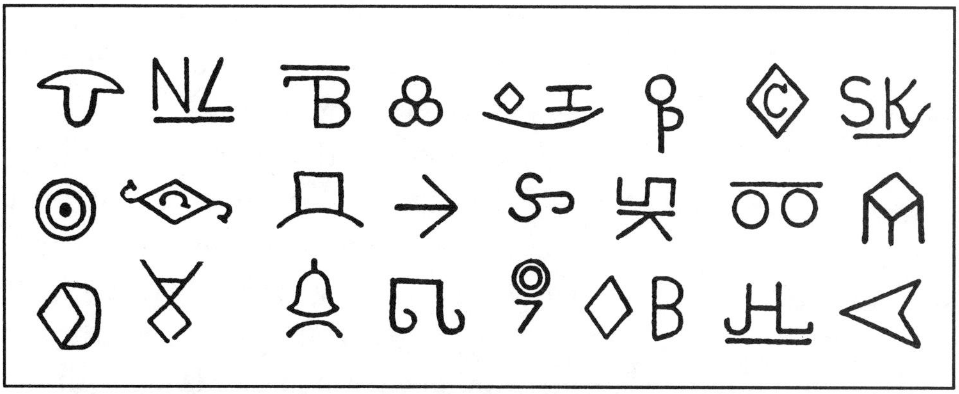

Nevada Brands. *A variety of brands from our state show the imagination and romance of stock-raising in the Silver State. Most of these brands have interesting stories behind them, too.*

Sheep

Raising sheep is the other main kind of ranching in Nevada. Other than wild mountain goats, the first sheep to enter Nevada came with the Workmen-Rowland emigrant party. They left New Mexico in 1841 on an overland trip to California. The emigrants carried 150 sheep with them to southern California by way of the Spanish Trail. The first commercial sheep drive took place eleven years later, in 1852. Richens Lacy "Uncle Dick" Wootton brought 9,000 head over the Humboldt section of the California Trail. Wootton described the reasons for the drive in his autobiography:

In New Mexico, where the Mexicans had large flocks, fine sheep could be bought for one tenth the price per head they were reported to be selling for in California and it looked to me as though a handsome fortune might be realized as profit on a large band of sheep driven through and disposed of at Sacramento or some other point on the coast. Up to that time nothing of the kind had been attempted, but I thought the scheme a practicable one and determined to try it.

Wootton's drive was a commercial success and was followed in 1853 by another successful drive led by Kit Carson. H.T.P. Comstock, for whom the Comstock Lode was named, also made a sheep drive into Nevada in 1856, but not with the same success as Wootton or Carson.

Sheep, like cattle, were shipped outside of Nevada to markets reached by the railroads. Some ranchers were opposed to sheep in Nevada. They thought the sheep competed with cattle for the range grass. By the late nineteenth century, however, ranchers often operated herds of both cattle and sheep.

"Uncle Dick" (Richens Lacy) Wootton, 1816-1893. Wootton was a fur trapper, Indian fighter, and pioneer who drove nine thousand sheep overland to California in 1852. He returned with a herd of mules, which he sold for $40,000 profit, and became a legend in his own time.
From Conrad's *Uncle Dick Wootton*

Sheep ranchers eventually gained an advantage over cattle ranchers. Prices for mutton remained relatively stable. By contrast, beef prices went up and down and the profit was uncertain. Sheep provided an additional and valuable source of income from wool. Unlike the production of leather hides, wool did not require killing the animal. The sheep were also better adapted to the extremes of climate.

Tramp sheepmen became a problem to the industry. They were men who owned no land and grazed their sheep on other people's property. The State Legislature solved this problem in 1895 by passing a special tax. It was levied on sheep but had an exemption for ranchers who owned land on which the sheep could be grazed. The tax was successful in driving the tramp sheepmen from the state.

SHEEP AND LAMBS:

Inventory, Supply

1987-97

Year	Sheep & Lambs Jan. 1 [1]	Lamb Crop	Inship- ments
	-- Thousand Head --		
1987	36	80	18
1988	96	74	4
1989	87	84	12
1990	101	80	13
1991	98	65	12
1992	35	62	29
1993	91	63	24
1994	91	62	24
1995	103	65	24
1996	87	54	24
1997	85	[2]	[2]

[1] Includes new crop lambs beginning in 1996.
[2] Data has not been released.

Courtesy of Nevada Agricultural Statistics Service

Inventory of Sheep and Lambs, 1900-1993

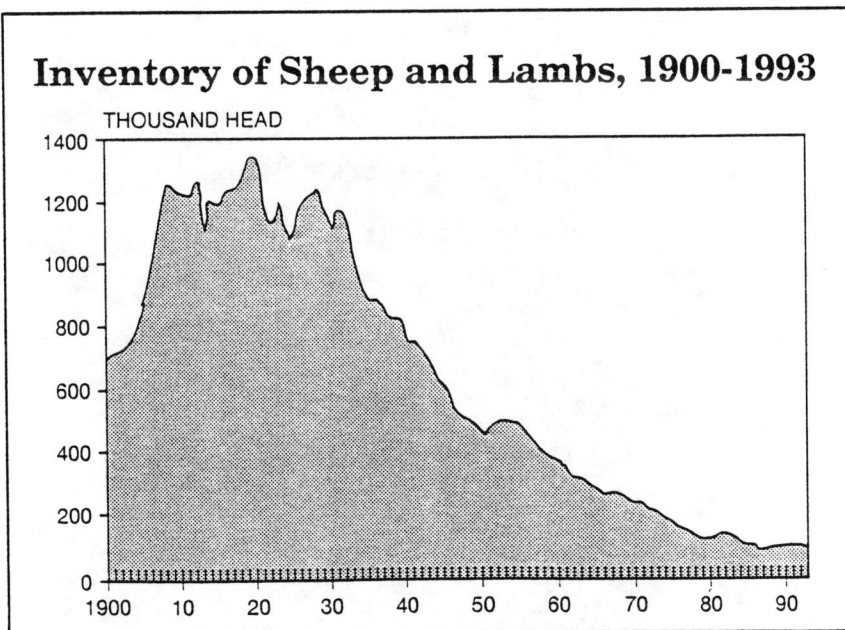

THOUSAND HEAD

The Basques

Pedro Altube, a six-foot, eight-inch tall Basque rancher, gave many of his fellow countrymen a start in Nevada. In 1870, the forty-three-year-old Altube began ranching in Elko County, where he operated herds of sheep and cattle. He employed Basque sheepherders who received their pay in livestock. Within four or five years, a good sheepherder could acquire his own band of sheep and go into business for himself. Many sheep ranchers in Oregon, Idaho, and Nevada got their start through Altube's activities. As a result, Altube gained the reputation of being the "Father of Basques in America."

A Basque Sheepherder and His Ever-vigilant Dogs. The nomadic ranchmen led lonely lives wandering the hills and valleys in search of grass for their flocks. Sheepherding first challenged the cattle ranchers in the 1870s and then surpassed them after 1890 as Nevada's principal livestock industry.
Courtesy of Special Collections, University of Nevada Reno Library

Today, the livestock industry provides just over one quarter of Nevada's agricultural income. Ranching now is much different than it was in the early days when the federal lands were open to settlement and use. The public lands have been administered by the federal government since 1934. When the Taylor Grazing Act was passed setting up the Grazing Service. The name of the agency was changed to the Bureau of Land Management in 1946. An Act of 1964 established a policy of multiple use of the public land. Most of Nevada's ranchers need the public rangeland to graze their livestock. They pay the federal government a fee to use the land from year to year.

Hard Times After 1880

After the mines closed down in the late 1870s, Nevada had a long depression. The state had almost no income except from the livestock industry. Ranchers continued to be successful most of the time because they could ship their animals to markets out of state in California and the Midwest.

However, there weren't many jobs on ranches. Without the mines, there was almost no place for men to find work. Thousands of people moved out of Nevada. Between 1880 and 1900, the population of the state dropped from 62,266 to 42,335.

With mining almost out of business, people turned to the land to make a living. If Nevada could just get more water on the land, the people would grow more crops and raise more animals. An effort was made to develop artesian wells, but the wells never produced enough water to be important.

The state's leaders looked at the success of irrigation projects in California and decided Nevada should build large irrigation projects. This effort took a long time and was only partially successful.

Reclamation

The first attempts at getting government support for irrigation projects in Nevada were made in the State Legislature. They were unsuccessful. Efforts of the western states to get federal support for irrigation projects were also unsuccessful until Theodore Roosevelt became president in 1900. He favored reclamation of desert lands. With his influence, the Reclamation Act of 1902 was passed; and, finally, the West had federal support for irrigation projects. The act was introduced by Representative Francis Newlands from Nevada, and the major irrigation project in Nevada became known as the Newlands Project.

Officials of the new U.S. Reclamation Service decided, in 1903, to build a huge irrigation system on the lower Carson River. The original idea was to irrigate more than 400,000 acres of newly reclaimed land in western and central Nevada. The plan involved the entire Truckee and Carson river basins, as well as Lake Tahoe. The lake storage was expected to add an estimated 100,000 acres to the land that could be farmed.

Between 1903 and 1917, the Newlands Project took shape. Great dams and canals were built on the Carson and Truckee rivers. Hundreds of families took up homesteads in the unbroken desert land. Construction of the Derby Dam and the Truckee Canal were done at the same time. The completed canal ended in a wooden chute which discharged the waters from the Truckee River directly into the Carson River.

Francis Griffith Newlands (1848-1917). Born in Mississippi, Newlands married Senator William Sharon's daughter and inherited much of Sharon's wealth and influence. With the help of Senator William M. Stewart of Nevada, Newlands started his political career in the Silver-Democratic Party and was elected to Congress in 1892 and to the U.S. Senate in 1903. In 1902, he was one of the leading backers of the Reclamation Act, which ushered in a whole new era of economic development in Nevada and the West. Courtesy of Special Collections, University of Nevada Reno Library

Opening of Derby Dam and the Truckee Canal on June 17, 1905. *This was the first reclamation project ever undertaken by the federal government. The photograph shows dignitaries standing around the newly-completed structure. The spillways at the left will divert the waters backed up by the dam across the Truckee River into the Truckee Canal. In the background, an excursion train of the Southern Pacific waits to take the celebrities away.*
Courtesy of Special Collections, University of Nevada Reno Library

Between 1904 and 1911, the U.S. Bureau of Reclamation provided the first parcels of land to settlers on the project. On June 17, 1905, a delegation headed by Senator Francis Newlands opened the gates at the Derby Dam and delivered the first Truckee River water destined for the farms in the Lahonton Valley. The first water actually received by settlers on the project was delivered to them on February 5, 1906. That season, 108 ranches were settled by 674 men, women, and children.

The Southern Pacific Railroad Company published a pamphlet in 1907 about the Newlands Project, describing the system to prospective settlers. It was called, "Uncle Sam's Nine Million Dollar Nevada Farm," and said:

Is he (Uncle Sam) going to farm it himself? No. He is going to give it away to the people of the United States. You need simply tell the agent at the land office in Carson or the agent

UNCLE SAM'S
NINE MILLION DOLLAR
NEVADA FARM

SOUTHERN PACIFIC

at the big farm at Fallon that you want eighty acres of good land. Pick out the eighty acres you want and just tell him where it is. Then pay eight dollars for the paper that gives you the land, if you begin living on it within six months and make it your home for the next five years. That is all for the land -- eight dollars. For the water he charges you $2.60 per acre every year for ten years. Then the water and the land belong to you and you will pay only a few cents per month to keep up the ditches and the reservoirs.

Only a part of the massive reclamation project was ever built, and that at great expense. Much of the project failed to work out as expected. The Bureau of Reclamation had greatly underestimated how much water would be needed and overestimated how much land could be reclaimed.

The experiences of the new settlers set the pattern for the future. They didn't have enough water. The land was hard to control. The settlers endured problems with land leveling, wind, and soil erosion.

The market was good, but it was several years before the farms were productive enough to provide a living for the settlers. Alfalfa, the leading crop, took two to three years to reach satisfactory production levels. Lawsuits became necessary for the project to obtain the amount of water it had to have from the Carson and Truckee rivers. Some settlers got discouraged. Others stayed and finally succeeded.

In 1911, the Bureau of Reclamation decided to build the Lahontan Dam to provide late summer irrigation water. It was completed in 1914, and the project was reopened to more settlers with sufficient water for full irrigation.

Lahontan Dam Near Completion in 1914. *The timber chute was later replaced by a concrete structure emptying above the power house.*
Courtesy of Special Collections, University of Nevada Reno Library

Aerial View of Lahontan Dam and Lake Lahontan on Carson River
Courtesy of Special Collections, University of Nevada Reno Library

In 1912, the settlers formed a water user's association and began to complain about the federal government's management of the project. In 1918, the local farmers formed the Truckee-Carson Irrigation District. They eventually took over the management of the project in 1926. With these actions, farmers started to control the use of water for irrigation.

Also, with the building of the Lahontan Dam, and the use of stored water, Fallon grew from a country crossroads town to become a leading agriculture producer. The Newlands Project now irrigates approximately 73,000 acres of land located below the Derby Canal and below the Lahontan Reservoir. This is the land that surrounds Fallon.

Ranch and Farm Communities

Because life on the range was often lonely, people got together for contests, dances and parties. Wherever there were enough children, they built schools. Ranchers would join together in an informal school district. They would choose a ranch house where the pupils were taught and then hire a teacher. The first school in the state was in 1854 in the Carson Valley, taught by Mrs. Issac Mott, who was assisted by a Mrs. Allen.

Nevada's principal ranching and farming communities are Elko, Fallon, Yerington, Minden and Gardnerville.

Major Crops in Nevada

Winter Wheat
Spring Wheat
Barley
Alfalfa Hay
Other Hay
Alfalfa Seed
Potatoes
Garlic
Onions

CASH RECEIPTS FROM FARM MARKETINGS, BY COMMODITIES, Nevada 1994-96

Item	1994		1995		1996	
	000$'s	% of Total	000$'s	% of Total	000$'s	% of Total
All Hay	64,612	21.7	66,367	23.5	66,915	23.4
Alfalfa Seed	7,480	2.5	9,770	3.5	10,400	3.6
Potatoes	14,460	4.9	16,286	5.8	20,471	7.2
Food & Feed Grains	3,196	1.1	3,964	1.4	6,928	2.4
Vegetables	12,883	4.3	16,141	5.7	21,652	7.6
All Other Crops	5,597	1.9	5,968	2.1	6,200	2.2
Total Crops	108,228	36.3	118,496	42.0	132,566	46.4
Total All Commodities	297,861	100.0	282,081	100.0	286,002	100.0

Today's Income from Farming and Ranching
1994

Cattle & Calves 54.8%

Courtesy of Nevada

Agricultural Statistics Service

Potatoes 3.9%
Alfalfa Seed 2.4%
Other Crops 1.5%
Vegetables 3.0%

heep & Lambs 1.3%
ther Livestock 2.0%

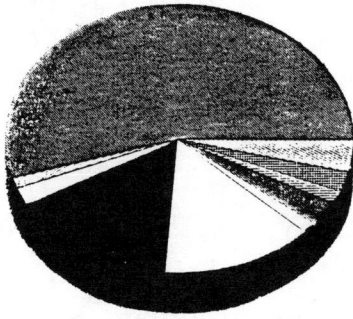

Dairy Products 15.8%   All Hay 14.1%

Cash Receipts from Farm Marketing of Commodities
1996

Sheep & Lambs 1.4%

Dairy Products 21.8%

Cattle & Calves 28.3%

Other Livestock 2.1%

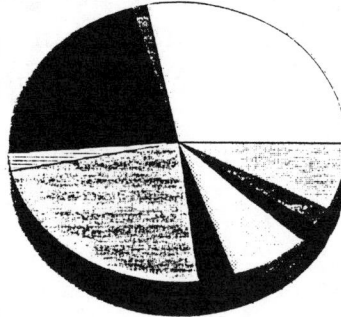

Vegetables 7.6%

Other Crops 2.2%
Food & Feed Grains 2.4%
Potatoes 7.2%
Alfalfa Seed 3.6%

Fallon   All Hay 23.4%

The first permanent building in Lahonton Valley was Ragtown Station on the Carson River. It began as a trading post for the overland emigrants at the southern edge of the Forty-Mile Desert. At first the men who kept the trading post lived in tents. Some people say their ragged canvas tents gave the place its name. Others say they called the place Ragtown because of the garments the emigrants had washed and put on the bushes to dry. In his overland diary for August 31, 1850, Bryon McKinstry of Illinois described the station:

When we first struck Carson River we found a village 8 or 9 stores (cloth tents). Flour sells at $2.00 per lb., Bacon $1., pies $1.25 to $1.75. small ones at that. Small biscuits at 50 cts. each, jerked beef at $1, coffee 12 ½ cts. per cup a meal of victuals, $3.00 and you are allowed only so much bread, beef and coffee. They tell the story of an emigrant that came yesterday and ate and drank $25 worth at a single meal.

AGRICULTURE 213

They cut hay and haul it up from the sink of Carson River and sell it from 25 to fifty cts. per bundle, about a large around as a man's arm. It would take $5 to feed a hungry ox. Oxen here sell for from $5 to $25 per yoke and the emigrants complain bitterly that traders steal their cattle and run them off.

Asa Levi Kenyon settled there in 1854 and recorded his land claim with the settlers' government at Carson Valley. Kenyon dug a well on the Forty-Mile Desert, about 15 miles from Ragtown, and did an excellent business selling water to the thirsty emigrants. Ragtown was just getting started as a transportation community when Captain James H. Simpson surveyed the Central Overland Route. His survey changed the road in 1859, bypassing Kenyon's station.

Ragtown Station, 1881. *This view, taken from Angel's <u>History of Nevada</u>, shows some of proprietor Asa Kenyon's various activities -- his horse-raising operation, several corrals full of cattle, a school, the station, store, saloon, ballroom, stables, and outbuildings, all inside a very neat and extensive fence.*

A new community started to the east of Ragtown, at Stillwater, in 1862. Stillwater began as a stage-coach station when the overland mail route was changed from the California Trail at Ragtown to the Simpson Wagon Road. Stillwater became the county seat of Churchill County in 1858. The county administrators there took a practical approach to law enforcement. This 1875 newspaper article from the *Austin Reese River Reveille* tells how one prisoner was jailed:

> *NOVEL PRISON -- We are reliably informed that a man who was arrested for some offense at Stillwater, the county seat of Churchill County, was confined in a shaft for lack of better accommodations. He was hoisted to the surface three times a day, and meals were placed on the edge of the shaft, and after he had eaten he was lowered back to his cell and the rope hoisted out. The shaft in which he is confined is 200 feet in depth, so there was not much opportunity for him to escape. Who says criminals are turned loose in Churchill County?*

Ranchers settled in Lahontan Valley and sold their produce to the freighting teams which were traveling between railroad supply points and the mining camps. By 1900, there were some ninety ranches in the area, and many of them had been operating for thirty or forty years. There was a substantial system of private irrigating ditches and dams in Lahontan Valley, carrying water to 15,000 acres of cropland and another 15,000 acres of pasture.

Where Fallon is today there was first just a small store run by Jim Richards, which the Indians called "Jim's Town." The present name of the location was adopted when Mike Fallon and his wife, Elizabeth Bruner Fallon, settled there in 1896. The post office at their ranch was named "Fallon," and that became the name of the future city.

Lemuel Allen and His Wife Sarah Ann, 1881. The Allens were among the earliest settlers in Lahontan Valley, when they stopped to live along the lower Carson River in 1862. Allen, a rancher and attorney, served Churchill County as its district attorney, then as its assemblyman, and finally as state senator. He was three times elected Speaker of the Assembly, and twice elected President of the State Senate. Of his ranch, Allen wrote: "In February, 1867, we rented a place which nowadays is four miles southwest of Fallon so we could sell our hay, it being on the main teamsters' road. In the fall of 1868, we bought that place and lived on it for forty-four years." From *Angel's History of Nevada*

A boom started in the Fallon ranch area when people realized that the U.S. Reclamation Service had plans for an irrigation project there. A Churchill County sheepman, Warren Williams, bought the Fallon ranch. He platted the land and advertised the lots for sale in 1903. Nearly everyone, businessmen and settlers, moved from Stillwater to the more centrally located Fallon. The State Legislature moved the Churchill County seat from Stillwater to Fallon.

In 1907, the Southern Pacific Railroad built a spur line from Hazen to Fallon. The U.S. Reclamation Service opened its office in Fallon,

Downtown Fallon on a Cloudy Day, about 1905. *Other than the small groups of townsfolk chatting on the wooden sidewalks, there's not much traffic; but, under the overhanging electric street lamp, lie the dirt, dust, and ruts of a heavily-traveled road.*
Courtesy of Special Collections, University of Nevada Reno Library

and the telephone company moved its offices from Stillwater to Fallon.

In addition to the Truckee-Carson Irrigation District, or Newlands Project, Fallon's economy got another big boost during World War II from the construction of the U.S. Auxiliary Naval Air Station nearby in 1942-44. The population doubled almost overnight. Thousands of people arrived in Fallon, creating a housing shortage. During the Korean War in 1951, the airbase was reopened and has been operating ever since. The naval airbase had a payroll of more than 2,000 people in the mid-1900s.

Fallon has been called "The Oasis of Nevada" for the fertility of its soil and the productivity of its agriculture. The region is nationally known for its "Heart 'O Gold" cantaloupes of jumbo size and matchless flavor.

Lovelock

At the time of greatest emigrant travel on the California Trail, the Humboldt River disappeared about two miles southeast of the present town of Lovelock. The water that was left spread out thinly over a good-sized area forming a natural meadow and tule swamp. This was known as the Big Meadows. It was a wonderful place where weary emigrants could camp. They could cut native grass for hay and rest their animals before the fearful trip across the Forty-Mile Desert to the Carson River.

James Blake built a stagecoach station there in the spring of 1861. Then George Lovelock, an Englishman, bought the station in September of 1866, giving the location its name. He lived there until his death in 1907.

The station became more important after the construction of the transcontinental railroad across Nevada in 1868-69. The Central Pacific Railroad set up a freight depot there. A little town grew up to serve the outlying ranches and mining camps. In the 1860s, irrigation ditches were built to tap the river upstream. The additional water was used to increase the hay acreage, resulting in heavy yields of native blue hay, much prized by the cattlemen as winter feed. By 1890, most of the valley was developed.

A rare incident of local violence occurred in 1885 when the Humboldt River was flooding. The Oneida Dam, a large earthen bulwark across the lower Humboldt River, backed up water onto the fields of local ranchers. The ranchers put on masks and destroyed the dam with dynamite in order to reclaim their flooded croplands.

After the turn of the century, a mining boom began and brought prosperity to the town. Pacific Coast stockmen also began sending cattle and sheep into the Lovelock Valley for pasture and feeding.

George Lovelock. In 1868, George Lovelock donated 85 acres for the new townsite at Big Meadows, and the town was named Lovelock after him. Lovelock, who was born in Wales in 1824, was a miner, carpenter, and rancher. In 1855, he pioneered a wagon road across the Sierra Nevada to Honey Lake Valley. He bought the ranch land where Lovelock is located, in Big Meadows, in 1866. He secured the first water right on the Humboldt River.
Courtesy of Nevada Historical Society

Lovelock's Classical Courthouse. *This beautiful building, designed by famous Nevada architect Frederick Delongchamps, attracts visitors to Lovelock. One of only two round courthouses in the United States, it features neoclassic elements such as the six Ionic columns. It was completed in 1921.*
Courtesy of Nevada Historical Society

Aerial View of Lovelock. *Nevada's unusual geography is captured in this aerial view taken southeast of Lovelock. The squared-off fields of Pershing County farms fill the foreground. Behind them, the Humboldt Sink stretches across the center of the photo. The West Humboldt Mountains separate the Humboldt Sink from the Carson Sink, which is the light area at the top of the picture. The Indian name for the West Humboldt Mountains was Tac-a-roy, meaning "Snow Mountains."*
Courtesy of Chuck Saulisberry for the U.S. Department of Agriculture

There were 20,000 cattle and 40,000 sheep feeding in the valley, and the stockyards had to be enlarged. By 1908, there were 100,000 head of livestock in the valley, and Lovelock was supplying meat to cities on the Pacific Coast.

When Pershing County was created out of southwestern Humboldt County in 1919, the Legislature made Lovelock the county seat. A spectacular courthouse, that still draws unusual attention, was designed by the prominent architect Frederick J. Delongchamps. Today, Lovelock is a farming and ranching community that also serves the mining enterprises in the area.

Minden-Gardnerville

Minden and Gardnerville are located together almost as one city in the historic Carson Valley. They are just a few miles across the valley from Genoa, where the first permanent white settlement was located in Nevada. Of the two cities, Gardnerville is the older. It began in 1878 as a hotel on land owned by John Gardner.

Ranchers and businessmen in the rich farm country of Carson Valley needed railroad service to the region. The ranchers persuaded the Virginia & Truckee Railroad to build into the valley, and construction started in April of 1906. The line went from Carson City into the heart of Carson Valley. The railroad planned, at first, to build its freight depot and station at Gardnerville. The prospect of the railroad there caused the price of land to go up. The railroad then accepted a site about a mile north of town that was donated by the H.F. Dangberg Land & Livestock Company. Minden was founded there in the spring of 1906, and the first locomotive steamed into Minden on August 1. Livestock men shipped their cattle and sheep by rail to San Francisco and Chicago.

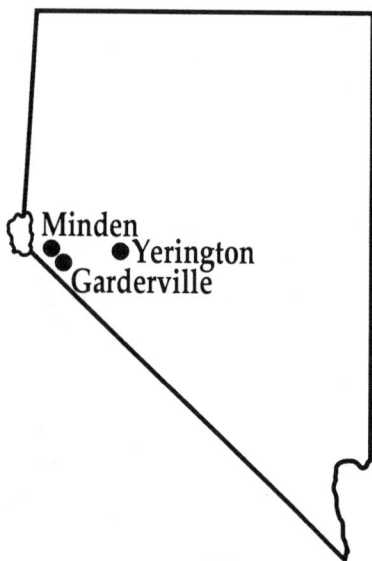

Minden
Yerington
Garderville

The Minden Flour Milling Company, about 1908. *The large cylindrical silos at left are used to store the wheat, which is milled in the brick building by grinding until the grain is turned into flour. The final product can be seen sacked and stacked under the shelter of the roofed loading docks, while horse-drawn wagons stand ready to distribute the flour to local markets. The V&TRR tracks immediately behind the mill allow the milling company to ship its output by rail to Reno. Paralleling the tracks is the future U.S. Highway 395.*
Courtesy of Nevada Historical Society

The V&TRR continued operations to Minden until the railroad went out of business in 1950.

Minden was named for the Westphalia town in Germany near where H.F. Dangberg was born. Minden became the county seat of Douglas County, replacing Genoa, in 1916.

Yerington

Yerington got its start as the little town of Greenfield. Greenfield's willow-thatched saloon was known as "Willows Switch." The liquor served there was sometimes called "pizen" by the cowboys. That was because when the bar owner ran short of whiskey, he added water and flavored it with chewing tobacco. This made it taste like poison to the cowboys, who would say to one another, as they rode along, "Let's switch off and get some pizen". Whether this account is just a story or not, the town was known as Pizen Switch for some time. It was later renamed in honor of Henry M. Yerington, a railroad official. This was done hoping that Yerington would run the Carson & Colorado Railroad through there. It never happened, but the town kept Yerington's name.

In 1911, after the Lyon County courthouse at Dayton was destroyed by fire, the county seat was moved to Yerington. The town served the surrounding mining camps as a distribution and shipping center. Yerington also outfitted prospectors. When a copper mining boom started in the area in 1901, Yerington enjoyed a marked increase in business.

Anaconda Copper Company made another major discovery of copper ore in 1951 at Weed Heights, not far from Yerington and operated a large open pit mine. The mine was closed in the late 1970s and reopened in 1996. While copper booms have enriched Yerington, its most stable income has come from agriculture. From when it first began in the 1860s, down to the present time Yerington has always been one of Nevada's steady and successful farming and ranching centers.

Downtown Yerington, 1881. This view from Angel's History of Nevada shows the beginnings of this Mason Valley community as a string of stores, shops and stables along the road to Bodie, California.

A True Story

This is the true story of John H. Sheehan, a Nevada boy, who left home in 1874 when he was 10 years old and worked as a hard-riding cowboy and ranch hand from the time he was 14 to 18. Mr. Sheehan told his story to the jury in a water rights trial in Fallon between 1923 and 1932, when he was in his sixties. The following story is in his own words. His words are rearranged to put them into story form.

SHEEHAN'S STORY

I ran away from home to work on a ranch when I was 10 years old. I was living with my parents at Gold Hill next to Virginia City in the mining towns. I wanted to be a buckaroo, not a miner.

Cattle Drive. A solitary cowboy rides trail on his herd as he moves the cattle away from their pasture in this Washoe County shot. The Mount Rose range dominates the scenic backdrop.
Courtesy of Special Collections, University of Nevada Reno Library

So I jumped on a train one spring morning in 1874 at Gold Hill. I went to Carson on that ore train. I hopped another train to Wadsworth. Then I got a ride on a team out to the John Luce ranch, where I went to work. It was easy to get a ride out of Wadsworth on a team in those days.

Wadsworth was the shipping point and distributing point for all the places east and for Ione and Belmont and as far east as White Pine. The merchants would order goods from San Francisco and Sacramento, and the goods would come there to Wadsworth. The teams would go and load those goods and haul them wherever they were to go. All those teams were no less than 16 mules -- from that to 24. There were 16, 18, 22 and 24 mule teams that ran on the road. And every so often there would be a station where they would stop overnight and get their meals and hay and grain. If they couldn't, they carried it with them. They would always load up enough at the ranches along the way to carry with them for their trips back and forth.

At John Luce's ranch I worked as a chore boy, doing just about anything a boy could do. Mr. Luce was a horse man. He raised and ran horses. I was back and forth between his place and the William Bailey ranch. During the time that I worked for him, Mr. Luce sold his own horse ranch and took up 40 acres on the Bailey ranch and moved his horses over there. Mr. Bailey also kept horses. He ran 200 to 250 brood mares and colts. Then he had 80 saddle horses and about 40 to 50 work horses on the ranch.

In the summer of 1878, when I was 14 years old, Mr. Bailey hired me. The first work I did for him was in the haying. Driving a hay *rake. After that, I rode for him and at times I worked on the ranch, riding and driving teams and doing whatever work came on.*

I kept the fence up: rode it every other day from the lake to the big corrals to see that the fence was up and the gates were closed. At times stock used to go through it, and people would come along and tear the fence down, and knock the wire down so their stock could get on the inside and run with Bailey's. During the first year I was there I rode that fence and repaired it and patched it with staples.

Mr. Bailey ran from 5,000 to 10,000 head of cattle. He was in the cattle ranching and butcher business. I used to drive the cattle from the ranch to Virginia City, to the slaughterhouse in Virginia City, and from the ranch to the slaughterhouse in Reno, and then I rode this country around here looking after his cattle.

Whenever he bought any cattle anywhere, I almost always went with him, and brought the cattle in and delivered them here for him. I made three drives south from his ranch at Warner Valley in Oregon to the ranch here. In the fall of 1878, I drove about 750 head of steers down from Oregon. Then in 1879 about 1,250 head of cattle and in 1880 about 1,650 head. On another drive from the Clark Station on the Truckee River I brought in about 1,250 head; and another time 800 head from the eastern part of the state.

As I said before Mr. Bailey was in the butcher business, selling cattle in Virginia City, and also in Reno. Generally in the spring of the year, or summer, or later in the summer, when the cattle began to get fat enough, we began driving cattle off the ranch to Virginia City for beef.

Well there would be times when I would practically be on the road there all the time, just as fast as I could drive, and other times when it could let up and I would not make a drive for probably two weeks.

At times I would deliver the cattle right to the slaughterhouse myself, and then there would be times that he wanted another drive at once, and he would come out and meet me, come out to Six Mile Canyon, and he would take the cattle or have men come out and meet me and take the cattle and send me right back to get another bunch of cattle to make another drive.

We would get them on the ranch, start them from what they called the big corrals over here across this pasture of the Big Bend.

We made the first day 26 miles, and the next day to the Cooney ranch on the Carson River, that was 18 miles. And then the next morning, we aimed to get up at 2:00 o'clock and start those cattle and get them up the Six Mile Canyon before daylight ... (The Six Mile Canyon was the main road into Virginia City) ... The cattle was all wild Spanish cattle that Mr. Bailey got from Texas. They were mean to handle and we had to get them by those houses in the canyon and by the teams before the traffic started in the morning. We would get them up there and turned them off and went up over the summit to the slaughter-house.

Mr. Bailey killed those cattle. He sold them to different butchers in Reno and Gold Hill, besides having two or three butcher shops of his own. And some of those cattle he would take to the Truckee Meadows. He had a slaughterhouse at Reno and killed cattle there and shipped the meat to San Francisco in his own refrigerator cars.

Historical Events

1851
Settlers Set Up First Government

1859
Territorial Government Attempted

1861
Civil War Began

Congress Created Nevada Territory

1864
Nevada Became 36th State

1870
State Capitol Built

1874
University of Nevada Started

1902
U.S. Reclamation Act

1926
Easy Divorce

1931
Legalized Gambling

1931
Divorce in Six Weeks

1935
Boulder Dam Completed

1941
Gunnery School Started, Later Nellis AFB

1945
State Began to Tax Gambling Revenues

SILVER
★★★★★★★★★★★
★★★★★★★★★★★
NEVADA
★★★★★★★★★★
★★★★★★★★
GOLD

Chapter Six

Government

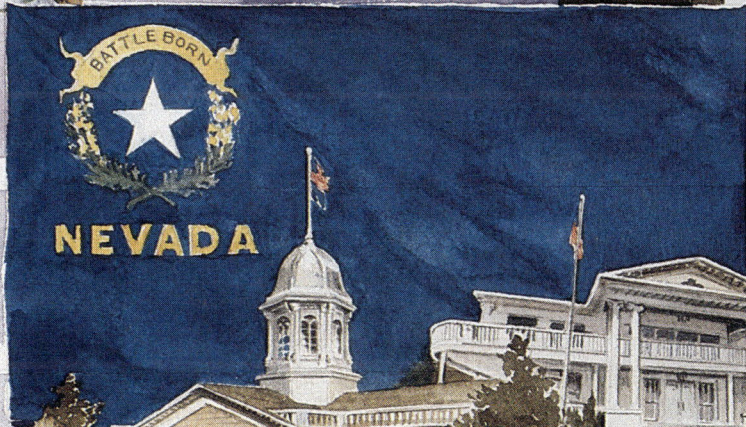

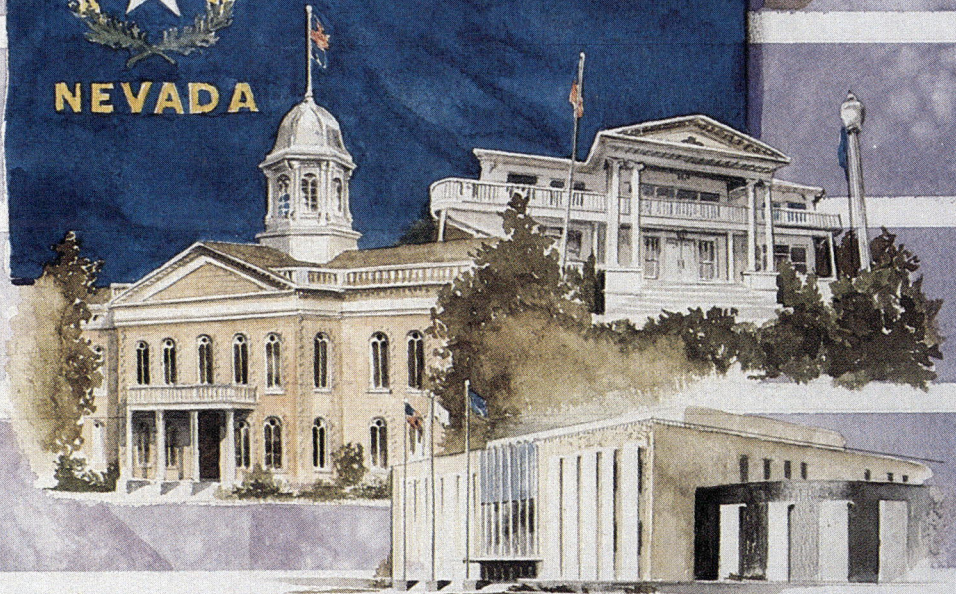

Government

Nevada's motto is "Battle Born" because our state government was born out of the Civil War. President Lincoln needed the great wealth from Nevada's silver mines to help pay for the cost of fighting the war. He also needed the support of Nevada to get the laws passed that would free the slaves, give them full citizenship rights, and give them the right to vote. In order to give the Union this support, Nevada became a state. Nevada has generally been much involved with the federal government -- in the purchasing of silver, in water development projects, in military projects, and in land use issues. Despite Nevada's small population, its U.S. Senators have often been very influential in the national government. In state government, Nevada has given its people low taxes and great personal freedom.

Courtesy of Nevada State Museum

There was no government in the early days of Nevada. Without government there were no laws for protection. The trappers, explorers, and early emigrants were strictly on their own. They traveled and camped in the valleys and the mountains of the Great Basin, hundreds of miles from sheriffs and judges. They had to protect themselves the best they could from bandits who could kill or steal without any fear of arrest because there was no law.

The overland emigrant parties had the worst problems. They had no one but themselves to enforce the law within their own parties. When a member of an emigrant party committed murder in 1846, the other members of the party formed a court and passed judgment on the killer. He was banished from the wagon train to wander alone in the desert with no weapons and no food.

The emigrants had to deal both with criminals within their own parties and with bandits who attacked them from the outside. The emigrants who held trials and executed these criminals were willing to admit doing it. They published letters in the newspapers stating what they had done and signed their names. No one questioned what they did. Most people thought the lynchings were necessary. People thought they were fair because the judgment, as well as the verdict, was decided by a jury who voted after hearing the evidence. The right to trial by jury is one of the fundamental principles of justice in the United States Constitution. This fundamental right was preserved and followed by the unofficial emigrant courts.

The Settlers' Government

The first settlers who decided to spend the winter in Nevada, in 1851, set up their own government.

On November 12, 1851, they held a public meeting at the Mormon Station in Carson Valley. Their purpose was "to consider the necessity of providing for the survey of claims and subdivision of the valley so as to secure all individuals in their rights to land taken up and improved by them, to agree upon a petition to Congress for distinct territorial government, the creation of public officers for the Valley, and the adoption of by-laws and fixed regulations to govern the community."

This meeting produced a local government which made laws relating to land claims. The newly established government consisted of a judge, his clerk, and a sheriff. It was supervised by a commission of 12 citizens -- a kind of grand jury. This government ruled over Carson Valley and surrounding areas until 1855.

Carson County

Just a few years before this time, the United States had won the war with Mexico. The war had ended in 1848 with the Treaty of Guadalupe Hidalgo. Under this treaty, the Great Basin area became United States territory. It had no government until 1850, when the U.S. Congress created the territory of Utah. Brigham Young was named the governor of the new territory. He was also the head of the Mormon Church. In addition to what is now Utah, the new Utah Territory included most of present-day Nevada, then called Western Utah.

The people who lived in Western Utah did not want to be ruled by authorities sent from Salt Lake City. They tried to get the state of California to annex Carson Valley. They also petitioned the United States Congress in 1851, 1857-58, and in 1859, asking for their own territorial government.

At first, the Utah authorities in Salt Lake City did not try to extend their rule into the Western Utah area. Then, finally, in January of 1855 the Utah government established Carson County and appointed George Stiles as the U.S. Territorial Judge. Stiles, Carson County Judge Orson Hyde, and other officials arrived at Mormon Station in June. Hyde, a Mormon Church official, had been ordered to establish a Mormon Church settlement in the area. He called for county elections to be held at Mormon Station on September 20, 1855. The voters decided the Carson County seat would be at Mormon Station. Hyde named the place Genoa, after the birthplace of Columbus.

This attempt by Utah territorial officials to govern Carson County failed. The Utah government could not get local support from the people who lived there. Several years later, in 1862, Orson Hyde recalled his failure. He denounced the people who lived in Carson and Washoe Valleys for "unceasing opposition ... in almost every form, both trivial and important, open and secret." Orson Hyde left Genoa and returned to Salt Lake City toward the end of 1856. Within just a few weeks -- on January 14, 1857 -- the Utah Territorial Legislature passed a law which essentially moved the government of Western Utah to Salt Lake City. By September 1857 the Church of Jesus Christ of Latter Day Saints had recalled its settlements in Western Utah, and the area was once again without any local government -- no judge, no sheriff, and no one to keep records.

Orson Hyde (1805-1878) of Connecticut. A senior official of the Mormon Church, Hyde established the first official local government in Nevada in 1855, when Nevada was still part of Utah Territory. The settlements he founded were abandoned in 1857.
Courtesy of Nevada Historical Society

Lynch Law in Carson Valley

Outlaws flourished in the wastelands of Nevada during the 1850s. In the summer of 1851, a force of California militia discovered the graves of six men.

They were supposed to have been murdered on the California Trail. In the spring of 1852, Utah Territorial Indian Agent Jacob H. Holeman wrote to the Commissioner of Indian Affairs. He said that there was "a company of white men and Indians who are stationed near the Carson Valley, and their object is to plunder and rob the emigrants." This condition was also described by the *Sacramento Union*. The newspaper reported that a murderer pursued to Carson Valley was found so strongly encamped that it was impossible to capture him. The newspaper also reported that the camp consisted of "a large party of Pah Ute Indians and about 150 white men, principally robbers and murderers who have fled from justice. The camp is situated about thirty miles from the emigrant trail and near the sink of the Humboldt."

In 1856, a group of white men disguised as Indians attacked a wagon train in the Deep Creek Mountains on the Utah-Nevada border and drove off a number of the emigrants' cattle. The overland emigrants reacted violently against these outlaws. The emigrants tracked them down, gave them a trial, convicted them, and shot six of them on the spot. In 1857, emigrants shot another man at the sink of the Humboldt. He was recognized by his victims as a "white Indian" -- a white man trying to blame his crimes on the Indians.

After the Utah government officials and the Mormon settlers withdrew from Carson Valley, there was no government. So, in 1857, the local ranchers formed their own government, or "People's Court." In 1858, this law and order group and the vigilante committee of Honey Lake Valley held a trial. They charged a gang of men with the murder of a ranchman from the Honey Lake country and with several other crimes. The vigilantes executed three men by hanging. They banished another from the area for life, fined several, and acquitted several more.

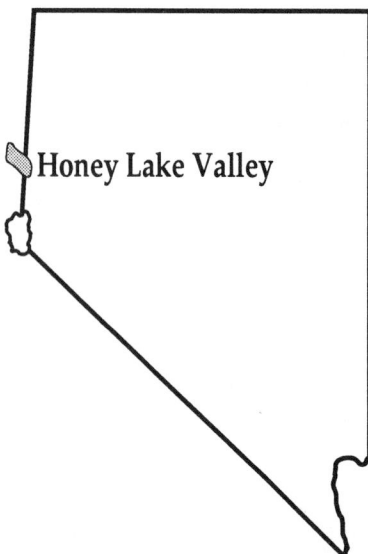

Honey Lake Valley

In some other trials, the "People's Court" acquitted the defendants, but on at least one occasion they cut off the ears of men who were convicted of stealing. The people who lived along this eastern slope of the Sierra didn't want things to remain that way. They petitioned Congress again and again to create a territorial government for Nevada. Congress, however, left the matter in the hands of the officials of the Utah Territory in Salt Lake City.

Two Governments

In 1857-58, a bill in Congress to set up Nevada Territory failed to pass. So, the ranchers of Nevada decided to create their own territory, breaking away from Utah. They didn't have the approval of either Utah Territory or of the United States Government, but they elected delegates to a territorial convention, which met at Genoa on July 18, 1859. The convention drafted a constitution for the unofficial Nevada Territory. The residents of Nevada approved the new constitution on September 7, 1859. They also elected a governor -- Isaac Roop of Honey Lake Valley -- and representatives to a territorial legislature. The legislature met for the first and only time on December 15, 1859. It was adjourned by Governor Roop, who declared in an address that the time was not right for the new territory's organization.

There was a good reason for Governor Roop to delay forming the new government. The Utah Territory had decided to reassert its authority. The Utah Territorial Legislature restored Carson County's representation in the Utah Assembly. This authorized the formation of a local Carson County government in January of 1859. This allowed the first court in two years to be held in Genoa.

Isaac Newton Roop. Roop was the first and only governor of the unofficial, breakaway Territory of Nevada, 1859-1861. Roop was active in the movement to create a separate political unit out of Western Utah but faded into obscurity after Congress created an official Nevada Territory in 1861.
Courtesy of Nevada Historical Society

Now there were two governments. The residents of Carson County were not enthusiastic about this second attempt by Utah Territory officials to govern them. There were charges of vote fraud at nearly all of the Carson County elections. At the beginning of the rush to the new silver discoveries in Virginia City in 1859, there were two different Carson County recorders holding office at the same time. Miners and others, not knowing which would eventually become the official recorder, had to file their papers with both recorders. Time ran out for Carson County, Utah Territory, in 1861. The county seat had just been moved from Genoa to Carson City when Congress finally established the new Nevada Territory.

Nevada Territory

Although the attempt of the ranchers to form their own territorial Nevada government in 1859 was a failure, it produced important results. It showed that a large number of Nevadans wanted a government of their own and did not want to be ruled from Salt Lake City. Other events of great importance soon caused Congress to create the Nevada territorial government.

The first of these events was the discovery of the rich Comstock Lode in 1859. This brought thousands of settlers to Nevada and added new importance to the region because of its mineral riches.

After Abraham Lincoln was elected President of the United States in 1860, the southern states began to secede from the Union. They formed the Confederate States of America in February of 1861. The Civil War had begun. This removed many southern votes from the United States Senate. The two governments divided the nation and caused disagreement on the formation of Nevada and other territories. Would they be slave states or free states?

Because Nevada had great mineral wealth, Congress did not want it to fall into the hands of the Confederacy. To keep control of this great wealth, Congress created Nevada Territory. On March 2, 1861, just two days before he left office, President James Buchanan signed the bill creating the new Nevada Territory.

Territorial Government

President Lincoln, who took office two days later, appointed the most important officers of the new territorial government. Most of these new officials were strong supporters of the Republican Party. The new governor, James Warren Nye, was a Republican from New York. He had helped deliver a large number of votes for President Lincoln in the 1860 national election. Other appointees were also Republicans. This assured Republican Party domination of Nevada for years to come.

Nye arrived in Nevada in July of 1861. He divided the territory into districts and directed the districts to send representatives to a legislature in Carson City. The legislature met from October 1 to November 29. The members passed laws to get the territorial government started, paid bills, and made plans for schools.

There was no room in Carson City large enough for the legislature to meet. To help the government get started, Abraham Curry, the founder of Carson City, let the legislature meet in his new Warm Springs Hotel. It was located two miles east of town. Curry constructed a two-car, horse-drawn railway for the legislators. It carried them from the Ormsby House, where they were staying in Carson City, out to their meeting room at the hotel. Curry, a great developer, did all this without charge.

James Warren Nye (1814-1876) of New York. Nevada's first governor, Nye studied law and was elected a judge in New York by the age of thirty. He joined the Republican Party in 1856 and became an influential politician in New York City, where he campaigned strongly for his friend Abraham Lincoln's election in 1860. Beginning in 1864, Nye served two terms as U.S. Senator.
Courtesy of Special Collections, University of Nevada Reno Library

The Nevada State Prison is now located where the Warm Springs Hotel was in 1861.

Even though Governor Nye had selected Carson City as the place for the legislature to meet, that did not make it the capital of the territory. William Stewart, the strongest leader in the new legislature, had his law office in Carson City. He wanted the capital there, and he was elected by the voters to get the capital for Carson City. Stewart worked quietly. He found out what each elected representative wanted for his district -- where he wanted the county seat and where he wanted the boundaries. Stewart then wrote a bill giving each of these representatives what he wanted and making Carson City the capital of the new territory. It passed, and that's how Carson City became the capital of Nevada.

Carson City was an ideal place for the territorial capital. It was well located to serve all of the main activities of the people. It was almost exactly half-way between the two busiest communities in the territory -- the wild, newly-rich Virginia City with its booming silver mines, and Genoa, the quieter, bustling business center of the state. The ranches of Carson Valley, Eagle Valley and the Truckee Meadows surrounded Carson City, giving the ranchers easy access to the capital. The forests that provided lumber for the mines were in the mountains around Carson City, giving the forestry industry access to the new capital.

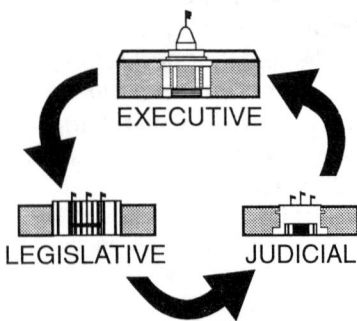

The territorial government organized by Governor Nye had the same system of checks and balances as the national government established by the United States Constitution. There were three separate but equal branches of the government -- the executive, the legislative, and the judicial.

EXECUTIVE

LEGISLATIVE   JUDICIAL

The executive part of the government consisted of the governor, appointed by the President and commissioned March 22, 1861. Other, lesser officials, charged with enforcing the laws of the territory, were appointed and sworn into office on July 11, 1861.

The legislature was organized as a bicameral, or two-house, system of elected officials. The people of Nevada elected senators and assemblymen from the various electoral districts.

The judicial branch of government was made up of a three-man Territorial Supreme Court. Each of the judges also held court in his own district of the territory. He rode a circuit through various counties assigned to him. The judicial organization of the territory was completed July 17, 1861.

One of the first and most important acts of the new legislature was to organize the Territory of Nevada into nine counties. They were Churchill, Douglas, Esmeralda, Humboldt, Lake, Lyon, Ormsby, Storey, and Washoe. Many of the features of territorial government formed the basis for the organization of state government. Through the years they have been changed and improved.

Statehood

It took Nevada just a little over three years to change from a United States territory to a state. There were several reasons why this change happened so quickly.

Many people in Nevada were dissatisfied with the territorial judges, who had a reputation for corruption. Under a state constitution, the judges could be elected by the people. This would give the citizens some control over the judges. They could vote corrupt judges out of office.

In order to become a state, Nevada had to first have a constitution ratified by the voters of the territory and approved by the U.S. Congress. The territorial legislature called for a constitutional convention, which met in November of 1863. The convention produced a constitution, but it was defeated by the voters in January of 1864.

This defeat did not stop Nevada from getting to be a state. An enabling act, permitting Nevada to become a state, was passed by Congress and signed by President Lincoln on March 24, 1864. This was done even though Nevada did not have the population required for other territories to become states. Territories were supposed to have a population of 127,000 to become a state. Nevada's population was only an estimated 25,000 people.

A new constitutional convention met during July of that year. The constitution produced by this second convention was ratified by popular vote September 7, 1864. The constitution was sent to Washington, D.C., by telegraph for approval. It is the longest telegram ever sent. Nevada then became the nation's 36th state. It was admitted to the Union on October 31, 1864, just in time for Nevadans to vote for President Lincoln's reelection.

William M. Stewart, the first U.S. Senator from Nevada, described one of the reasons Nevada became a state in his *Reminiscences*:

> *When the enabling act was passed by Congress on March 21, 1864, authorizing Nevada to enter the Union, it was understood that the Government at Washington was anxious that Nevada should become a State in order that her Senators and Representative might assist in the adoption of amendments to the Constitution to aid in the restoration of the Southern States after the Union should be vindicated by the [Civil] war.*

William Morris Stewart (1827-1909) of New York. *Stewart served as Nevada's first U.S. Senator. A teacher, prospector, lawyer, and politician, Stewart served as senator for almost thirty years. In the Senate, Stewart put Nevada first in his efforts to stabilize the economic structure of the Silver State.*
Courtesy of Nevada Historical Society

When Stewart was elected U.S. Senator in December of 1864, he traveled to Washington, D.C., to attend his first session of Congress. Once there, he met President Lincoln:

The morning after I took my seat in the Senate I called upon President Lincoln at the White House. He received me in the most friendly manner, taking me by both hands and saying:

"I am glad to see you here. We need as many loyal States as we can get, and, in addition to that, the gold and silver in the region you represent has made it possible for the Government to maintain sufficient credit to continue this terrible war for the Union. I have observed such manifestations of patriotism from your people as to assure me that the government can rely on your state for such support as is in your power."

The wealth from the mines of Nevada did help to secure victory for the North in the Civil War and thus helped to preserve the United States.

The State Government

As a state, Nevada had the same three branches of government that it had as a territory -- executive, legislative, and judiciary -- but some things changed. The governor was now elected by the people instead of being appointed by the President. As a state, Nevada now had two U.S. Senators and one U.S. Congressman as part of the national government in Washington, D.C.

The State Legislature continued to function as it had under territorial government. It remained a two-house system. Senators were elected from the counties. Assembly members were elected according to population.

State laws are passed by the two-house Legislature from bills introduced into either house. The bill is assigned to a committee in the house where it is introduced. The committee holds hearings to get information for and against the proposed law. After these hearings, the bill is sent back to the full house into which it was introduced. The committee generally gives the bill a "pass" or "do not pass" recommendation. If the bill is passed, it is sent to the other house where the same process is repeated. After the bill is approved by both houses, it is sent to the governor for his signature.

If he signs it, the bill becomes a law. If he doesn't like the bill and vetoes it, the bill then goes back to the Legislature. It can still become a law, if it is approved by a two-thirds majority of each of the houses.

The county governments continued in the same locations with the same county seats. They operated then much as they do today. Each county is run by a board of county commissioners. Each county has officials: a sheriff to enforce the law, a district attorney to prosecute criminals, and a county assessor to assess and collect taxes. There is a district judge to serve each county, sometimes several judges, and a clerk of the court to keep the court records. As Nevada grew, new counties were added by breaking up the existing counties. Nevada now has 17 counties.

Inside the counties, there are city governments with elected city councilmen who make the city laws and set city policy. Each city has an executive, sometimes a mayor, sometimes a city manager, and sometimes both. Each city or city-county government has a police department, a fire department, and other departments and officials to provide public services. Each county in Nevada is a school district.

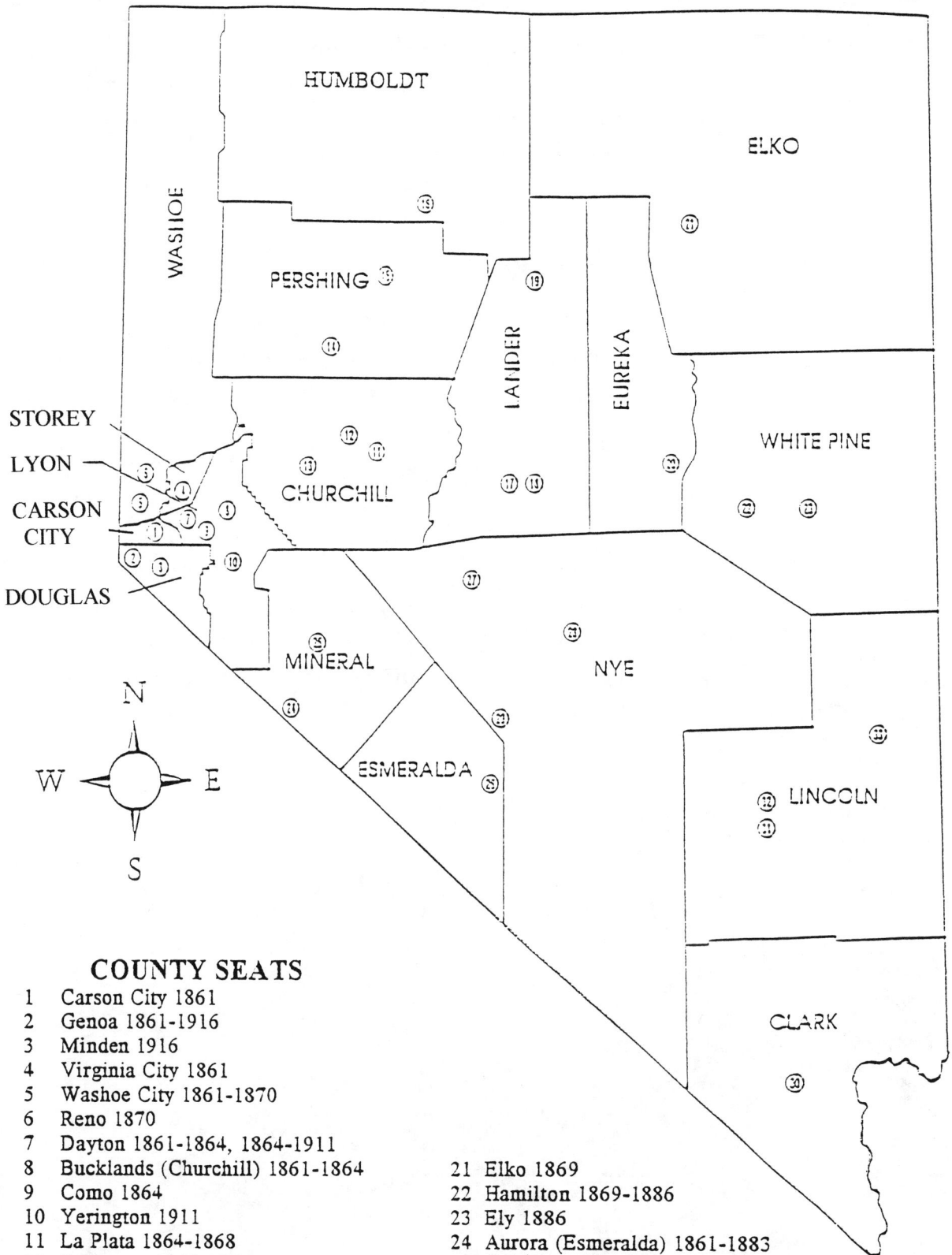

Map of Nevada counties with compass rose (N, W, E, S).

County labels on map: HUMBOLDT, ELKO, WASHOE, PERSHING, LANDER, EUREKA, WHITE PINE, STOREY, LYON, CARSON CITY, DOUGLAS, CHURCHILL, MINERAL, NYE, ESMERALDA, LINCOLN, CLARK

COUNTY SEATS

1 Carson City 1861
2 Genoa 1861-1916
3 Minden 1916
4 Virginia City 1861
5 Washoe City 1861-1870
6 Reno 1870
7 Dayton 1861-1864, 1864-1911
8 Bucklands (Churchill) 1861-1864
9 Como 1864
10 Yerington 1911
11 La Plata 1864-1868
12 Stillwater 1868-1903
13 Fallon 1903
14 Lovelock 1919
15 Unionville (Humboldt) 1862-1873
16 Winnemucca 1873
17 Jacobsville 1862
18 Austin 1863-1980
19 Battle Moutain 1980
20 Eureka 1873

21 Elko 1869
22 Hamilton 1869-1886
23 Ely 1886
24 Aurora (Esmeralda) 1861-1883
25 Hawthorne (Esmeralda) 1883-1907;
   (Mineral) 1911
26 Goldfield 1907
27 Ione City 1864-1967
28 Belmont 1867-1905
29 Tonopah 1905
30 Las Vegas 1909
31 Crystal Springs 1866-1867
32 Hiko 1867-1871
33 Pioche 1871

In addition to the counties, cities, and school districts, there are other local divisions of government such as irrigation districts, development districts, and improvement districts.

The Right to Vote

At first, Nevada's constitution gave the right to vote only to adult, white males. In 1880, the rule was abolished in a state election which extended the right to vote to all adult males.

Women did not get the right to vote, even though they were very active and effective in Nevada government. Bills that would have given women the right to vote were introduced into the State Legislature repeatedly but failed to pass. Finally, a group called the Nevada Equal Franchise Society was formed, with Anne Martin of Carson City as its leader.

Anne Martin, President of the Nevada Equal Franchise Society. *Martin (in the front passenger's seat), a native Nevadan, was largely responsible for women winning the right to vote in Nevada. She was the first woman to be nominated for the U.S. Senate, in 1918.* Courtesy of Nevada Historical Society

Miss Martin traveled to all parts of the state, appealing to men in the mines and on the ranches. They responded by supporting women's right to vote. An amendment establishing women's suffrage in Nevada was passed by the Legislature in 1911 and 1913 and approved by the all-male voters in 1914. This was six years before women got the right to vote nationally in 1920.

The Teenage Vote

Eighteen-year-olds were given the right to vote in the United States in a U.S. Constitutional amendment adopted in 1971. Before that, people had to be 21 or older to be qualified to vote. Now, older teenagers play a regular citizen role in government.

Reapportionment

For the first century of government in Nevada, the representation in the Legislature was on the same basis as in the U.S. Congress. In the Senate, the members were elected from political districts in the same way U.S. Senators are elected from the states. The members of the Assembly were elected according to population.

Then, in 1964, the U.S. Supreme Court ruled that all the members of state legislatures should be elected according to population. This meant that each member of the legislature should represent about the same number of people.

A suit was filed by Flora Dungan of Las Vegas which forced the Nevada Legislature to be re-apportioned according to this ruling. This gave Las Vegas control of the Legislature because they had more votes. The rural counties and Reno lost control of the Legislature that, together, they had held for 100 years. Since that time, the balance of political power has moved more and more into Clark County.

The 26th Amendment to the U.S. Constitution

"The right of citizens of the United States, who are 18 years of age or older, to vote shall not be denied or abridged by the United States or by any state on account of age."

Flora Dungan. *Ms. Dungan's lawsuit against the state forced Nevada to adopt representation by population in the State Legislature. As an assembly-woman from 1962 to 1967, she was the first woman to serve on the state's judiciary committee. Ms. Dungan was a leading advocate of prison reform, drug abuse education, welfare rights, and civil rights.*
Courtesy of Nevada Historical Society

State Government Services

Education

Education started in Nevada in 1854. Mrs. Isaac Mott taught the first group of children seated around her kitchen table. She lived a few miles south of Genoa. Private classes were soon held in other homes. The first teacher of these classes was Miss Hannah K. Clapp of Carson City, who soon organized her own private school, the Sierra Seminary. The first school district in Nevada was organized at Franktown by Orson Hyde in 1856. The first schoolhouse was also built at Franktown.

Education these days is the largest activity of government in Nevada. More than half of the state budget is spent on public schools and the University of Nevada System.

Each county in Nevada is a public school district, with an elected board, separate from county government. The school board hires teachers and administrators, builds schoolhouses and athletic fields, buys and runs buses, and does whatever is necessary to operate the public schools.

The University of Nevada System started with a preparatory school in Elko in 1873 and was moved to Reno in 1886. The University of Nevada at Las Vegas started in 1957 as a branch of the University of Nevada at Reno but soon became a complete university in its own right.

Community colleges were added to the University of Nevada System in 1970 and are located in Elko, Reno, Las Vegas, and Carson City with branches in a number of smaller cities and towns.

Nevada's schools are growing more rapidly in the 1990s than those of any other state. A national study in 1993, to forecast the needs of higher education, predicted that the number of high school graduates in Nevada would triple by 2009.

PIONEER EDUCATOR

Maude Frazier served Nevada for more than fifty years. She was a teacher, administrator, legislator, and lieutenant governor. She was born, educated, and started teaching in Wisconsin. In Nevada, she taught school in Genoa, Lovelock, Seven Troughs, Beatty, Goldfield, and Sparks. She became deputy state superintendent for southern Nevada in 1921. In order to travel long distances over rough roads to reach her schools, she bought and learned to repair a car. Later Miss Frazier was super-intendent of the Clark County School District during the years of rapid growth brought on by the building of Boulder Dam. After "retiring," she served for ten years in the Nevada State Legislature. In 1962, at the age of eighty-one, she was appointed lieutenant governor. She died in 1963.

Courtesy of Nevada Historical Society

One-Room Schoolhouse and Class, about 1890. *In Nevada's sparsely populated rural communities, one-room classes were the rule and not the exception. Here, a mixed collection of students and their dapper instructor are frozen in time by the photographer.*
Courtesy of Special Collections, University of Nevada Reno Library

University of Nevada at Elko. *Established by the State Legislature in 1873, Nevada's university system was a monument to the state's committment to education. In 1885, the University was relocated to Reno. Since that time, the Legislature has added a campus at Las Vegas; and in 1970 it created a system of state community colleges.*
Courtesy of Nevada Historical Society

Jean Ford   **Mary Gojack**   **Sue Wagner**

These women legislators traveled the state giving speeches and seminars that urged women to take part in government. They held workshops showing women how to get elected to public office.

How Women of Nevada Became a Strong Force in State Government

In the 1960s the importance of women in public affairs finally became recognized. President Kennedy appointed a commission on the status of women. Betty Friedan wrote "The Feminine Mystique." The National Organization for Women and the National Women's Political Caucus were formed. Nevada women responded to these events in a variety of ways. One way was in getting elected to the Nevada Legislature.

Their first concern was to get equal treatment for women -- equal pay, equal job opportunities, equal chances to be promoted on the job, and equal opportunity to obtain credit. They also wanted the needs of children met, particularly health and safety, with adequate medical care for all children. They wanted children protected from drug abuse, physical abuse, and sexual abuse. Their concerns extended to racial minorities and to the poor and handicapped. They worked for fair housing.

The first notable achievement of a woman legislator in this period of time was that of Flora Dungan from Las Vegas, whose lawsuit against the state resulted in representation by population being applied to both the Assembly and Senate (as described in Chapter 6). She also advocated prison reform, drug abuse education, welfare rights and civil rights, and programs for juvenile assistance.

Later in the 1960s and 70s came a group of women legislators: Mary Frazzini from Reno, Eileen Brookman and Jean Ford from Las Vegas, Mary Gojack, Sue Wagner and Nancy Gomes from Reno, and in 1980, Helen Foley from Las Vegas. These women worked together for their objectives, across party lines and without regard to north/south interests. Three of them -- Ford, Gojack and Wagner -- traveled the state giving speeches and conducting workshops on "Practical Politics for Women." They ran seminars for potential women candidates and urged young women to become involved in government.

Perhaps the most popular accomplishment of these women was the law first advocated by Gojack to get the sales tax removed from food. Ford and Gojack introduced the Parkland Bill, passed in 1973, authorizing local governments to collect funds from developers to be used for building neighborhood parks. Other efforts of the women's group opposed secrecy in government by requiring that more meetings be kept open. Once attention was focused on the need of women, children, and minorities to get fair treatment, many male legislators supported the women's proposals.

In 1993 Nevada had 17 women serving in the State Legislature, making it 9th among the 50 states in the number of women lawmakers. It also had women as lieutenant governor, secretary of state, attorney general, and a member of the U.S. Congress. Women in politics have made state government more responsive to the needs of people in Nevada.

Human Welfare

The first state agency established in the history of Nevada was a welfare service. The State Orphan's Home at Carson City was opened in 1870. It eventually became the Children's Home of Northern Nevada. The home was closed in 1992, after 122 years of service. The last children living there were moved to foster homes.

Today, human welfare services are the second largest activity in state government. Next in size is education. Human welfare services are also the second largest item of expense, using approximately 20 percent of the state budget.

Most of these services are under the Welfare Division, which is part of the Human Resources Department. Nearly all of the services help people with either no income or a very low income. Also, because of a large transient population, Nevada has a great need for these services.

The Welfare Division provides the following services:

1) Aid to single mothers, pregnant women and pregnant, unmarried teenagers with no other means of support.

2) Medical aid to these women and also to the unemployed and to some families with income below the poverty level.

3) Food stamps to these people and to some others of very low incomes; and

4) Health care programs and various other social services to mothers, pregnant women and some families of low income.

Another department, Child and Family Services, provides for protection from child abuse and sexual abuse. It also supervises the correctional institutions for juveniles.

Frankie Sue Del Papa.
Elected secretary of state in 1986 and attorney general in 1991, Frankie Sue Del Papa has been an outstanding example of women in Nevada government. She is a strong advocate of women's causes and humanitarian causes. Nationally she has been the secretary of and an officer in the National Association of Secretaries of State.
Courtesy of Frankie Sue Del Papa

Law Enforcement

Another important service of government is law enforcement. It protects people and their property. Most of the police work for this protection in Nevada is done by city policemen and county sheriff's officers. The city police provide protection within the city boundaries. The sheriff's officers provide protection in the county areas that lie outside of city limits. These city and county officers answer complaints and investigate crime scenes and traffic accidents. They make the arrests for felony offenses such as murder, armed robbery, or arson. They also make arrests for misdemeanors such as a violation of curfew or truancy.

These city and county officers are much involved with the safety and protection of young people. They enforce the curfew laws. They check on parked cars to see if the occupants are safe. Preventing the sale or possession of drugs is an important part of their work. They keep their eye on youth gangs and try to prevent gang violence.

When an adult is arrested, he or she is taken into the regular court system made up of justice courts, municipal courts, and district courts. Adults who are held for trial or a hearing are kept in a city or county jail. If convicted and imprisoned, they are sent to a city or county jail, or a state prison.

When juveniles (persons under 18 years of age) are arrested, they go into juvenile court where their cases are heard or tried. While awaiting a hearing or a trial, they are held in a juvenile detention center. If convicted and sentenced to do time, they are either placed in a local detention center or sent to one of the state's youth correctional centers.

Although persons under 18 are almost always dealt with as juveniles, if their crime is extremely violent (such as murder), they may be tried as adults and sent to adult jails or prisons.

The Nevada Highway Patrol is another police agency that enforces the laws on the state and interstate highways in Nevada. Their principal duty is the enforcement of the traffic laws and the investigation of traffic accidents. If other crimes, violent crimes such as a shooting or a robbery, are committed on the highways, they may be dealt with by the Nevada Highway Patrol in the same way they would be handled by city or county officers.

The Environment

Protecting the environment to save planet earth may be the most important work of government today. This is especially true for young people who will have to live in an environment that seems to be getting worse in many ways every year. In state government, it is the Environmental Protection Division that enforces the controls to make the environment as safe as possible for Nevadans.

Air quality is controlled to meet the standards of the federal Clean Air Act. This act provides for the air to be clean to breathe and clear for visibility. The division issues permits to ensure that the emissions that industry puts into the air do not violate the standards of the Clean Air Act.

The Environmental Protection Division also enforces the state standards for water quality. The water must be kept clean for people to drink and to protect fish and other aquatic life. The state issues permits to industry, and to cities and counties, to ensure that waste water discharged into rivers and streams does not violate clean water standards.

The environmental division also controls the disposal of hazardous waste, usually chemicals, produced by industrial processes. The division regulates where and how the waste is disposed.

In a separate program, not connected with pollution control, the environmental division also protects the ground water reserves. In Nevada, the driest state in the nation, protection of ground water reserves is especially important to the future of the state.

Ties to Federal Government

The policies of the United States Government have always had a tremendous effect on Nevada, perhaps more than on any other state. Nevada has always needed federal government support in order to get along. Examples are the purchase of silver, the building of irrigation projects, and the many military projects with their large payrolls. The federal government has also needed much from Nevada, particularly its mineral production and its wide-open spaces for military projects. Federal needs have created a sort of love-hate relationship between Nevadans and our national government.

The people of Nevada love the money they get from the federal government, but they hate the controls that come with it.

To begin with, the mines of Nevada supplied much of the money for the Union to pay for the Civil War. Nevada representatives helped President Lincoln get the laws passed to free the slaves. For many years, the federal government bought the silver and gold from Nevada to mint the coins that made up the nation's money supply.

Most of Nevada has always been federal land. It is land that belongs to the United States Government, rather than to private individuals. This government land makes up 87 percent of the area of Nevada. Since this land belongs to all the people, it is open land, and it supports Nevada's two oldest industries -- mining and ranching. It is open to miners for mining and to ranchers for grazing their livestock.

The open land of Nevada has provided the space needed for many military projects. It was Nevada's wide-open space that was used for developing the atomic bomb for World War II, and it has been used for nuclear testing for 30 years.

Without all this U.S. Government involvement, Nevada would have been a very poor state; and without Nevada's unique resources, the nation's economy and military strength would have suffered.

When Nevada first became a state in 1864, William Stewart, Nevada's first senator, worked closely with President Lincoln to get the Thirteenth, Fourteenth, and Fifteenth amendments passed. These are the amendments that freed the slaves, established their citizenship, and ensured their right to vote.

"Senatorial Courtesy." *This 1893 cartoon from the humor magazine, Puck, shows that not everyone was sympathetic to the cause of silver. Here, Nevada Senator William M. Stewart declaims the merits of silver coinage, while his fellow senators snooze.*

Key Pittman (1872-1940). *Pittman left his native state of Mississippi for Alaskan gold fields before he settled in Nevada. When U.S. Senator George S. Nixon died in office in 1912, the State Legislature chose Pittman to replace him. Re-elected to the Senate four times, Pittman spent much of his career fighting to stabilize silver prices.*
Courtesy of Nevada Historical Society

Senator Stewart also strongly supported the government purchase of Nevada's silver. For more than 100 years, the U.S. Government's policy on buying silver to make coins was vital to the well-being of Nevada. When the federal government bought large quantities of silver, Nevada was well off. When the United States bought little or no silver, times were bad in Nevada.

At the time that gold and silver were discovered on the Comstock, the government used gold and silver coins for money instead of paper. The national government had a great need for money to pay for the Civil War. This made gold and silver sell at a high price.

Then, in 1873, Congress decided to stop buying silver and adopt an all-gold system for the nation's money. The western states called this the "Crime of '73." This had a disastrous effect on Nevada. The act ended the market for silver, and by 1880 the Nevada silver mining industry had shut down. Congressional acts were passed to buy limited amounts of silver in 1878 and 1890 but were repealed in 1893. After that, the government bought almost no silver for 25 years.

The effort to get the government to buy silver again dominated politics in Nevada. Silver clubs were formed. A new political party, called the Silver Party, was organized. This new Silver Party included both Democrats and Republicans, and it gained complete control over politics in Nevada. In 1896, William Jennings Bryan ran for president. He promised that, if he was elected, the government would buy silver again. He was defeated.

After that, nothing was done in government to benefit the silver industry until 1918. In that year, Congress passed the Pittman Act. It was sponsored by Senator Key Pittman from Nevada.

The law was a promise of the federal government to buy a certain amount of silver until 1923. Other western states backed Nevada, but they were unable to renew the government commitment to buy silver when the act expired in 1923.

Ten years later, in 1933, President Franklin D. Roosevelt accepted an international silver agreement. The federal government eliminated gold coins and began to purchase and mint all the silver mined in the United States. It was used to make dimes, quarters, half dollars, and dollars. Again, Senator Pittman helped an act to get passed in 1934 that increased the number of silver coins in circulation. This lasted for more than 30 years until 1965, when Congress stopped making dimes and quarters from silver. In 1970, the last of the silver coins, the half dollar, went out of circulation when Congress stopped minting silver coins altogether. This final act had a devastating effect on the silver industry in Nevada.

*The **United States Mint at Carson City.*** *This nineteenth-century photograph shows the structure where the silver and gold produced by Nevada's mines was minted into coins by federal government employees. Today, this imposing building houses the Nevada State Museum, with its wonderful collection of exhibits and information.*
Courtesy of Special Collections, University of Nevada Reno Library

Senator Stewart also wrote the Mining Act of 1866, giving miners special rights in the use of public lands. This law is still in effect 125 years later.

In his second term (1887 to 1905), Stewart also organized the western representatives in Congress to support national projects that would develop arid western lands, but without immediate success. Instead, it was Francis G. Newlands, a U.S. Congressman from Reno, who wrote the National Reclamation Act of 1902. Newlands also got the Truckee and Carson river basins approved for what became the Newlands Project described in Chapter Five. Newlands was soon elected to the U.S. Senate and served there from 1903 to 1917.

Other Nevada Senators

Senator Tasker L. Oddie, one of the partners in the great Tonopah gold discovery and a former governor of Nevada, was responsible for getting the federal government involved in the building of interstate auto highways. After he was elected to his second term in 1927, Oddie began building support for federally funded interstate highways. On May 21, 1928, Congress passed the Oddie-Colton Highway Act, which provided federal aid to states building interstate highways. Oddie also was able to get federal aid for other state road projects. By 1931, the Nevada section of the federal highway system was completed and surfaced with gravel.

Other Nevada senators have been influential in national affairs sometimes unrelated to Nevada. Patrick McCarran, a Democrat from Tonopah and Reno, was responsible for the Civil Aeronautics Act, the Internal Security Act, and the McCarran-Walters Immigration Act. He was largely responsible for getting the original location in Nevada of what became Nellis Air Force Base.

Tasker Lowndes Oddie (1870-1950) of Brooklyn, New York. Oddie came to Nevada to practice law in 1898. In 1900, he was one of the original partners in the great Tonopah ore discovery. Oddie served as governor of Nevada from 1911 to 1914, and as U.S. Senator between 1921 and 1935. Oddie brought the interstate highway system to the United States.
Courtesy of Nevada Historical Society

In more recent years, Senator Paul Laxalt, a Republican from Carson City, was influential nationally because of his close personal ties with President Ronald Reagan. The friendship began when both were governors of the adjoining states of Nevada and California. Laxalt was Reagan's spokesman in the U. S. Senate and was the campaign manager for all three of Reagan's campaigns for the presidency.

The Boulder (or Hoover) Dam

One federal project of great importance to Nevada is Boulder Dam. Located in Boulder Canyon on the Colorado River about 15 miles southeast of Las Vegas. It is 727 feet high, 660 feet thick, 1,244 feet long. Is considered one of the engineering wonders of the United States. The dam is officially named the Hoover Dam. It was the great project of President Herbert Hoover's administration. However, it has always been called Boulder Dam. It took six companies working together between 1931 and 1935 to build the huge structure. The dam creates Lake Mead, which is 115 miles long and one of the largest artificial lakes in the world. It covers the lost city of the Anasazi Indians. Lake Mead has become a great attraction for water recreation.

Boulder Dam was an economic bonanza for southern Nevada. It brought inexpensive electric power to the region. This lowered the cost of electricity for refining ore and brought a mining boom to southern Nevada. Cheap electricity also made it possible to cool buildings with air conditioning in the hot climate of Las Vegas. This made hotels more attractive to visitors. It also helps power the neon signs needed for Las Vegas to become the great entertainment center of World.

Paul Laxalt. Laxalt was *governor of Nevada in 1967 when the state legalized corporate ownership of gaming establishments. The son of a Basque rancher from France, Laxalt was later elected to the U. S. Senate.*
Courtesy of Nevada Historical Society

Distribution of Electrical Power from Hoover Dam

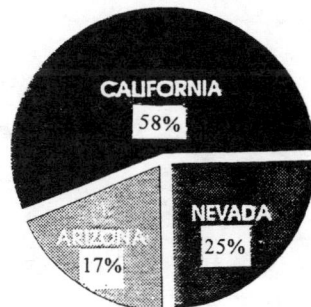

CALIFORNIA
58%

NEVADA
25%

ARIZONA
17%

Hoover Dam. *An engineering wonder, the Hoover Dam tamed the turbulent Colorado River and harnessed its energy for generations to come. Started in 1931 during the Hoover administration and completed in 1935, this dam became a symbol of constructive use of national power. A truly heroic engineering project, the dam provided inexpensive power to southern Nevada and benefitted all of the surrounding states.*
Courtesy of Special Collections, University of Nevada Reno Library

Technological Achievement. *This magnificent sight greets motorists on U.S. 93 as the highway takes them over the top of Boulder Dam. This is where the highway crosses the border between Nevada and Arizona. Tours of the dam are provided daily, and an exhibit building houses a model of the river basin.*
Courtesy of Las Vegas News Bureau

U.S. Military Services

The military services of the United States Government have been a very important part of life in Nevada. In total, from the very beginning of the early explorations, all through the early years of Nevada history, and again in modern times, military activities have had a tremendous influence on Nevada.

Before Nevada was ever settled, it was the explorations of Capt. John C. Fremont that described Nevada's Great Basin region to the rest of the nation. Capt. Fremont named Pyramid Lake and the Truckee, Carson, Walker and Humboldt rivers. Then it was Capt. James H. Simpson of the Army Engineers who, in 1859, surveyed the central route across Nevada. This became the Pony Express Route and the Simpson Wagon Road. It is roughly the route of present U.S. Highway 50. In 1860, Fort Churchill was built to protect the settlers. Soon other Army forts were built in Nevada. Fort McDermit had the longest service, from 1865 to 1888.

However, it was in the next century that military programs made great changes in the state of Nevada. World War II brought huge military projects that poured millions of dollars into the Nevada economy and created jobs for thousands of people. Nevada was an ideal location for military air bases. Good flying weather the year around and millions of acres where almost no one lived made Nevada a perfect place to train pilots.

It all began in 1941. Influenced by Nevada Senator Pat McCarran, the Army chose a small airport nine miles northeast of Las Vegas for a gunnery school. Gunnery training at the Las Vegas Army Airfield began in January of 1941.

Patrick Anthony McCarran (1876-1954) of Nevada. McCarran served his native state for twenty-two years as U.S. Senator. He was responsible for a good deal of important national legislation, including the Civil Aeronautics Act, the Internal Security Act of 1950, and the McCarran-Walters Immigration Act. His life was dedicated to an unrelenting fight against communism. Courtesy of Nevada Historical Society

Top Gun, F18
Courtesy of Gordon Bean

Activity died down after World War II, but the base was never closed. In May of 1950, the Las Vegas Army Airfield was renamed Nellis Air Force Base. The name honored Army Air Force First Lieutenant William H. Nellis of Searchlight. He was killed in combat in the skies over Europe in 1944, after 89 successful missions. Training was revived at the outbreak of the Korean War in June of 1950.

Nevada's newest military aviation activity is the nation's TOP GUN SCHOOL. The school moved from Miramar NAS, San Diego to Fallon in 1996. Its mission is to further train fighter pilots. The pilots come to Fallon in groups, are trained for a period of time and then they return to their military units.

Training at Tonopah. *World War II bomber and fighter pilots were trained at Tonopah. Here, Bell P-39 Aircobras, used to train fighter pilots, stand on the field in front of a hanger at Tonopah in July of 1942. B-24 bomber pilots who flew over Europe were also trained here. Bomber pilots who flew over Japan were trained at Wendover and many fighter pilots were trained at Nellis Air Force Base.*
Courtesy of Central Nevada Historical Society

The air base at Fallon started out in 1942 as an Army facility but was transferred to the United States Navy in 1943.

The Reno Army Air Base was operated by the Air Transport Command. In 1945 it became an Air National Guard facility and was later named Stead Air Force Base during the Korean War.

After the war atomic weapons of the United States were tested on islands in the Pacific Ocean. This was not satisfactory. The U. S. Government needed a new place for testing. It chose a part of the large Las Vegas gunnery range, using locations at Frenchman and Yucca Flat. Experimental work began in 1950 and the first bomb detonated in Nevada was in January of 1951. The now famous Nevada Test Site has been the location of nuclear testing since then. Many people disapprove of the testing of these nuclear devices.

The ammunition center at Hawthorne was built in 1928 to 1930. It is still very much in use.

The Yucca Mountain Project

Most Nevadans are opposed to a federal installation that has been proposed for the state. It is the Yucca Mountain project that would make Nevada the storage place for the nation's nuclear waste. This has been opposed by Nevada officials at both the state and national levels and in both political parties. They argue that it is an attempt, by the rest of the nation, to solve the national nuclear waste problem at the expense of Nevada. It is known that Yucca Mountain is on an earthquake fault.

Sen. Richard Bryan states, "There can be no compromise when it comes to the health and safety of Nevadans. Designating Nevada as a dump site for nuclear waste was a decision based on politics, and not science and we will continue to fight it".

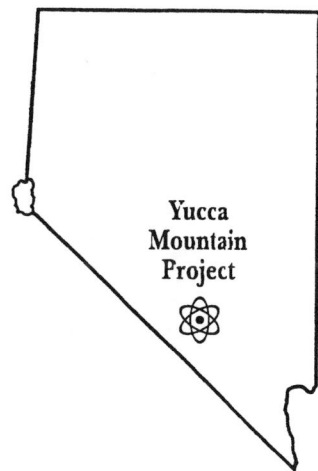

Yucca
Mountain
Project

Nevada scientists fear that leakage from a nuclear waste deposit would contaminate underground water and the soil over a large area of central Nevada. This project is still being studied by Congress.

State Boundaries

Nevada has artificial boundaries. That is, the state boundaries are not set by rivers, lakes, the ocean, or mountain ranges, as is the case in many states. Nevada's northern boundary is at the 42nd Parallel. This was the dividing line between United States and Spanish territory agreed upon after President Thomas Jefferson made the Louisiana Purchase in 1803. Nevada is in what was then part of the Spanish territory.

The southern boundary of Nevada was set at the 37th Parallel by both the territorial and the state constitutions. Later, it was moved south to where the Colorado River intersects the 35th Parallel.

The eastern boundary was taken from Utah Territory in three pieces, a little more each time, until it reached the present line at the 114th Meridian.

The western boundary is the 120th Meridian south to the 39th Parallel at Lake Tahoe, California. Then the boundary goes in a direct line southeast to the intersection of the Colorado River. The river forms the boundary north and east to the 114th Parallel.

The western boundary with California was unsettled for more than 100 years. At first it was set on a meridian that was thought to represent the summit of the Sierras. The mountains were so rugged that no agreement could be reached as to just where the boundary should be. There was even a gun battle, in Susanville in 1863, between a sheriff's posse from California and a posse from Nevada over who had authority in the area. There were similar disagreements, without violence, in Esmeralda County, Nevada, and Mono County, California. Lines were repeatedly drawn and changed. The line finally accepted was one made by the U.S. Coast and Geodetic Survey conducted between 1893 and 1899. It was challenged by both California and Nevada but finally set as the permanent boundary by a U.S. Supreme Court decision in 1980.

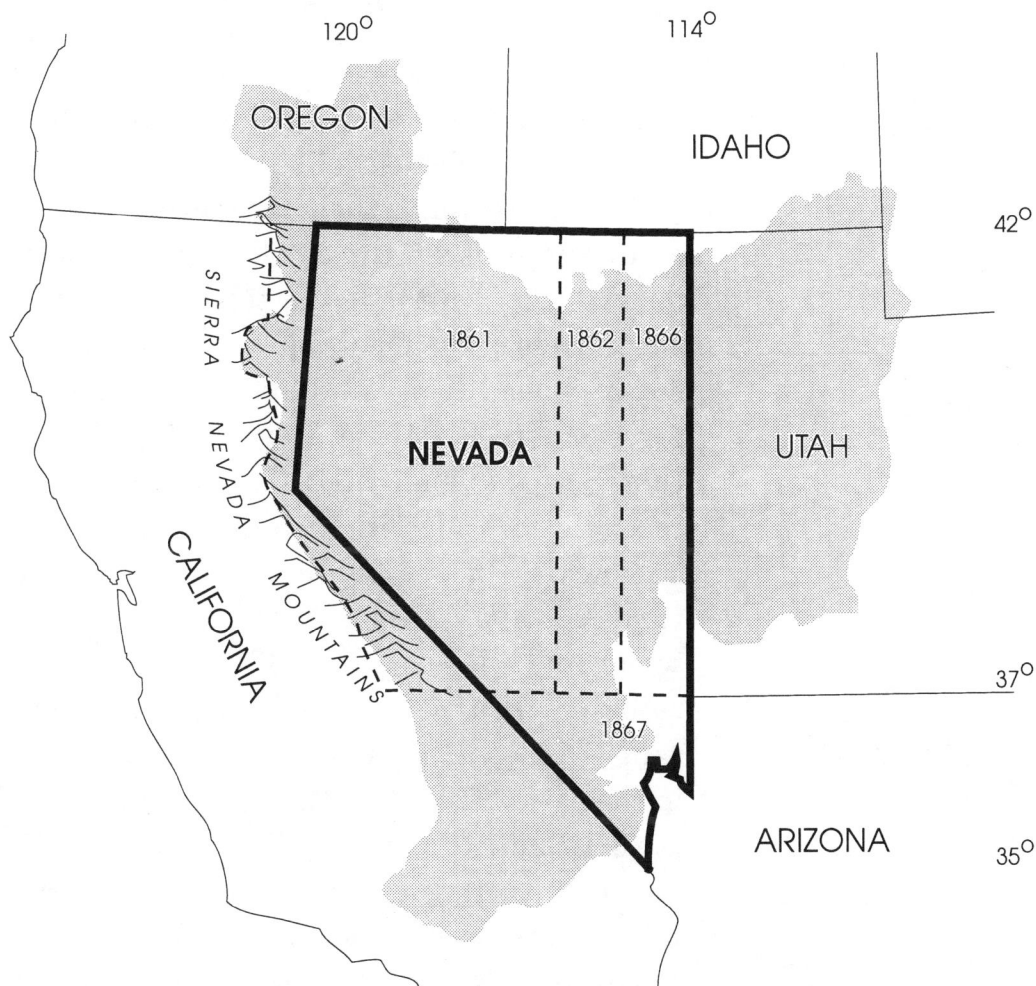

The Political and Geographic Boundaries of Nevada. *This map shows the political boundaries of the state and the dates of its territorial enlargements, superimposed over a map of the Great Basin region. Unlike most borders, the Nevada-California state line does not run along the summit of the mountains. Note that most of the Sierra Nevada lies within the state of California.*

The Great Seal of Nevada

The Great Seal of the State of Nevada was adopted by the State Legislature in 1866. The design is described as follows.

In the foreground there are two large mountains at the base of which, on the right, is located a quartz mill. On the left, a tunnel penetrates the silver leads of the mountain with a miner running out a carload of ore and a team loaded with ore for the mill. Immediately in the foreground there are emblems indicative of the agricultural resources of the state including a plow, a sheaf, and sickle. In the middle ground there is a railroad train passing a mountain gorge and a telegraph line extending along the line of the railroad. In the extreme background there is a range of snow-clad mountains with the rising sun in the east. Thirty-six stars (to signify Nevada as the 36th state to join the Union) and the motto, "All for Our Country," encircle the entire illustration. In the outer circle, the words "The Great Seal of the State of Nevada" are engraved with "Nevada" at the base of the seal and separated from the other words by stars. The Great Seal above is also displayed in color at the front of this chapter.

Home Means Nevada

'Way out in the land of the setting sun,
Where the wind blows wild and free,
There's a lovely spot, just the only one.
That means home sweet home to me.

If you follow the old Kit Carson trail,
Until desert meets the hills,
Oh you certainly will agree with me,
It's the place of a thousand thrills.

Whenever the sun at the close of day,
Colors all the western sky,
Oh my heart returns to the desert grey
And the mountains tow'ring high.

Where the moon beams play in shadowed glen,
With the spotted fawn and doe,
All the live-long night until morning light,
Is the loveliest place I know.

Chorus:

Home means Nevada,
Home means the hills,
Home means the sage and the pines.

Out of the Truckee's silvery rills,
Out where the sun always shines,
There is the land that I love the best,
Fairer than all I can see.
Right in the heart of the golden West,
Home means Nevada to me.

Frances C. McDonald

The State Flag

Nevada did not have a state flag until 1905. Changes from that first flag were made in 1915 and 1929. Finally, in 1991, the State Legislature made minor changes resulting in the flag we have today.

The new flag is on a field of blue with two sprays of sagebrush crossed to form a wreath in the upper left-hand corner. A scroll across the top of the wreath carries Nevada's motto, "Battle Born," which signifies that Nevada entered the Union during the Civil War. A five-pointed star occupies the center of the wreath and, under the star, the word "Nevada" is spelled out in clear, distinct letters. The flag is displayed in color at the beginning of this chapter.

1905 State Flag
Courtesy of Nevada Historical Society

State Buildings

The Legislature decided to provide for a state capitol building in 1869. The members chose an unlikely spot to build it, according to pioneer Allen Bragg, who recalled the site in a 1915 newspaper article for the Carson City News:

The Capitol grounds was an unsightly place called the Plaza, without a blade of grass or a tree of any kind, but a little sagebrush in spots. The place was fenced with unpainted six by six timbers, two timbers high, and for years a half burned wooden structure called the pavilion, which was never finished, stood by where the capitol now stands. Later in the [eighteen] sixties the plaza was used by the Silver Star Baseball Club.

The ground was cleared, the design approved, and the cornerstone celebrations took place on June 9, 1870. The stone was cut at the Nevada State Prison and hauled to the site. The workmen finished construction by the end of that year, and the Legislature of 1871 was the first to get to use the building.

In 1875, it was decided that a new fence should be built around the capitol grounds. Cattle grazed freely over the grounds, and the Carson City ladies claimed that manure was damaging their long skirts. The work to build the fence was put out to bid. At $6,450, H. Clapp was the lowest bidder. When the legislators discovered that H. Clapp was Hannah Clapp, the school teacher who operated the Sierra Seminary, they had reservations about giving her the work. But Miss Clapp fought for her rights and was awarded the contract. She had the materials preconstructed and shipped to Carson City. The fence, now more than 115 years old, still surrounds the capitol building. The capitol building itself was extensively reconstructed in the 1970s, preserving its great historic value.

Hannah Hezekiah Clapp. In her time, Ms. Clapp was Nevada's foremost career woman. She founded Nevada's first school, the Sierra Seminary, in Carson City in the 1860s. She was the contractor who built the iron fence that still stands around the State Capitol. Ms. Clapp was the first faculty member of the University of Nevada at Reno and was its librarian. She also founded Reno's first kindergarten.
Courtesy of Nevada State Museum

The Famous Capitol Fence. The iron fence, with some of the State Capitol visible through the trees, was built in 1875 on a contract let to Hannah Clapp, the local school teacher. It still stands, strong and solid, and lends a touch of elegance to the Capitol grounds.
Courtesy of Susan Bean

The State Capitol of Nevada at Carson City, 1871. *This photograph shows the capitol building shortly after its construction was completed. The Legislatures of the state met here for one hundred years, and the governor of the state also had his offices inside this building. Today, the structure, which formerly housed all of the government of the state, is too small for many administrative departments.*
Courtesy of Special Collections, University of Nevada Reno Library

The Governor's Mansion dates from 1908-09. Governor Denver S. Dickerson and his family were the first to occupy it. Before that time, the governors had lived in their own private homes.

The legislative building south of the capitol was built in 1970, one hundred years after the capitol was built. The Legislature of 1971 was the first to meet in the new building.

A new 17-million dollar, three-story Nevada Supreme Court Building, designed by Susan Eismann Pence, opened in 1992. It is expected to meet the state's needs until sometime after 2050.

The Governor's Mansion at Carson City
Courtesy of Susan Bean

The Legislative Building at Carson City
Courtesy of Susan Bean

**Nevada Supreme Court
Building.** This dramatic exterior
marks the entry to Nevada's new
17-million-dollar Supreme Court
Building planned to meet the
state's need until after the year
2050.
Courtesy of Susan Bean

**Nevada's New
State Library and
Archives Building.**
All of Nevada's
official archives and
state library materials
are now collected in
this new building
which opened in
1993. The old annex
at right was
combined with the
new structure. The
annex is built of
locally quarried
stone.
Courtesy of Susan Bean

A new 14.1-million dollar Nevada State Library and Archives Building opened in January of 1993. All of the state's library and archives records, which had been scattered in several places, were brought together in the new building. The new library was designed by Las Vegas architects Edward P. DeLorenzo and Mark Sitka. The library offices are located on the second floor. An exhibit gallery on the first floor displays the Nevada State Constitution and other historical documents.

Carson City, The State Capital

An unusual combination of two things made Carson City the place for the capital of Nevada. It was the gateway to Virginia City, the richest place on earth and the largest city in the West; and the land at Carson City belonged to Abraham Curry, a very skillful developer and promoter.

Carson City was the crossroads for travelers and very close to the rich mines of the Comstock. All the travelers enroute to Virginia City passed by Carson City. From Carson City, they went down the Carson River to Dayton and up the Six Mile Canyon into Gold Hill and Virginia City. Coming into Carson City, they came up from Nevada's other principal community, the business and farming center at Genoa. They also came by wagon down from Susanville to the north, and by stagecoach up through Placerville and over the Sierras from California. All these conditions made Carson City the ideal location for a government capital. But it was the skill of Curry, who owned the land, that developed the city there. Curry bought the land just a year before silver was discovered on the Comstock. Without Curry there would not be a Carson City as we know it.

Abraham Z. Curry. *The founder of Carson City, Curry was also a warden of the Nevada Territorial Prison and first superintendent of the U.S. Mint at Carson City.*
Courtesy of Nevada Historical Society

The very first settlement of the land was made by a group of miners who came from California seeking gold. Failing to find any gold, they set up a trading post. One of the men, Frank Hall, shot an eagle, skinned it, and nailed the skin on the front of his cabin. The trading post was then called Eagle Station. The ranch that developed around the trading post was known as Eagle Ranch. Eagle Valley became the name of the valley surrounding the ranch, and it is still Eagle Valley today.

In 1858, Curry came to Western Utah with the intention of investing in the business community at Genoa. The price of land was too high, and he decided to "build a town of his own." He moved to Eagle Valley, bought the ranch there, and founded Carson City.

By that time, the ranch had several owners. Curry bought it from them for $500 and some mustangs. By the end of 1858, the site for the city had been platted, and Curry had set aside a plaza area for the future construction of public buildings. He had started a city right where it needed to be.

The great silver discovery was made on the Comstock in 1859. Thousands of miners poured into Virginia City. The nation needed the wealth from the mines, and, on March 2, 1861, Nevada became a territory. President Lincoln appointed James Nye as territorial governor. Nye arrived in July and named Carson City as the place for the territorial legislature to meet. Under the powerful influence of Senator William Stewart, the legislature passed an act making Carson City the territorial capital and future state capital.

Two developments in 1869-70 added greatly to the importance of Carson City as a commercial center. In 1869 the Virginia & Truckee Railroad was built down the mountain from the mines to Carson City, and the new United States Mint was built in Carson City. Both began operating in January of 1870.

Today, Carson City is remarkable for its historic attractions. Besides the government buildings described earlier, there are more than 60 points of historical interest along a walking tour of the city. The trail passes historical churches built in the gold rush days and still in service. Homes of many famous people are scattered along the trail. You can see where Mark Twain visited his brother Orion, where John Wayne made his last movie, and the building where Dat-So-La-Lee wove her world-famous Indian baskets.

Carson City is a wonderful place for students to visit.

A Field Trip to Nevada's Capital

Let's take an imaginary tour of Nevada's capital. Imagine that your class is visiting Carson City on a field trip for historical study. Your class is gathered together on the lawn in front of the State Capitol. Here is what your teacher might say:

This is the center of state government in Nevada. Here, almost in a line, are the main buildings of government. You've read about them at the end of the chapter on government in your history book. We are in front of the State Capitol [1], which was built in 1870. Here is the famous fence that was built by Hannah Clapp in 1875. As we walk through the State Capitol building, you will notice how big and heavy and roomy everything is. That is the way public buildings were built 125 years ago. To the south, you will recognize the Legislative Building [2], built in 1970, just 100 years after the capitol was built.

By contrast it is very modern and convenient, a wonderful place to work.

The other two buildings we will visit in this mall area are the new Supreme Court Building [3], which is to the back, southeast, and between the capitol and the Legislative Building, and the new State Library and Archives Building [4], which is built next to the former State Printing Building. It is just east of the capitol. You will enjoy visiting these new buildings. Both were built in 1992. They are absolutely beautiful and well constructed to serve the needs of the state for the next half century or longer. You have read about all four of these public buildings in your government chapter.

Later, to students gathered on the lawn in front of the Presbyterian Church, the teacher says:

The old churches we will now visit are a very special part of Nevada history. They were all built during the silver mine bonanza days, when Virginia City was the richest place on earth and larger than San Francisco. Wealth from Virginia City built these fine old churches. This First Presbyterian Church (5), where we are gathered, was the first church built. That was in 1864. We will walk only a few blocks to visit the other old churches. We will stop to see the First Methodist Church (6) built in 1865; then St. Peter's Episcopal Church (8) built in 1867-68. As we walk between these two churches, if we look east, we can see the modest house of Dat-So-La-Lee (7), the world famous Indian basket maker whom you have seen pictured with her baskets in your history book. Finally, we will visit St. Teresa of Avila Church (9) built in 1870-71. As you visit these great historic churches, try to visualize what they have seen in the past 120 years -- the weddings, the baptisms, the funerals of Nevada's great leaders, and all the community that surrounded them in Carson City.

On our way to the Governor's Mansion, we will visit some historic houses. The first will be the Stewart-Nye house (10) which William Stewart built in 1860, at about the time he became the most powerful political figure in Nevada. Soon, he sold it to James W. Nye, who was appointed Territorial Governor by President Lincoln in 1861. The Krebs-Peterson house (11), built in 1914, this is where John Wayne's last move, "The Shootist," was filmed in 1976. This is a particularly emotional film. The lead character in the story, played by Wayne, was dying of cancer; and Wayne himself was also dying of cancer at the time the film was being made. From here we will go a short distance to the Governor's Mansion (12).

On the lawn at the Governor's Mansion, the teacher says:

This beautiful, southern-style colonial mansion is the home of Nevada's governor. It was not built until 1908-09, when the state was more than 40 years old. It is a great showplace. The governors have been very generous in allowing its garden and lawn to be used for many important public and social occasions.

We will be passing another house built by William Stewart (13) which he built in 1887, long after he had become Nevada's U.S. Senator. The beautiful old homes of Henry Yerington (14), Orion Clemens (15), whose brother, Samuel, was better known as Mark Twain, Abe Curry (16) and Alfred Chartz (17) will

*be seen on our way to the U. S. Mint (18).
Here, millions of Nevada's famous silver
dollars were coined from 1870 to 1894. This
building now houses the Nevada State Museum,
with a replica of a Nevada mine and dioramas
of Nevada's land, animals and Native
Americans. We will go on to the old Virginia &
Truckee Railroad Station (19), which was
headquarters for the railroad from 1872 until
1950 and our tour will end at the Carson City
Auditorium which now houses the Children's
Museum.*

*After their busy day visiting the State
Capital, the students were tired. They slept in
their seats on the way home. Tom, who
generally pestered everyone else, dreamed that
he would be a Nevada senator. Kate, knowing
women could be anything they wanted,
dreamed that she would be governor of
Nevada.*

**The New Legislative Building at Carson City, refaced
in 1997.**
Courtesy of Susan Bean

CAPITAL CITY TOUR

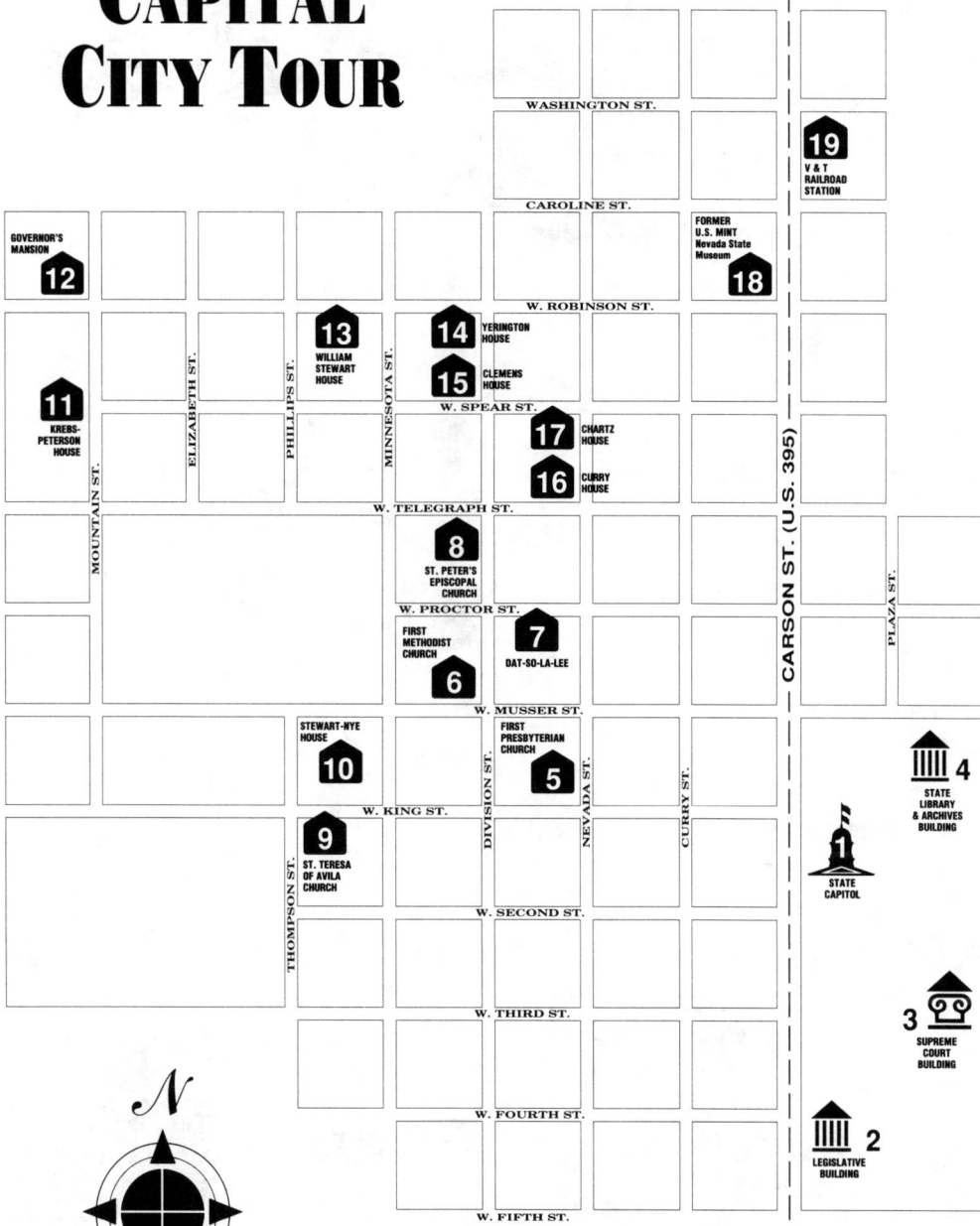

WASHINGTON ST.

CAROLINE ST.

19 V & T RAILROAD STATION

12 GOVERNOR'S MANSION

18 FORMER U.S. MINT Nevada State Museum

W. ROBINSON ST.

13 WILLIAM STEWART HOUSE

14 YERINGTON HOUSE

11 KREBS-PETERSON HOUSE

15 CLEMENS HOUSE

W. SPEAR ST.

17 CHARTZ HOUSE

16 CURRY HOUSE

W. TELEGRAPH ST.

8 ST. PETER'S EPISCOPAL CHURCH

W. PROCTOR ST.

FIRST METHODIST CHURCH

7 DAT-SO-LA-LEE

6

W. MUSSER ST.

STEWART-NYE HOUSE

FIRST PRESBYTERIAN CHURCH

4 STATE LIBRARY & ARCHIVES BUILDING

10

5

1 STATE CAPITOL

W. KING ST.

9 ST. TERESA OF AVILA CHURCH

3 SUPREME COURT BUILDING

W. SECOND ST.

W. THIRD ST.

W. FOURTH ST.

2 LEGISLATIVE BUILDING

W. FIFTH ST.

MOUNTAIN ST.
ELIZABETH ST.
PHILLIPS ST.
MINNESOTA ST.
THOMPSON ST.
DIVISION ST.
NEVADA ST.
CURRY ST.
CARSON ST. (U.S. 395)
PLAZA ST.
STEWART ST.

N

Historical Events

1857
First Hotel In Nevada

1897
Corbett-Fitzsimmons Fight

1927
Divorce Made Easy in Nevada

1931
Gambling Legalized in Nevada

1905
Slot Machines Legalized

1936
Harold's Club Started in Reno

1940
Great Entertainers at Commercial Hotel in Elko

1945
State Government Began to Tax Gambling

1946
Harvey Gross at Tahoe

"Bugsy" Siegel in Las Vegas

1955
Gambling Control Board Created

1967
Corporate Ownership of Casinos Approved

1983
Commissions on Economic Development
and Tourism Established

Chapter Seven

Business

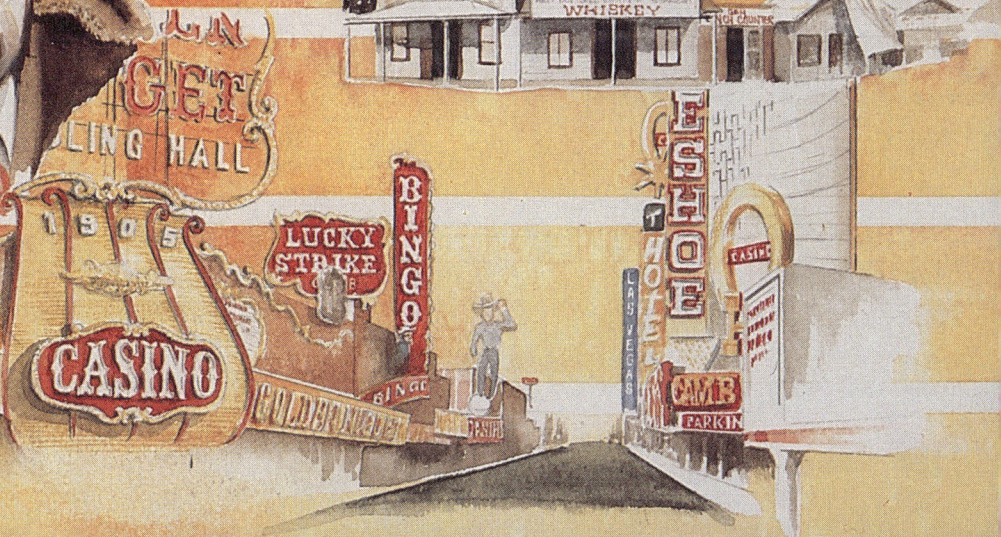

Business

The business of Nevada has been mining, ranching, and tourism. Too often it has been "boom and bust." In Nevada's first 100 years, business boomed when there were great silver and gold mining strikes. It also prospered in areas where copper was mined. In between the boom times, ranching kept the economy alive, but it didn't provide many jobs. People moved out of Nevada. Population dropped. Then, after World War II (in the past 50 years), tourism, supported by legalized gambling, has made Nevada the fastest growing state in the nation. Now, in the 1990s, business in Nevada is threatened again by the increasing popularity of gambling in other states.

Verne Horton

We have seen in previous chapters how the business of Nevada developed through the years. The business of the Indians was self-support through hunting, gathering, and small agriculture.

The first business of the white people who came to Nevada was fur-trapping, followed by raising livestock and some crops, and then, very soon, by mining.

After the discovery of gold in 1850 and silver in 1859, mining became the main business of Nevada. The development of copper mining in the early 1900s sustained mining as the principal business of the state.

Ranching, with the raising of livestock and the growing of field crops, became the secondary business of Nevada. When rich ore deposits were discovered and developed, Nevada prospered. In the periods of time between mining activity, ranching kept the state going. This was the pattern of business in Nevada for nearly a century.

Important changes in the business of Nevada began to occur in the 1920s and 1930s. At first, it was easy divorce that brought celebrities to Nevada to dissolve their marriages. The celebrities attracted other visitors. Easy divorce was followed by the legalizing of gambling in Nevada in 1931. It took some time for these changes to have their full impact. Finally, after World War II, about a century after gold was discovered in Gold Canyon, Nevada found a new income in gaming and tourism.

Tourism

Tourism has been a part of Nevada's history from the earliest days of settlement. The first tourist in Nevada was probably Lola Montez, the Countess of Landsfeld, an internationally famous actress and celebrity living in Grass Valley, California.

Lola Montez, Countess of Landsfeld (1818-1861). This Irish-born celebrity blazed the trail to Nevada for tens of millions of tourists when she and a party of friends and guests visited the Truckee Meadows on a sightseeing trip in July, 1854.
Courtesy of California State Library

Nevada's First Hotel. *The Rogers & Thorington House, built at Genoa in 1857, provided lodging for travelers on the California Trail and especially for passengers on the transcontinental stagecoaches which began operating that year. This Douglas County photograph, taken some years later, shows the California Trail (Genoa's main street), the overland telegraph, developing shade trees, and a new wing added to the back of the freshly-painted hotel. As road traffic increased, so did the hotel business.*
Courtesy of Nevada Historical Society

Her excursion to Donner Lake and the Truckee Meadows in the summer of 1854 is the first such sight-seeing jaunt to Nevada that was reported in the newspapers.

Nevada's first hotel was built in Genoa in 1857 by William B. "Lucky Bill" Thorington and William D. "Uncle Billy" Rogers. They took advantage of the increase in travelers brought over the Sierra stagecoach routes which opened that year. It was also known as the "White House" hotel, where many a card game was played.

Nevada's first resort was opened in 1862 by David Walley, at the hot springs in Douglas County which bear his name. Still in operation today, the original resort has been reconstructed and improved.

Nevada's First Resort. *Opened in 1862 on the California Trail near Genoa, Walley Hot Springs offered a well-appointed hotel, curative mineral springs, and a superior climate to persons seeking healthful relaxation. Many of Nevada's natural hot springs have provided the site for a resort hotel.*
Courtesy of Nevada Historical Society

During the nineteenth century, the International Hotel in Virginia City had a reputation to match its name. It was the most sophisticated and cosmopolitan hotel in Nevada. A towering skyscraper in its day, the six-story International Hotel for years had the only elevator between the Mississippi River and the Pacific Coast. President U.S. Grant and General William T. Sherman were guests there. Many foreign dignitaries and financial kingpins spent the night in the tastefully furnished, gas-illuminated rooms.

The early Nevada hotels and restaurants set a pattern for later days. Mary McNair Mathews, a resident of Virginia City, remarked in her 1880 book, *Ten Years in Nevada:*

> *Every restaurant table groans with food of every kind gathered from every kingdom of the globe. From eight to twelve different kinds of vegetables, and nearly as many kinds of meat, are on the table three times a day. Cakes and every kind of pastry and puddings you will find; there are also fruits from every country and clime.*

The International Hotel at Virginia City. *This morning scene from the 1870s depicts the finest eating, drinking, and sleeping establishment in nineteenth-century Nevada. Everything about it was modern and up-to-date, from its richly-furnished rooms illuminated by gaslight, to its shining brass elevator. A hotel of this class provided special areas, or rooms, for its patrons who cared to gamble.*
Courtesy of Special Collections, University of Nevada Reno Library

This lavish nineteenth-century tourist industry came to an end when the mining boom played out in 1880. Nevada was to wait for nearly half a century before tourism really flourished again. In the meantime, there were occasional episodes of successful tourist activity.

Tolerant Nevada

Nevada's great tourist industry of today was built on the state's tolerant attitude toward human behavior. Nevada passed laws to benefit from its tolerant attitude. When Nevada began holding prizefights, they were considered a savage form of entertainment in most other states. When divorce was first made easy in Nevada, it was still considered sinful in other states and discouraged by their laws. At the time that gambling was legalized in Nevada, it was against the law in other states. It was almost universally considered a destructive vice that discouraged work and made men lazy. All these activities that were first accepted publicly in Nevada -- prizefighting, easy divorce, and legalized gambling -- have gradually become commonplace in other states.

Laws to Help Nevada Grow

The people of Nevada have passed laws to help the state grow and prosper in ways different from any other state. They began doing this because Nevada often suffered from hard times.

Nevada's two main businesses, mining and ranching, were boom and bust industries. When mining and ranching prospered, Nevada was well off. When they had hard times, the state was very poor, and people moved away to other states.

In 1880, at the end of the greatest mining boom, the population of Nevada was 62,266. The silver mines closed down, and nearly a third of the people in Nevada moved away. Population had dropped to 42,335 by 1900. Then rich ore deposits were discovered at Tonopah and Goldfield, creating new wealth and activity. The copper mines opened up in White Pine County, and Nevada was prosperous. Population nearly doubled. The boom ended.

Mining Camp Social Center, 1902. *The Northern Saloon, in the newly-founded tent town of Tonopah, had a large sign and frame construction in a place where most citizens played and slept under canvas. Jim Butler, discoverer of Tonopah's silver mines, stands in front of the open door. The proprietor of the Northern, legendary western lawman and gunfighter Wyatt Earp, is just to the right of the sign and behind the lady on horseback. A saloon was usually one of the first permanent buildings to be constructed in a new town or camp.*
Courtesy of Nevada Historical Society

Times were bad again and people moved away as they had done before. Population dropped from 81,885 in 1910 to 77,405 in 1920.

It was always easy to get a divorce in Nevada. Judges were tolerant and granted divorces more freely than in other states. Members of the Legislature decided to make divorce even easier in order to attract more people to Nevada. In 1926, they shortened the residence requirement for divorce to three months. Then again, in 1931, they shortened to only six weeks the time that people had to wait in Nevada to get a divorce. For many years, during the 1920s and 1930s, wealthy easterners, stage and screen celebrities, and foreign nobility came to Nevada for divorces. These rich people spent money freely, and they attracted other couples who wanted easy divorces. This activity brought additional visitors to Nevada. The state's economy improved.

Gambling Boosted Growth

Nevada, with its mining camp heritage, was always a gambling society. In 1910, because of pressure from reformers, officials turned against gambling. The Legislature made it illegal to gamble, as it was in other states. But the restriction was never really enforced.

Then, in 1931, the Legislature passed a law to legalize gambling in Nevada. Since gambling was illegal in most other states, the gamblers came to Nevada where it was legal. Investors moved to Nevada to open gambling establishments, and this stimulated business. In 1945, the Legislature put a one percent tax on the winnings of gambling houses. Over the years, this tax was gradually raised to more than six percent.

Soon this tax revenue from gambling paid much of the cost of government. Officials in Nevada encouraged the growth of gambling for its tax revenues. Visitors came to Nevada in rapidly increasing numbers. The construction industry boomed as investors built larger and larger hotels and casinos to serve the growing number of visiting gamblers. Other industries of all kinds developed to serve the influx of people.

Visitors found that Nevada offered great outdoor recreation. They came here to hunt and fish, and simply enjoy the wide open spaces. With all this increased activity there were thousands of new jobs, and the population grew rapidly.

Warren Nelson, a Nevada Gaming Pioneer. Nelson, co-founder of the Club Cal-Neva in Reno, came to Nevada in the mid-1930s from Montana. He is credited with having introduced the game of keno, one of the more popular forms of gambling today.
Courtesy of Cal-Neva Casino

Low Taxes Helped Growth

People of Nevada have always opposed taxes, even more than in other states. A combination of constitutional provisions and state laws have put severe limits on property taxes, making them lower than in other states. They also made it impossible for the State Legislature to enact a personal income tax.

State's Population

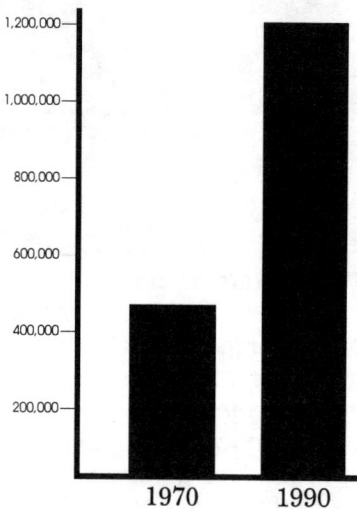

1,200,000	
1,000,000	
800,000	
600,000	
400,000	
200,000	
	1970 1990

1997 estimated population

1,700,000

There are no taxes on merchandise stored in Nevada warehouses, as there are in other states. These low taxes have attracted industries and investors to Nevada.

With low taxes on property and no income tax, the state has depended on gambling taxes to pay more than half the cost of state government and has gradually raised the sales tax to meet increasing costs.

As a result of all these government actions -- easy divorce, legalized gambling, low taxes or no taxes -- Nevada has gone from near poverty to prosperity. Nevada has become the fastest growing state in the nation. The state's population more than doubled from 1970 to 1990 -- increasing by 123 per cent from 488,738 in 1970 to 1,201,833 in 1990.

This rapid growth has not been entirely beneficial. There have been some unhappy side effects. The great number of unskilled jobs in the hotel and casino industry has brought tens of thousands of transient workers to Nevada. At the low rate of pay, these workers can scarcely make a living. Many are often unemployed, waiting for work, or laid off in a slack season. This has given Nevada a high percentage of people who need welfare services.

At the same time, the revenue from taxes on gambling and retail sales have not been very dependable. In the early 1990s, tax income to pay for state government fell rapidly. It became impossible for the state to maintain all its usual services to the people.

Prizefighting

The first great crowds of tourists came to Nevada to attend prizefights. In 1897, a prize-fight between heavyweight champion "Gentleman" Jim Corbett and challenger Bob Fitzsimmons was cancelled in San Francisco. Seeing a chance to bring the fight to Nevada, the State Legislature passed a law legalizing prizefighting in Nevada. The resulting fight in Carson City was set for March 17, St. Patrick's Day, a lucky day for Fitzsimmons who was an Irishman.

Corbett was a great favorite with sports fans in San Francisco. Special trains were run to Reno to bring the crowds to the fight. Thousands of visitors came to Carson City. The hotels were jammed, and people rented rooms in their homes. Everyone made money. It was a man's event. Prizefighting was considered too rough for the ladies.

That didn't keep Nellie Verill Mighels, the *Nevada Appeal*'s famous woman journalist, from covering the fight. She reported "the feminine angle" for the *Chicago Tribune*. But she signed a man's name to the article because she didn't want her women friends in the East to know she had attended a prizefight.

Later, Nellie Mighels recalled:

I was so ashamed that I had seen this terrible display. Only Fitzsimmon's wife, two girls from the red light district and myself represented the feminine element in the audience. In the second round, Corbett gave Fitzsimmons a bloody nose. Fitzsimmons rubbed the bloody glove down Corbett's back and then turned and grinned at the audience. I was so afraid someone would get hurt that I was just petrified. Fitz' back was toward me. Corbett slid gently down to the floor. Fitzsimmons let him down easy and Gentleman Jim took the count.

In 1906, George L. "Tex" Rickard, a Goldfield saloon keeper, decided to recreate the excitement aroused in Carson City in 1897. To do that, he put up the largest prize ever offered for a prizefight up to that time, a purse of $30,000. The fight matched two famous lightweight boxers -- Oscar M. "Battling" Nelson, a white man, and Joe Gans, a black man.

George Lewis "Tex" Rickard.
Rickard, a Texas cowboy, rancher, town marshal, and gambler, got his start in Goldfield, Nevada. He went on to make millions of dollars for himself and his backers as an international-class sports promoter.
Courtesy of Nevada Historical Society

After unprecedented publicity, the fight was staged on Labor Day in 1906. There was extensive betting on the match. Perhaps the contest between races added to the interest. Gans won in the 42nd round, when Nelson was disqualified for foul blows. Tex Rickard went from Goldfield to New York City to become an internationally famous sports promoter and gambler.

After Tex Rickard's great success with the fight in Goldfield, Reno decided to try a similar event. On July 4, 1910, Jim Jeffries, former heavyweight champion, was matched with Jack Johnson, the first black man to become heavyweight champion. The contest caused great excitement, attracting crowds from everywhere. There was a huge attendance of sportswriters from across the nation to see the fight. Hotel rooms were filled. Special trains with sleeping cars were parked in the railroad yards. The sense of conflict in the crowd ran high, perhaps again, because of the contest between races. Johnson inflicted a severe defeat of Jeffries, ending in the 15th round of the 45-round fight. After the Johnson-Jeffries match, prizefighting became more acceptable in other states; and it became less important in Nevada for about 50 years.

Then, in 1963, Las Vegas hosted a world heavyweight boxing championship match on July 22. Sonny Liston retained his title with a knockout victory in one round over Floyd Patterson. Two years later, Mohammed Ali, boxing under his given name of Cassius Clay, came to Las Vegas as the new champion. In another world heavyweight boxing championship match on November 11, 1965, he defeated former champion and perennial challenger Floyd Patterson after a twelve-round bout.

Downtown Reno During the Johnson-Jeffries Fight, 1910. *The streets are crowded with some of the thousands of reasons why popular national sport promotions are good for business. Just before and during the fight, Reno's hotels were full to capacity, and rooms were nowhere to be had.*
Courtesy of Nevada Historical Society

Gradually, in recent years, Nevada has become more and more a national center for boxing. Both Las Vegas and Reno now have matches every few months that bring large crowds of fight fans into Nevada. Championship boxing and matches that develop future champions have become a mainstay of tourist entertainment in Nevada today.

Easy Divorce

Beginning in the early 1900s, Nevada became known for "easy divorces." Gradually, over a period of about 20 years, easy divorces became a major attraction bringing people to the state. Nevada had only a six-month waiting period for divorces. Most other states required a much longer wait.

In 1906, Laura Corey, the wife of William Corey, who was president of the U.S. Steel Corporation, won a two-million-dollar divorce settlement in Reno. The story about her divorce ran in newspapers everywhere. The whole nation learned that Reno judges were lenient in granting divorces. In 1920, the famous movie star, Mary Pickford, obtained a divorce in Reno so she could marry Douglas Fairbanks.

Magazine stories began to tell about what an exciting time the rich and famous ladies had in Reno while they waited for a divorce. They lived at luxurious dude ranches and went for horseback rides with handsome cowboys as guides. They could gamble in lavish, exclusive clubs at night. For every famous person who came to Reno for a divorce, there were hundreds of ordinary people who came to Nevada to end unhappy marriages. To make it even easier to get a Nevada divorce, the Legislature shortened the waiting period to three months in 1927 and to six weeks in 1931. A small but very profitable trade built up in the Reno-Tahoe-Carson City area as result of the easy divorce attraction.

Elegant Society Women Amuse Themselves Gambling. *Nevada's most sophisticated casino of the 1920s, Graham and McKay's The Willows, was a favorite spot for out-of-state divorcees waiting to satisfy Nevada's residency requirements for a "quickie divorce." This fashionable trio are having mixed reactions to their fortune. They are playing "chuk-a-luck," as a poker-faced dealer stands in the shadows.* Courtesy of Nevada Historical Society

Gambling in the Early Days

The urge to place a bet is nearly as old as man himself. The earliest histories and myths mention gambling as a common pastime in almost every known culture. In Nevada, the Paiute, Shoshone, and Washo Indians have played and bet on games since prehistoric times. Legends of these tribes mention wagers and betting among the earliest inhabitants and mythological figures.

When the first fur trappers and explorers came into Nevada, they reported that many of the Indians liked to gamble. In *The Big Bonanza*, Dan DeQuille mentioned it also:

> *Young Winnemucca (Numaga) never gambled, but Old Winnemucca was an inveterate gambler -- that is, among his own people. The Paiutes do not gamble with white men. Old Winnemucca has been known to lose all his ponies, all his blankets and, in fact, everything he possessed, down to a breech-clout, at a single sitting.*

Poker-Playing Paiutes. *These Paiutes gamble their earnings on the turn of a card in a camp outside Rhyolite. Betting played an important part in Indian society, where even mythical characters liked to play games of chance.*
Courtesy of Nevada Historical Society

One of Nevada's famous gamblers of the earlier years was William B. "Lucky Bill" Thorington. Lucky Bill was a sure-thing gambler -- that is, he cheated. He didn't always keep it all for himself, though. There are many stories about Lucky Bill's charity and his skill at "thimble-rig" (the shell game). Here is one example from Angel's *History of Nevada*:

In 1854 a couple of California-bound emigrants stopped at Mormon Station, and had a falling out, and it transpired that they were partners, one of them owning the wagon and the cattle that hauled it, while the other, who had a wife, supplied the provisions. The expense of this provision supply and incidentals along the route had exhausted the husband's finances, and the owner of the train refused to take the bankrupt emigrants any further. Lucky Bill passing, saw the woman weeping disconsolately by the wagon, and his sympathies were at once aroused. Upon inquiry he learned the state of affairs, and told the husband and wife to borrow no further trouble for he would see that they reached the Sacramento (river) without further delay.

That night the owner of the outfit was induced to bet against Lucky Bill in his thimble-rig game, and in the morning he had neither an outfit nor a dollar in money left. The winner gave him back fifteen dollars of his money, bought him a new pair of boots to travel in, told him to "lite out" for California on foot, and to never after that bet against anyone who was playing his own game. To the bankrupt family he gave a cow, spent the loser's money in buying them provisions, and then hired a man to drive the team with them to California.

Unfortunately, Lucky Bill came to an unhappy end. He was tried and convicted of murder in 1858 by the Carson Valley "People's Court," or vigilance committee. Thorington and two other men were hanged for the crime.

Legalized Gambling and Tourism

The territorial legislature and the first State Legislature both made gambling as illegal in Nevada as it was in other states. Gambling was widely considered a "back room" sport that made men lazy and impoverished families. However, at this time, Nevada was populated by single men. There were very few women in Nevada during the mining town boom days. Many of these women were employed as entertainers. Thousands of men without wives or families had nothing to do when they were not working. So, many ignored the laws against gambling and gambled in the saloons at night and visited the women entertainers. Then, in 1869, the State Legislature passed a law, over the veto of Governor Henry Blasdel, which made gambling legal in Nevada.

There were problems with the new law about who should be permitted to play, admitting minors, licensing fees, hours of play, and cheating. In 1905, the Legislature legalized "nickel-in-the-slot" machines.

After forty years of legalized gaming in Nevada, the Legislature decided to make a radical change. In 1909, it again passed a law prohibiting all gambling in the state. The prohibition took effect October 1, 1910. Crowds of curious and sentimental people packed Reno's gambling halls, but wagering stopped promptly at midnight. The new law was not widely respected.

The total ban on gambling in the state was ineffective. Law enforcement agencies found it difficult to enforce the law. People who chose to break the law did so willingly. There were few complaints about gambling, unless it involved cheating. Sheriffs' departments and city police enforced the law unevenly. The state's gambling operations produced no revenue in licenses or taxes. The illegal games flourished and made a mockery of the law.

In 1931, after much discussion over the question of whether to allow legal gambling in Nevada, Assemblyman Phil Tobin, of Humboldt County, introduced a bill in the State Legislature. It was termed a "wide-open gambling bill." The bill drew strong opposition from religious, temperance, and other groups. Despite this opposition, Tobin's bill passed both the Senate and the Assembly and was signed into law by Governor Fred Balzar on March 19, 1931.

One of the major factors behind the legalization of gaming in Nevada was a desire to regulate the industry. The Legislature also hoped that legalized gaming might encourage the local economy. The Great Depression, which started at the end of 1929, had ruined many businesses in Nevada, and tourism had almost stopped. No one seemed to have any money, and the Legislature bet that legalized gaming might pay off.

The payoff did come. Eventually, it paid off far beyond the Legislature's wildest dreams. In fact, tourism based on gaming finally became most of the state's economy and, for many years, has paid for approximately half the cost of government in the state.

It took almost a half century for all this to happen. It was nearly 20 years before the gamblers understood the opportunity offered by having gambling legalized. The Nevada gamblers had been operating, in back rooms because gambling, though permitted, had been illegal. This was what they were used to. When it became legal, they were afraid to really go public. Legalized gambling had been tried before and the reformers had it stopped. So, although the gambling clubs could now operate legally, they did not operate quite openly.

Reno

It was an old-time carnival barker, Raymond I. "Pappy" Smith and his son, Harold Smith, who demonstrated how to prosper from legalized gambling. The Smiths came to Reno in 1936. They used a carnival gimmick (mouse roulette) to attract people. Then they gave them old slot machines to play. The Smiths put up signs reading: HAROLD'S CLUB OR BUST, each sign listing the distance to Reno. At first, the signs did not mention gambling which might have led to disapproval.

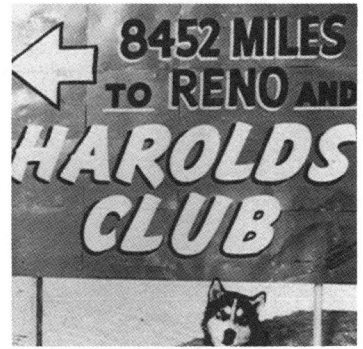

Publicity Put Nevada Gaming on the Map. In 1941 to promote the fun of gaming. After Harold's Club began to provide a free evening to graduates of the nearby U.S. Air Force Survival School, the servicemen put up Harold's Club signs as far away as the Congo and both the North and South Poles, even in combat zones.
Courtesy of Nevada Historical Society

In his book I Want to Quit Winners, Harold Smith, Sr. wrote: *The advertising campaign we started that year was to make our name known on every continent of the world. Now that we'd got our feet wet we weren't happy with Nevada's reluctance to promote its legal gaming. We started building roadside billboards extolling the FUN of playing at our club. The 25 signs we put up within 500 miles were to grow in the years ahead to more than 2,000 scattered over much of the civilized world. (I understand one was even raised inside the Antarctic Circle)... We made it and expanded the club more. It was still pretty a rough gem, however, to sightseers expecting a deluxe casino. As Daddy admitted, "It took us five years to catch up with our advertising".*

The Smith Family. Three generations of gaming innovators, Harold Smith Sr., Raymond I. "Pappy" Smith and Harold Smith Jr., ponder the pros and cons of gambling at Harold's Club. The casino was posted with signs which said, "No one can win all the time. Harold's Club advises you to risk only what you can afford".
Courtesy of Special Collections, University of Nevada Reno Library

Another California gambler, William F. Harrah, moved his operation to Reno in 1937. Like Harold Smith, Harrah became disgusted with government harassment in California and decided to try his luck in a state where gaming was legal.

He came to Nevada from Venice, California, where he ran a game similar to bingo. He had bought the game there from his father for $500. Six employees came with him from Venice. They opened a bingo parlor in Reno. It failed at first and then moved to a new location. In the new place, the business survived and grew slowly until, finally, it became a large casino-hotel.

Distinctive Casino Architecture. As tourism and gaming became big business in the years following World War II, large profits meant expansion for the older casinos with modest storefront beginnings. Harold's Club has taken over several adjoining shops and buildings in this view of the intersection of Virginia Street and Commercial Row in the mid-1950s. The largest signs emphasize the historical link between the modern casino and the gambling saloons of the Old West. Over the main entrance to the original club, there is a large mural showing the overland trek of the pioneers by covered wagon, "Dedicated in All Humility to Those Who Blazed the Trail".
Courtesy of Nevada Historical Society

DOWNTOWN RENO, January 1, 1997

The "Great Reno Flood of '97" was what is called a "Hundred Year Flood" because floods of this magnitude occur on an average of about every 100 years. In this view the Truckee River has flooded deep into downtown Reno. You look up South Virginia Street at the right and up Sierra Street at the left. At the bottom of the picture the river stays in its channel and runs right through the flood.

Courtesy of Marilyn Newton, Reno Gazette Journal

William Fisk Harrah (1911-1978) of California. *Harrah got his start at the age of twenty, when he ran a commercial bingo game. Attracted by Reno's legalized gambling, he relocated there in 1937. He told a friend, "That's a place! Look at that; they don't close the bars and they don't close the games. They leave you alone." Harrah was the first casino owner to use modern sociology and psychological studies to attract tourists, and he built a multi-million-dollar empire with advertising and charter buses.*
Courtesy of Nevada Historical Society

Harrah often emphasized his belief in absolute honesty, friendliness, courtesy, and in offering a variety of entertainment. He said, 40 years later, that he never foresaw how successful the business would become.

Reno began a boom period immediately after the end of the Second World War. When the twelve-story Mapes Hotel opened in 1945, it was the tallest skyscraper in Nevada. Built by Gladys, Gloria, and Charles Mapes, the business was the first major hotel to be constructed in the U.S. after the defeat of Germany and Japan.

The next year, 1946, Lincoln Fitzgerald opened his Nevada Club casino in downtown Reno. It became a landmark in the town, and in Nevada's gaming history, and has now evolved into Fitzgerald's Casino-Hotel.

The Famous Reno Arch as It Appeared in the 1930s. *Built in 1927, the arch quickly became the widely-known landmark for Reno. It was highly visible to travelers on the railroad trains and to drivers on old U.S. Highway 40 (now Fourth Street). Although the arch was built in 1927, the slogan, "The Biggest Little City in the World," wasn't added until 1929. The framework and the lighting have been remodeled many times, most recently in 1987.*
Courtesy of Nevada Historical Society

The Reno Skyline. *This view of Reno greets the tourist who drives into the city from Interstate 80. The beautiful new Silver Legacy Hotel is the highest building to the right. The great ball you see is part of the hotel and contains a tremendous exhibit of Nevada's historic mining industry. At left, stands Harrah's world famous hotel. Harold's Club is buried behind a building at about the center of the picture. Reno's spectacular mountains provide the backdrop.*
Courtesy of Reno News Bureau

Elko

Meanwhile, it was a smaller Nevada city in which the great value of live entertainment was first demonstrated. Newt Crumley built a theater in his Commercial Hotel in Elko and brought the first famous celebrities to Nevada. Later booked the world-famous to play in the small town in northern Nevada.

Lake Tahoe

Lake Tahoe is a major contributor to business in Nevada. It attracts tourists by the thousands from all over the world and brings millions of dollars into the economy of Nevada. Although tourists come to the lake to gamble, the greater attraction to Lake Tahoe is the recreation it offers. Boating is a major business, fishing, swimming and scuba diving attract additional people everyday, all summer long.

LAKE TAHOE is located on the state border between Nevada and California. It is named from a native American word. Tahoe means "Big Water" in the language of Nevada's Washo Indians who once lived in a camp at the lake for many years. The first white person to report seeing the lake was the famous western explorer, John C. Fremont. In 1844, from a mountain top to the south he looked through the trees and saw the beautiful oval-shaped lake.
Courtesy of Susan Bean

In 1955, William Harrah bought the Gateway Club and opened Harrah's Hotel Casino at South Lake Tahoe. Since then most of the other major casino operators in Nevada have opened hotels at South Lake Tahoe making it one of Nevada's principal gambling centers.

Las Vegas

At first, Las Vegas paid limited attention to the 1931 law that legalized gambling in Nevada. It did license six small casinos. Clark County was booming from the construction of Boulder Dam. Eventually, the city did began to develop a gambling center called "Glitter Gulch" along Fremont Street. This was the oldest business street in Las Vegas. It was the street that newcomers first beheld when they got off the train at the Union Pacific Depot.

The earliest development of what was to become the world-famous Las Vegas "Strip" was unimpressive. It started in a small way in 1940-1941 with the construction of El Rancho Vegas, a motor court and roadhouse with gambling attractions, located a few miles south of the city on the highway to Los Angeles. The Last Frontier, built along the highway in 1941-42, was an establishment similar to the El Rancho. It featured an additional attraction, an amusement park in the form of an Old West-style village. Both the El Rancho and the Last Frontier were designed to attract the business of travelers passing through Las Vegas on their way to other places.

About four years later, the gangsters of the underworld moved in with the construction of the Flamingo Hotel-Casino. At first, Nevada officials failed to realize that it was gangster money developing the gambling industry in Las Vegas.

LLOYD KATZ operated four movie houses when he first came to Las Vegas in 1951. He immediately became a leader in work to benefit the community. He let the churches use his theaters for fund raising events. At the time movie theaters were still segregated. He integrated his theaters at once. He traveled nationally on behalf of the Civil Rights movement and supported the Fair Housing Act for Nevada. He was a member of the Advisory Board for the Nevada Medical Center. His wife, Edythe, worked with him on his efforts and on her own on behalf for education and for children. Both also supported Jewish causes. This husband and wife career of public service was recognized in the founding of the Lloyd and Edythe Katz Elementary School, a part of the public school system in Las Vegas. His friends and the University of Nevada, Las Vegas, honored him by creating an Honors Lounge in his name for honor students.
Courtesy of Edythe Katz

The El Rancho Vegas. *This hotel-casino, south of Las Vegas on the highway to Los Angeles, was opened in 1940 by Thomas E. Hull. This was the first hotel-casino to be built along the Las Vegas Strip, which has become internationally famous as a symbol of legalized gaming.*
Courtesy of Nevada Historical Society

Nevada's leaders apparently thought when they legalized gambling that they were simply removing the restrictions from the existing back-room operations. Common sense should have told them that legalizing gambling would open the door to wealthy gangsters who had been operating illegal gambling on a large scale in eastern cities. In Nevada, they could run wide open without being bothered by the law.

The first such operation was the Flamingo Hotel-Casino. It was the inspired creation of Benjamin "Bugsy" Siegel, a New York gangster. Siegel came to the West Coast in the late 1930s to organize a wire service for reporting sports events. He also was interested in gambling operations in California, which were illegal.

Early in 1947, Siegel told world-famous gambling authority John Scarne why he had come to Las

Vegas to build his resort-casino. Scarne recounted
Siegel's story in his *Complete Guide to Gambling*.
Siegel told Scarne:

> *I owned a piece of those gambling ships that
> were getting plenty of action three miles off the
> coast of Southern California. And just when I
> thought I had it made, Governor Warren came
> along and closed gambling up tight as a drum,
> not only in the state [of California], but on the
> boats too. Overnight my dream of Monte Carlo
> in the Ocean is killed.*

> *So I'm thinking about where I can find
> another spot away from any other casinos -- a
> place like the ocean so when people come to
> gamble they can't go anyplace else but have to
> stick with me. There were too many sawdust
> joints in Vegas, Reno and other Nevada towns,
> but I figured it this way. If people will take a
> trip out into the ocean to gamble, they'll go the
> desert, too -- especially if its legal and they don't
> have to worry about getting pinched.*

> *So one day I drive into Nevada looking for a
> nice desert spot and picked this one because the
> price is right and it's on the main road to L.A.
> Then I took a trip around the country and tried
> to interest some of the boys in the proposition.
> Some of them thought I was nuts. But I dug up
> the dough, and here I am with a five-million
> dollar hotel and a casino full of customers.*

Siegel never lived to enjoy his casino. He
quarreled with his associates and was killed.
Three other gangsters assumed control of the new
Flamingo Hotel-Casino. It was a great money-
maker.

The successful example of the Flamingo Hotel-
Casino was soon imitated. A large building boom
began in Las Vegas during the Korean War (1950-53).

The Fabulous Flamingo. *High-rolling tourists from southern California stroll into the main entrance of the world's first modern hotel-casino, against a backdrop of orange and purple twilight. Built on the Las Vegas Strip in 1946 by gangster Benjamin "Bugsy" Siegel, the Flamingo was the prototype of the multi-million-dollar gambling resort .*
Courtesy of Nevada Historical Society

By this time, the hotel-casino industry in southern Nevada was "on a roll" which was to make Las Vegas the biggest city in Nevada. Tourism excursions to Las Vegas by car made these gambling emporiums and night spots immensely profitable, and a number of casinos were built through 1955.

Nevada's naive public officials were shocked when they realized that many of the new hotel-casinos were owned by gangsters. The gangsters hid their ownership by hiring apparently honorable people to pose as owners in order to appear respectable.

One after another, Nevada's governors gradually dealt with the gangster problem. Governor Vail Pittman saw trouble coming and moved the licensing of casinos away from city and county government and put it under the State Tax Commission. In 1955, Governor Charles Russell created a Gambling Control Board to investigate the background of applicants for gaming licenses.

The Las Vegas Strip. *This view looks down the famous Las Vegas Strip. The pyramid shaped Luxor Hotel is in the left foreground, guarded by the face of an Egyptian pyramid. Midway along the right side of The Strip is the MGM Hotel where so many entertainers have started their careers. The Strip runs 24 hours a day with its hotels always open for the tourists. Las Vegas claims to be the entertainment center of the world. The Strip supports that claim. New hotels are constantly being built along The Strip.*
Courtesy of Las Vegas News Bureau

Then Governor Grant Sawyer created a new state gaming commission with special powers to grant or deny gaming licenses.

In 1966, Howard Hughes came to Nevada and bought 14 percent of the Nevada Casino industry including many of the largest casinos in Las Vegas. He also bought a television station, a large ranch and 2700 mining claims. Other investors then recognized the opportunities in Nevada and bought many of the other Las Vegas casino resorts and hotels.

By 1970, he was the state's largest private employer, with 800 people working for him.

Howard Hughes was also the richest man in Nevada. Eventually he became worth $2 billion dollars making him the richest man in America.

Howard Hughes, 1936.
Courtesy of Summa Corporation

McCARRAN INTERNATIONAL AIRPORT at Las Vegas. *Las Vegas claims to be the entertainment capital of the world. The arrivals at the airport support that claim. Tourists arriving at the airport numbered 30 times as many in 1997 as there had been in 1960. The tourist travel to McCarran Airport gives boost to the state's entire economy. Tourism provides tax income for state government that helps the entire state economy. McCarran Airport is a major contributor to Nevada's prosperity.*
Courtesy of Clark County Department of Aviation

Nevada is the model for gaming regulation throughout the nation. More than half the states now have some kind of gaming. Promoters of its tourism claim that Las Vegas is the best known city in the world. Las Vegas is now the leader in Nevada government because it has more than half of the state's population.

GOVERNOR ROBERT J. 'BOB' MILLER. *After serving two years of Gov. Bryan's term, then being elected to two full terms of his own, Gov. Miller will have served as Nevada's Governor longer than any other person in the state's history. He led the state to great reforms in education, including classroom size reduction and education standards for students.*
Courtesy of Bob Miller

Nevada Business Today

In 1983, Governor Richard Bryan saw the need to rebuild the Nevada economy. He urged the state to completely reconstruct its Department of Economic Development. The State Legislature agreed. Two separate commissions were established: the Commission on Economic Development and the Commission of Tourism. The state was then divided into seven economic regions. Each of these regions has a commission made up of local business leaders who work to improve the economy. Their efforts are financed by a combination of government funds and private business funds.

Nevada has enjoyed prosperity in business for many years. Then, the recession of the 1990s hit the state hard. Government services had to be reduced because of low tax revenue. As more and more states adopted legalized gambling, Nevada leaders became worried. Gambling in other states may damage Nevada's major industry—tourism and gaming. For a long time, Nevada leaders have known that the state is too dependent on legalized gambling. Nevada is rebuilding its economy to make it more diversified.

Gaming in Nevada is big business. Nevada has been the national leader in gaming since it legalized gambling in 1931, more than 60 years ago. Now this is changing. More and more states are adopting state lotteries or some sort of gambling. They want the revenue that government gets from gambling. Gambling has become the fastest growing industry in the United States. With this competition from other states, gambling has become a less dependable source of income for Nevada.

Richard Bryan. As governor, Bryan led the state in the 1983 reconstruction of the Department of Economic Development. Bryan was elected to the U.S. Senate from Nevada in 1988.
Courtesy of Nevada Historical Society

Harry Reid. Elected to the U.S. Senate in 1986 and reelected in 1992, always fought to protect Nevada from nuclear waste either on deposit or in transit. He helped create the interstate water agreement with California and is strong on the wise use of water. At age 30 he became the youngest lieutenant governor in Nevada history. He was born at Searchlight, was raised in a small cabin and attended a two-room elementary school.
Courtesy of Harry Reid

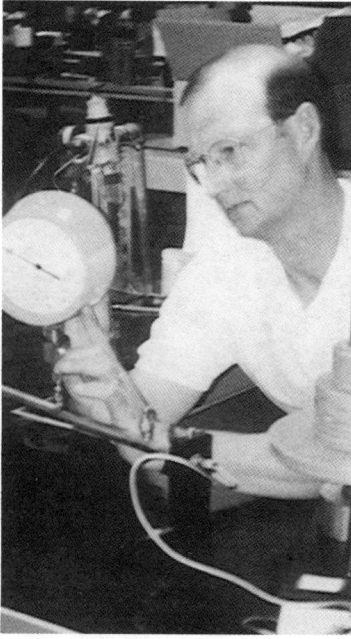

Making pressure gauges.
*Alan M. Jones is checking the
quality of a gauge produced
by Perma-Cal Industries, Inc.,
of Minden. He is the Quality
Assurance Manager. Perma-
Cal is one of many small
industries flourishing in
Nevada. Others are moving
into Nevada each year from
other states.*
Courtesy of Economic Development
Authority of Northern Nevada

The seven regional development commissions of local businesspersons have specific goals. One is to develop as much new non-gaming business as possible. Another is to improve the state's existing gaming industry. A third goal is to improve the income of existing non-gaming business.

These regional commissions have been unusually successful in bringing hundreds of new businesses into Nevada and creating thousands of new jobs. Many of these new businesses are small manufacturing and large distribution (shipping) companies. Nevada has two great advantages in the warehousing and distribution business. One is that Nevada is centrally located to serve all of the Pacific Coast and mountain states. The other is that it has a Freeport Law, which eliminates the inventory tax on some goods stored in warehouses.

To improve gaming income, the huge casino-hotels in Nevada have started adding theme parks to appeal to families. These are areas filled with theme entertainment features (something like those at Disneyland). Gaming and theme hotels account for nearly 400,000 jobs statewide.

The latest and greatest improvement in gaming revenue has been at Laughlin, a new city of large hotel-casinos located 80 miles south of Las Vegas on the Colorado River. It now exceeds Lake Tahoe in gaming revenues.

Nevada leaders are working in every way possible to make up for the future loss of business because gaming is becoming legalized in most other states.

Many of the existing non-gaming businesses have been growing and prospering. In total, the efforts of Nevada's Department of Economic Development are successful. Nevada leads all other states in percentage of job and population growth. Manufacturing is a strong industry in Nevada with regular annual growth of 2 to 4 percent.

Excalibur Hotel-Casino. *The 4,000 room Hotel-Casino is one of the many theme resorts in Las Vegas. In the early 1990s, they were being built rapidly in Las Vegas to attract families to the resort city. The Excalibur transports visitors into a fantasy castle where King Arthur's knights of old lend enchantment to the visitors' vacations.*
Courtesy of Las Vegas News Bureau

The Luxor. *One of the great family destination resorts built in Las Vegas in the mid-1990s; the Luxor is a replica of ancient Egypt. It is a 30-story pyramid that contains the world's largest atrium and has a replica of the River Nile running through it. The huge Sphinx that greets visitors is even larger than the original in Egypt.*
Courtesy of Las Vegas Convention Center and Visitors Authority

Mushroom Cloud from an above ground test at the Nevada Test Site, October 1958.
Courtesy of University of Nevada, Las Vegas Special Collections Department

First railroad depot in Las Vegas – was housed in a railroad coach car. (c1905)
Courtesy of University of Nevada, Las Vegas Special Collections Department

Wilbur Clark's Desert Inn Hotel. (c.early 1950s)
Courtesy of University of Nevada, Las Vegas Special Collections Department, Manis Collection

Fremont Street, C. 1940s.Las Vegas
Courtesy of Manis Collection University of Nevada, Las Vegas

Historical Events

1855
Chinese Laborers Came to Nevada

1870
40% of Nevadans Were Foreign Born

Peter Altube Brought Basques to Nevada

1900
Central Europeans Came to Nevada

1934
Taylor Grazing Act Enacted

1940
Nevada's Population Reached 110,247

1971
Fair Housing Act

1990
10% of Nevada's Population Were Hispanic

1993
Survey Finds 4 Out of 5 Nevadans
   Came from Some Other Place

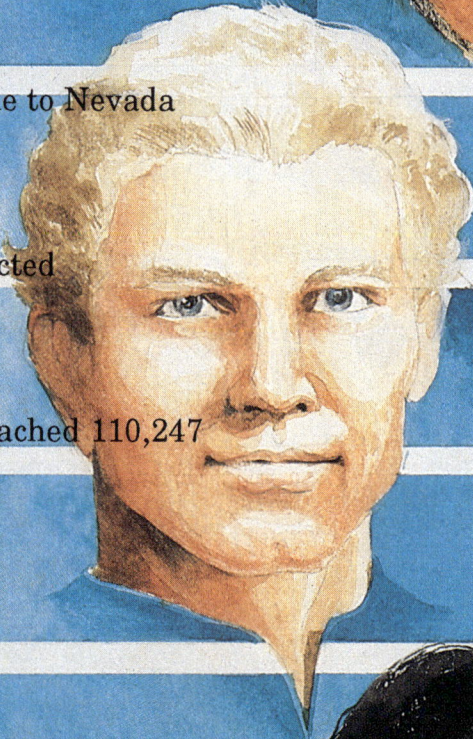

Chapter Eight

The People of Nevada

The People of Nevada

The people of Nevada are the result of an unusual history of strong outside influences. The institutions and the people of Nevada were shaped by a wide variety of forces that intruded from outside. Even today, a greater percentage of outsiders live in Nevada than in any other state. Four out of five residents of Nevada came here from some other place.

A Basque woman dances the "Jota."
Courtesy of Reno News Bureau

Like almost all Americans, the people of Nevada are hard-working, patriotic, and independent. However, Nevada people also have their own special characteristics that are different from the people of many other states.

All Americans, except Native Americans, are descendents of people who came to America from someplace else. In Nevada, this connection with foreign ancestry has always been very strong. Many people have come directly to Nevada from foreign nations. In the very early days, more people came to Nevada mines and ranches from Europe and China than from other parts of the United States. In the middle years of Nevada history, people came to Nevada from the Slavic nations to work in the copper mines at Ely and the gold mines at Tonopah and Goldfield. Now they are coming from Mexico, Central America, South America, and Asia.

These foreign-born Nevadans bring their national cultures with them. They form societies to observe their national customs -- societies such as the Italian-American, the Mexican-American, the Irish-American, the Slavic-American, the Greek-American, etc. They hold festivals to celebrate Columbus Day, Cinco de Mayo, St. Patrick's Day, the Basque Festival at Elko, and many others. These festivals are attended by large numbers of the general public. People see new ideas they like, and some of the customs of each of the various nations becomes a little part of life in Nevada.

The percentage of Nevadans today who were foreign born is still very high. Also, the number of foreigners moving into the state continues to remain very high. Both of these influences -- the historical foreign influence and the modern foreign influence -- make Nevada representative of many parts of the world.

FANNIE GORE HAZLETT, TYPICAL SUCCESSFUL EMIGRANT

There were many entire families who came to Nevada by wagon train. Many of them were seeking opportunity in a new land, more than mining riches. Thousands of widows and single women made up 20 percent of the settlers who took up land under the Homestead Act, and they were at least as successful as the men. The experience of Fannie Gore and her two brothers, who came to Dayton in 1862, is an example of a family coming west by wagon. Here is how Fannie described her trip:

FANNIE'S MEMORY OF HER TRIP

Crossing the plains was in no sense a picnic or a pleasure trip. I crossed the plains in 1862 with the usual experience of terrific thunderstorms on the Platte River, when the lightning could be seen at night playing around the iron work of the wagons; riding all day in the drizzling rain, knowing there was no warm fire or comfortable bed at night; our supper the remnants of some former meal; walking miles every day; cooking over fires of brush or anything else we could find; tending sick people; sometimes a funeral; sometimes a little fun; sometimes an Indian scare; fording swollen streams. We were from 7 in the morning until 10 at night getting across the Green River which had overflowed its banks. Plodding over the Nevada deserts, often traveling at night to avoid the fierce heat of the sun and refection of the sand; people tired and irritable, teams worn out. So we toiled along averaging about 15 miles a day.

At last we arrived at Fort Churchill on the Carson River. A company of soldiers was on parade. We thought we had never seen anything so clean and white; we were very dirty, and very happy; the long road, 2,000 miles of it, lay behind us -- all the way from northern Iowa which we had left sixteen weeks before.

Courtesy of Nevada Historical Society

Dayton was a booming supply center. The Gore brothers acquired wooded land and harvested wood for the mines. Fannie cooked for their wood camp crew. Her house was a 10 X 14 ft. tent with half of the front open. She had a dry goods box for a table and empty molasses kegs for chairs. Her tin dishes had come west in the back of their wagon. Fannie said she was treated with the "proverbial respect shown to women in the early mining days."

Two years later Fannie married Dr. J. C. Hazlett, who practiced medicine in Dayton until he died in 1895. After that, Fannie became postmaster at Dayton for a time and then retired to Reno to live near her grandchildren. She lived on until 1933, when she was 95 years old.

Another thing that is different about Nevada is that it is an urban state. Urban means that most of the people live in cities. In the 1990 census, 88 percent of the people in Nevada lived in cities. This makes Nevada the fourth most urbanized state in the whole United States. Although Nevada is famous for its wide open spaces, there are not many people living out there in all that empty space. We Nevadans live mostly in the cities.

We live in the cities because that is where the jobs are. There are more jobs in tourism, and in other businesses that serve the tourist industry, than in any other kind of employment. There are also a great many people employed in stores, wholesale houses, warehouses, transportation, utilities, and construction. Almost all the jobs in these industries are in the cities. While most of the work of mining is done outside of the cities, miners tend to live in the cities closest to the mines.

Although ranching and farming are a large part of Nevada's economy, they do not provide many jobs for workers. Those who are employed by ranchers and farmers usually live on the ranch or farm, or near it. Here is where you will find the working cowboy. Many people in Nevada dress like cowboys, but not many of them are real cowboys.

In modern times, by contrast with early days, a great many people from other states in the United States have migrated to Nevada. A study of people made in 1993 by the University of Nevada, Reno, found that four out of every five Nevadans came here from someplace else. Less than half the people in any county in Nevada are native Nevadans. Census figures show how rapidly the state has grown. The population in Nevada today is 10 times what it was 50 years ago. In 1940, the state's population was just 110,247. Fifty years later, in 1990, it was 1,201,833.

State's Population

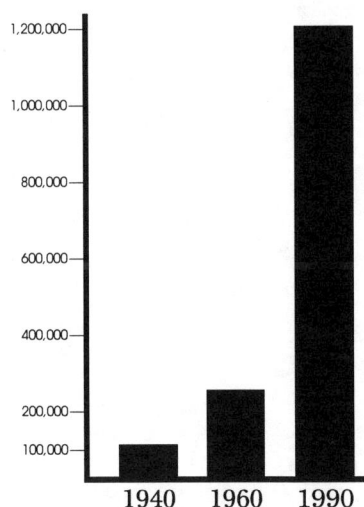

The population today is four times as much as it was just 30 years ago. In 1960, the population was 285,278. In 1990, the population of over 1,200,000 was more than four times as great as in 1960.

Live and Let Live

Nevada people have always had a "live and let live" attitude. Nevada people are very tolerant of the behavior of other people. This is sometimes called an "anything goes" attitude. Perhaps Nevadans have this tolerant attitude because they came from so many different nations. In order to get along, they had to accept the customs of one another, and they all learned to live together.

To Find Jobs

From the very beginning, most people came to Nevada for one of two reasons:

(1) They came to Nevada to escape from extreme unhappiness or misery somewhere else. They often came from other countries to escape from starvation, religious persecution, military conscription (the draft), violent revolutions, or other intolerable conditions.

(2) They came to Nevada to improve their living; they came to make more money so they could live a better life.

In both these cases, they came to Nevada to find jobs. Many people have always come here to find work or to gain greater income opportunity in some other way. This movement of people to Nevada to find jobs is still going on at a rapid rate.

Many have succeeded in their hopes, but others have been disappointed. Life in the mining towns was hard and often failed to produce much income.

The emigrant settling of land was also a hard life, uncertain and often disappointing. Today, ordinary people who come here to find a job may wind up in a poverty cycle from which they cannot escape. Jobs are sometimes easy to get; but they are often seasonal and low paying, with no job security. In recent years, Nevada has been an easy place to get a job but, at the same time, often a hard place to make a living.

Nevada's Ethnic Mix

Nevada has a large ethnic population. More than one fourth of the residents of Nevada, 26 percent to be exact, belong to ethnic groups. In the 1990 U.S. Census, the word "ethnic" refers to racial difference, not to being foreign born. Many of the people belonging to these ethnic groups were born in America. They are Americans by birth. The ethnic statistics include blacks, Indians (Native Americans), and Hispanics who were born in America. These people certainly are Americans, the Indians being even more American than the whites. The other ethnic groups which are neither black, Indian, nor Hispanic make up about 18.6 percent of Nevada's population.

Here is the population of Nevada's ethnic groups as they were listed by the 1990 federal census:

Hispanics	124,419
Blacks	78,771
Asians, Including Pacific Islanders	38,127
Indians (Native Americans)	19,637
All Others of Ethnic Origin	52,603
Total	313,557

Ancestry

In the 1990 census, Nevadans also listed their ancestry. They listed the countries from which their ancestors came to America. This is the way the non-ethnic ancestries were listed:

German	280,052
Swedish	31,301
English	207,062
Dutch	30,751
Irish	199,953
Scotch-Irish	27,950
Italian	87,525
Norwegian	23,229
French	60,218
Welch	14,266
Polish	33,591
Slovak	6,311
Scottish	32,601
Yugoslavs	3,592
Total	1,038,402

Foreign Born in Early Nevada

When we think of the people who settled Nevada, we most often think of Americans coming from the Midwest down the California Trail to get rich in the gold country or to settle on a ranch and develop the land. This was not usually how the settlers got here. The truth is that far more settlers came to Nevada from foreign nations than came west from other parts of America.

In the nineteenth century, people from many nations wanted to come to America. They had to come to a place in America where they could get a job and make a living. Nevada offered more job opportunities for foreigners than most other states offered.

So, they came to Nevada. In 1870, only six years after Nevada became a state, 44 percent of the people in Nevada were foreign born. That made Nevada have the highest percentage of immigrants of any state in America.

Foreigners worked in the mines and cut the timber for the mines. They built the railroads that carried ore from the mines and livestock from the ranches to markets out of state. They operated, maintained, and repaired the railroads. They held public office and helped make the laws. They were labor leaders. Foreigners built the schools and churches, and many of them were the teachers and the preachers for these institutions. They printed and edited the state's newspapers.

The first wave of immigrants was the Germans who came to the mines, but soon left mining to become highly successful as ranchers, farmers, and businessmen. The next wave was the Irish who worked in the mines. After that came the Chinese, the Italians, and the Central Europeans (from the Slavic nations). Quite a few Mexicans came to Nevada in the early mining days. The Irish and the Chinese came to America to escape famine. Other foreigners came to America to escape revolutions, persecution, prejudice, military conscription (the draft), or poverty. Sometimes they came for adventure.

Virginia City in 1875

A good idea of the extent of foreign-born activity in Nevada can be gained by looking at Virginia City at the start of 1875. After midnight on New Year's Eve, in the early morning hours of the new year, the Germans were dancing and singing at the Athletic Hall. The French and Italians had joined together to sing each other's songs at Gregorie's Saloon in the heart of downtown at Union and C streets.

CORNISH BALLADEER

Richard Jose, the blacksmith balladeer, started singing in public as a little boy in Virginia City. He was sent there from Cornwall, in England, to live in the care of a relative. But the relative had moved away. Left alone with no support, the nine-year-old boy wandered into a saloon and began singing "Where Is My Wandering Boy Tonight?" The miners loved it and gave him money to live on. A women's reform group soon stopped such a little boy from singing in saloons. He moved to Reno and went to work for an uncle who was a blacksmith. Richard continued to sing for churches and public benefits. His beautiful voice was heard by a booking agent, and soon he was singing in San Francisco. He went on to perform in Europe and Africa and achieved world-wide fame. Jose became a recording artist for the Victor Talking Machine Company. His record, "Silver Threads Among the Gold," made the company its first million dollars.
Courtesy of Nevada Historical Society

Later in the week, the sixteen-piece Cornish orchestra and the English Choral Society greeted the new year more reverently at the Methodist Church. The Swiss also helped to usher in 1875 with their minstrel show; and, late in January, the British Benevolent Association held its first semi-annual election.

Professional Men

Among the important foreigners who settled in Nevada were many professional men. Nearly all of the doctors were from other nations. The priests and preachers came from the European nations. Many of the newspaper editors and printers (men and women) were from other nations.

The doctors in Reno were German, French, Canadian, Italian, English, Russian and Swiss. A French doctor served White Pine and Eureka counties. French-Canadian and English doctors practiced in Esmeralda County. A Scottish-Canadian doctor was in Rawhide, and Humboldt County was served by a New Zealander and a Welshman.

In Nevada churches, many of the ministers were foreigners. For more than two generations, Catholic priests trained in Dublin came to Nevada. Almost all of the priests and their assistants who served Virginia City (then the center of Nevada's population) were from Ireland. Protestant ministers also came from Ireland. In Virginia City in 1870, all the priests and all the protestant ministers were from Ireland, and there was one from Ireland at Gold Hill.

Methodist preachers came to Nevada from many cities in England and Wales before World War I. There were also Episcopal ministers who came to Nevada from England. Many served their apprenticeship in Nevada. John Brown traveled from Scotland to organize the first Presbyterian church here.

St. Mary's of the Mountains (right). *Virginia City's most famous church was rebuilt after the great fire of 1875. Bishop Patrick Manogue, then a young priest, was pastor of the church. Fr. Manogue was a "giant of a man" who had been a miner before he became a priest. He was much loved by the miners of Virginia City. John W. Mackay put up much of the money for rebuilding the church. St. Paul's Episcopal Church (background), a classic example of Gothic architecture, was built in 1876. A musical version of "Ghosts of the Comstock," the play at the end of Chapter Four, was presented in St. Paul's Church by Virginia City students. A video tape of this musical is available.* Courtesy of Nevada Historical Society

Immigrant preachers, priests, and rabbis came from non-English speaking countries such as Holland, Belgium, Norway, Italy, Denmark, Germany, France, Poland, and Greece. They also came from Brazil, India, China, Peru, the West Indies, and the East Indies.

At least a score of immigrant writers became journalists in Nevada. Among them were Englishmen and Frenchmen. Immigrant journalists also founded Nevada newspapers in their own languages. There were German language and Italian language newspapers published in Nevada.

Among all these foreigners who arrived in Nevada in the very earliest days, the influence of the Germans and the Irish drew special attention. A famous writer of the time, J. Ross Browne, said of Nevada, "Unless you were born in Ireland, which is so much the better, or born in Germany, which is still better ... do not rush headlong to Nevada."

Inventor of the Ferris Wheel Lived in Nevada

George Washington Gale Ferris, inventor of the Ferris wheel, lived in Carson City as a boy and attended school there. He became a very successful engineer, specializing in steel and concrete construction. Sponsors of the World's Columbian Exposition in Chicago in 1893 wanted something new and dramatic to draw crowds to the fair. George Ferris remembered a water wheel on the Carson River. He had spent many hours watching it run when he was a boy. He came up with the idea of a big wheel for the fair -- one that would carry people up into the sky. Sponsors for the fair liked the idea, and Ferris built the magnificent, huge wheel. It was 250 feet high and carried 36 cars. Each car was 24 feet long, had 38 chairs, and glass windows on all sides. Every ride carried 1,368 people high in the air to view the countryside. The wheel served 1,453,611 customers in its nineteen weeks of operation at the fair. When the fair closed, the wheel was moved to another place in Chicago, where it ran for several years. It was duplicated for the Paris Exposition in Europe in 1900. The big wheel was moved from Chicago to St. Louis in 1904, where it drew crowds to the Louisiana Purchase Exposition. After that, it was dismantled and sold for scrap. But George Washington Gale Ferris never lived to see this happen. He died of typhoid fever in 1896 when he was only 37 years old. Since then, all over the world at fairs, carnivals, and amusement parks, Ferris wheels have continued to give pleasure to millions of people.

Germans

The German settlers of Carson Valley showed how Europeans could fit into Nevada better than most Americans did. They resisted Americanization (giving up old country ways for American ways). Instead, they set up an excellent society of their own.

They maintained their native language and formed German social organizations. This made Carson Valley much like a farm community in Germany. Their energy made their farms a model of how to develop the new land. They cleared the land, dug irrigation canals, and made Carson Valley the most stable and consistently productive community in Nevada.

Italians

There were also many successful Italian settlements in the Truckee Meadows and around Dayton. There, the land-hungry immigrants from Italy secured land holdings. They kept the thrifty practices learned in Italy, and in the second generation as Americans, many of the Italians had become bank executives, doctors, and leading businessmen.

When news of the gold and silver strikes reached Italy, Italians came to Nevada. Some of them worked in the industries that served the mines such as lumbering, transportation of supplies, and retail trade.

Albert A. Michelson. A German-American who lived as a boy in Virginia City, Michelson became a professor of physics at the University of Chicago. In 1907, he was America's first winner of the Nobel prize in physics for his work with light and in meteorological investigation. He was also a military officer and a talented violinist and artist.
Courtesy of Nevada Historical Society

Columbus Day Parade. This 1992 Reno parade was spectacular as the Sons of Italy celebrated the 500th anniversary of the discovery of America by Christopher Columbus. It featured many floats like this one. Italian descendants in Nevada, first as miners and farmers and now in all walks of life, have been remarkably successful and have kept alive a strong cultural identity.
Courtesy of Reno News Bureau

However, the most attractive occupation to the Italians was agriculture. They produced vegetables, dairy products, wheat, hay and grain. They brought with them the right experience for use in Nevada because they knew about irrigation for the production of crops. The Truckee Meadows appealed to the Italians. It gave them an opportunity to acquire cheap, undeveloped land. Virginia City provided a market that was nearby for their crops. The Italian farmers soon moved into Mason Valley and Smith Valley, where there was fertile undeveloped land with adequate water. There they produced potatoes, alfalfa, and grain, hogs, and dairy cattle.

Chinese

The first Chinese came to Nevada in the mid-nineteenth century to work in mining, railroad construction, and related industries. They developed little Chinatowns throughout the state. In 1855, a group of about fifty Chinese left San Francisco to work on the Carson Valley irrigation projects. Because the Mormon bosses in charge of the projects were impressed with the industry and willingness of the Chinese to work for low wages, they allowed them to stay on as placer miners in Gold Canyon near Carson Valley. These two characteristics -- hard work and low pay -- became the hallmark of Chinese in America. People in Nevada, like California, organized anti-Chinese movements and lobbied for legislation that discriminated against the Chinese. This discouraged the Chinese from staying in Nevada. Many left by the early 1900s (or even earlier). Some, however, stayed and became permanent residents. They have worked in mining, railroading, tourism, food services, land development, and education.

The finest example of a pioneering Chinese-American in Nevada was Gue Gim Wah, who lived in Lincoln County. For 70 years she cooked for the miners and the public. Her fame as a wonderful cook and a loyal American spread. Her life symbolized the struggles, contributions, and achievements of the Chinese in Nevada. Finally, recognized as a great Nevadan, she led the Nevada Day parade as its grandmarshal in 1980.

Gue Gim was born near Hong Kong in 1900 and came to America with her father when she was 12 years old. A Chinese man named Tom Wah ran the boarding house for the miners at the Prince mine east of Pioche. When he decided to get married, he went to San Francisco to find a bride. There he met with Gue Gim's father, whom he had known in China. He saw Gue Gim, and she was the girl he wanted. Gue Gim's father gave her to Tom in marriage. Tom was 43, she was 16. But like other Chinese girls, she followed her father's direction. She said, "Of course I afraid, but what I do? No ask, just do. Tom and I run boarding house and cook. I learn English." Tom died in 1933. Despite the pleas of relatives who wanted Gue Gim to move to San Francisco, she decided to stay in Castleton. Her Wah's Cafe, with its huge American kitchen filled with Chinese and American objects, was an example of the two cultures that make up a Chinese-American's life. In 1987, when she died, she was hailed as "Pioche's most famous resident."

Courtesy of Special Collections, University of Nevada Las Vegas Library

Yugoslavs in Nevada

Compared to other foreign groups in Nevada, Slavs were a distinct minority before 1900. Then, in 1900, and for many years thereafter, the mining booms in Tonopah and White Pine counties brought an influx of South Slavs into Nevada. These people became permanent citizens and brought their Slavic culture into Nevada. Descendants of South Slavs in these two communities are the nucleus of the Yugoslavs in Nevada today.

Whole communities from the Balkan peninsula were transplanted to Nevada towns. Single males made the journey first. Word from them about job opportunities in Nevada went back to their home communities. Wives and sweethearts joined the men in Nevada.

Although Catholic Croatians and Greek Orthodox Serbs had lived close together on the Balkan Peninsula, they were very unfriendly to one another. Their stormy relationship continued in Nevada. In Tonopah, the Slavs were sometimes called Sclavonians or Slavonians, terms not meant to be respectful.

White Pine County received an influx of South Slavs soon after 1900. Croatians and Serbs joined Greeks and Italians and others who came to work in the copper mines near Ely and Ruth. The large copper companies of White Pine County closely controlled the lifestyle of their workers. Company towns were established, where housing was provided according to ethnic groups. The groups were segregated into separate communities. As "foreigners," the whole area occupied by these groups was separated from the "whites."

World War I brought about a change in the attitude of Nevada people toward the Slavic community. The initial attack by Austria on Serbia evoked sympathy for the Serbs in Tonopah and also in White Pine County.

School sports also helped to break down the barriers between the races. As the youngsters reached high school and played together in teams on the athletic fields, the differences melted away.

Many workers came from the Slavic nations to work on the Nevada Test Site during World War II. Today, the largest community of Slavic people in Nevada is in Las Vegas, which is now home to approximately four hundred Yugoslavs. Many of them came to Las Vegas from other American cities.

Basques

There are more Basques living in California and Idaho than in Nevada. But Nevada is the center for Basque-American activity. Nevada has the advantage of being centrally located in the Basque community that spreads over the three states. Nevada also has the Basque Studies Program.

This national center of Basque culture is part of the University of Nevada in Reno. The national Basque festival has been held in Elko for the past 30 years. At this celebration, thousands of Basques keep their Old World traditions alive and share their New World culture.

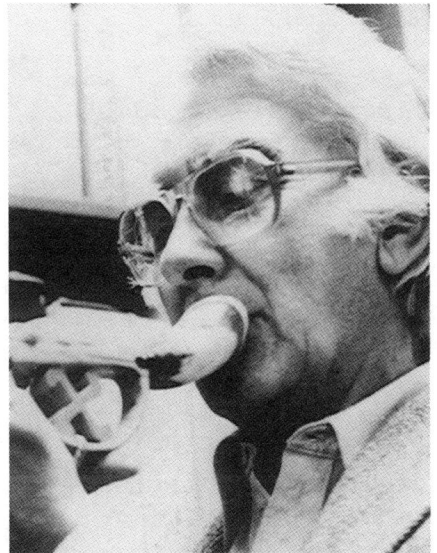

The Late Professor Jon Bilbao of the Basque Program playing an ancient Basque horn, the Alboka.
Courtesy of Basque Studies Program, UNR

Basque Children. These young Basques present the Basque flag and the American flag at one of their many outdoor celebrations. Both flags are always featured to symbolize the union of Basque culture with life in America.
Courtesy of Reno News Bureau

We learned in Chapter Five how opportunity in the sheep industry brought the Basque immigrants to Nevada. Cattlemen fought the enterprising Basque sheepherders. Ranchers opposed letting the Basques graze their herds of sheep on the open range. The cattlemen got laws passed restricting grazing on rangelands. This made it difficult for the roving sheepherders to operate. But it never stopped them. Finally, the Taylor Grazing Act in 1934 brought all public lands under federal regulation and the itinerant sheep bands could no longer operate.

Today Basque ranchers who own their own land continue to dominate the sheep industry. Other Basques in Nevada are notably successful in small businesses and in the professions.

Hispanics

In this century, Hispanics have become the largest minority group in Nevada. In 1996, Hispanics made up 16.6 percent of the state's population. Hispanic population was expected in 1996 to reach 20 percent by the year 2000 and it will continue to increase. This means that, at the turn of the century, one in every five persons in Nevada will be Hispanic.

Nevada Hispanics trace their ancestry to more than 20 Spanish-speaking nations. Mexican-Americans are the dominant Hispanic group, but there are many with Central American or Cuban ancestry. The Central Americans came in the 1980s, particularly from Guatemala and Nicaragua. The Cubans came earlier to flee from Castro's revolution. Including the Cubans, most Hispanics came to the United States for political reasons or to escape from poverty.

Emma Sepulveda, Latina Woman of The Year for 1997, is a strong advocate for women's causes and for equal rights and community action. She is a Latino, who as president of Nevada Hispanic Services, founded Latinos for Political Education. She was awarded the Thornton Peace Prize in 1994 for promoting resolution of conflicts through non-violent means.

Following the explosion in 1997 of a chemical plant in Sparks where Mexican-American workers were killed and wounded, she helped the Mexican families to understand and cope with the tragedy. Born in Argentina and raised in Chile, Emma came to Reno in 1974. She is a professor of Spanish at the University of Nevada in Reno and she gives public lectures on Hispanic topics and women's causes.

Courtesy of Emma Sepulveda

Cinco de Mayo Festival. *Mexican-Americans maintain their culture with many festive events. Here Mexican dancers celebrate the Mexican Independence Day, in Victorian Square in Sparks.*
Courtesy of Sparks Redevelopment Agency

Mexicans have some good reasons for coming to Nevada.

Nevada's tourist industry offers many jobs where workers may not have to be able to speak English. Mexican immigrants can usually find housing or they can live with friends or relatives already in America.

Mexicans came into Nevada in the earliest days of its settlement, soon after the Mexican-American War ended in 1846. They came to Nevada to work in the mines. Another migration of Mexicans came in the early 1900s to work on the railroads, in the mines and on the farms. There were colonies of Mexicans around Elko, Ely, Winnemucca, Sparks and Las Vegas. The descendents of these early Mexican-Americans are now established successful members of Nevada society.

A Mexican-American woman sings at the Cinco de Mayo Festival.
Courtesy of Sparks Development Agency

Luther Mack is an black man who has risen to the top level of accomplishment, both in public service and business. In 1974 he started his first McDonald's Restaurant in Reno. He was Chairman of the Foundation Board at the University of Nevada in 1996 and 1997. He served as chairman of the board for the Reno-Tahoe International Airport. He has received the "Small Business Award". He was awarded the degree of "Doctor of Humane Letters" at the University of Nevada Commencement Ceremonies in 1998. Mack is a graduate of Reno High School.
Courtesy of Ries Photography

The Hispanics of present times have settled mostly in Clark County. They have participated in the services of the University of Nevada system, the public schools, the churches, businesses, offices, hotels casinos and the building industry. The largely non-English speaking Mexican population has created a need to offer services in Spanish as well as English. For many years the Nevada Department of Motor Vehicles has given tests in Spanish.

By the mid 1990s, almost all information given to the public was bilingual. This was true in retail stores and services, in hotels and casinos, in agencies of government and institutions such as hospitals.

Black Americans

From the earliest beginnings, black people have contributed to the state of Nevada. But most of the time, they have had to live with unfair prejudice against them. Over the years much of that prejudice has slowly been overcome. Many black Nevadans are now leaders in business, government, education and social institutions.

Blacks were involved in the very earliest history of Nevada, even before it began to be settled. In the 1820s, Black men were with Jedediah Smith, the first explorer to cross Nevada from east to west. We learned in Chapter Two about James Beckwourth, the black explorer for whom the Beckwourth Pass is named and who lived in Nevada for a long time.

One of the wealthiest farmers among the early settlers in Carson Valley was Benjamin Palmer. The first non-Indian baby born in Carson Valley was a black child. The mother was Charlot Barber, Palmer's sister.

The first Baptist Church in Nevada was founded by a black congregation in Virginia City. There were black businessmen, often barbers, living in Virginia City during the years of great prosperity from 1860 to 1880. And in Elko, a black barber, Thomas Detter, wrote the first book published there.

Despite all of this, the new government of Nevada was prejudiced against black people. At first, blacks were not permitted to vote, hold office, serve on juries or be in the militia. They could not testify against whites in court and their children could not attend public schools. Finally, black men were given the right to vote in 1870 by the Fifteenth Amendment. Most racist laws in Nevada were repealed in the 1870s, but in actual practice, strong prejudice remained.

Although there were black workers in the crews that built Boulder Dam, the first substantial black population in Nevada developed at Henderson near Las Vegas. During World War II, Basic Magnesium, Inc., hired black workers and there was an influx of blacks from the South. Black workers stayed in Las Vegas after the plant closed in 1944, but they suffered severe prejudice from employers for the next 25 years.

Very few black people were employed in hotels and casinos in either Las Vegas or Reno. They were not even welcome as customers in the casinos. They could not stay at the hotels. Black entertainers were not even permitted to stay in hotels where they were performing on stage. The 1960 session of the legislature banned discrimination against black people by public agencies and by contractors doing work for the state. But no effective legislation was passed to enforce these laws.

The black people in Nevada received little relief until the 1964 federal Civil Rights Act was passed.

Senator Joe Neal. A lawyer, an engineer and a legislator, Senator Neal of Las Vegas has been Nevada's leading black man in public affairs for more than 30 years. Elected to the Nevada State Senate in 1972, he served at various times as acting governor of Nevada, president of the senate and as minority floor leader for many years. He received the American Civil Liberties Award and the Lifetime Achievement Award from the NAACP. A Las Vegas elementary school bears his name and he teaches Constitutional Democracy at the Clark County Community College.
Courtesy of Joe Neal

Bernice Martin Mathews.
Bernice Mathews of Reno was elected to the Nevada State Senate in 1995. She was the first black woman to serve in the State Senate and holds the highest position in state government ever held by a black woman. She serves on the Finance, Human Resources and Legislative Affairs committees. Previously, in 1991, she was elected to the Reno City Council as its first black member. She is also a successful business woman in Reno where she has a long record of community service.
Courtesy of Karen Inc.

The next year, the Nevada Legislature passed a similar but weaker law making racial discrimination against the law in public accommodations and employment. Then, in 1971, the legislature passed a fair housing act. Despite these changes in the laws, it has taken vigorous action by black leaders to gain respect. They continued to strive for equal treatment and equal opportunity.

Eventually, blacks began to make real progress. Woodrow Wilson was elected to the State Assembly in 1965 and Joe Neal has been a state senator since 1973. The number of black members in the state legislature is gradually increasing.

Black people are now strongly involved in leading positions in government, the professions and in business, social and community organizations. The influence of black people in Nevada is growing steadily.

Asians

There's a modern wave of Asians coming to Nevada. These new Asians are very different from the Chinese who played such an active role in early-day Nevada. Many of the Asians are medical professionals, highly trained technicians or scholars with advanced degrees. The early day Asians came mostly from the Chinese countryside. The new Asians are coming from various cities and countries of the Orient.

The Asian population in America and in Nevada is changing dramatically. The Chinese and Filipino populations have more than doubled in the past 30 years. The numbers of Koreans and East Indians are 10 times what they were. During the same years, the percentage of Japanese in the population has dropped by two-thirds. The new Asians come to America because of crowded conditions and lack of career opportunities in their homelands.

With all their education and skills, many of these newcomers face a serious language barrier because they don't speak English. This makes it very difficult for them to find the work they have been trained for. In order to survive, these skilled professionals have to go to work in the service or tourist industries. A Filipino medical doctor may wind up making change for slot machine players. Others survive by getting into their own small businesses where everyone in the family can work. Koreans have been especially successful in their own business enterprises.

Nevada has another population of new Asians who are here, not because they want to be, but because they had to flee from their homeland. They are the refugees from the Vietnam War.

Many of these Vietnamese, Laotians, and Cambodians can speak English because they learned it in their schools. This helps them find employment. However, many of these refugees would like to return to their homeland but see no prospect of being able to do so.

Wing and Lilly Fong. *The Fongs are major community leaders in business and public service in Las Vegas. Mr. Fong is a very successful restaurant owner who, for many years, has given generously of his time and money in support of community projects. Mrs. Fong was a regent of the University of Nevada for many years. The Lilly and Wing Fong Elementary School in Las Vegas is named for them.* Courtesy of Special Collections, University of Nevada Las Vegas Library

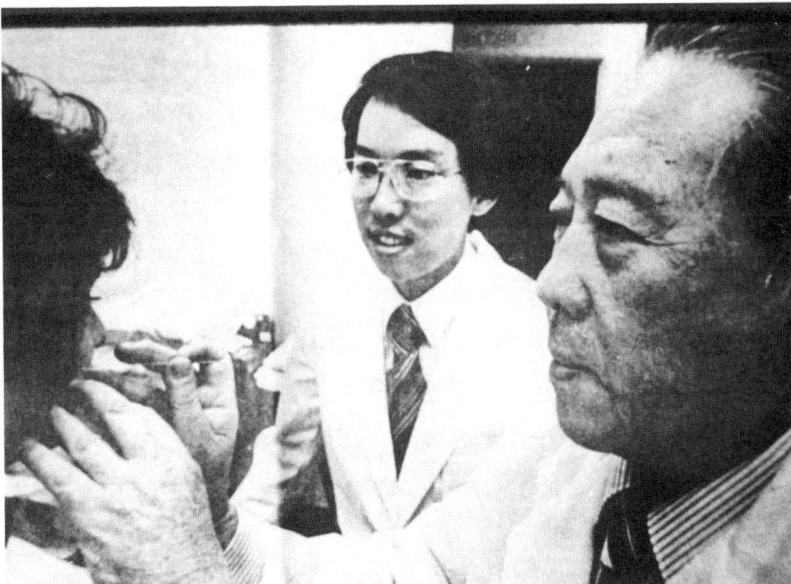

Dr. Yee-Kung Lok. *A leader in the field of Oriental Medicine in Nevada, Dr. Lok established the state's first acupuncture clinic. His influence helped get the law passed in 1973 that legalized acupuncture, herbal medicine, and other Asian health practices. He was chairman of the State Advisory Board of Oriental Medicine. His son Steven, at his right, has taken over the operation of the clinic since Dr. Lok retired.* Courtesy of Nevada State Museum

This new population of Asians in Nevada shows one very important characteristic. Their children are often at the top of their classes in American schools. A very high percentage of them earn advanced professional and academic degrees in the colleges and universities. Today, they are often held back by prejudice against them. This will change in the future. Many of these new Asians will be among the intellectual and social leaders of Nevada.

Nevada's Native Americans

Nevada's Native Americans want to become more independent of the federal government. In order to do this, they have to create revenue. They also want to revive and preserve the knowledge of their tribal language and their culture and traditions.

Some tribes have established businesses in order to generate income and create jobs for tribal members. They nearly all have smoke shops. Some have gas stations and convenience stores. In addition, the different tribes operate a variety of other businesses. For instance, the Reno-Sparks Colony operates a major printing plant. In other places, the tribes own farms where livestock and alfalfa are raised. They also own and run other businesses.

The greatest extent of tribal activity has been in Yerington. There, under the 14-year leadership of Tribal Chairman Linda Howard, the Yerington Paiute Indians developed a variety of businesses and published a number of tribal educational publications. They established a smoke shop, a fast-food restaurant, a convenience store, an alfalfa farm, a land-leveling business, and a land lease venture. Their publication initiative produced books on tribal government, on the Paiute language in both English and Paiute versions, and books of tribal customs, heritage, and superstitions.

Linda Howard. *Ms. Howard was the tribal chairman of the Yerington Paiute Tribe during a period of very active development of tribal businesses and educational enterprises. She believes young people must learn the skills of the business world and also respect and preserve their Native American language and cultural heritage.*
Courtesy of Patrice Bingham Photography

Historical Indian Dancing. *An Indian powwow to celebrate their national heritage is held each year by Native Americans at the Stewart Indian Museum in Carson City. The celebration features historic tribal dances done in beautiful Indian costumes.*
Courtesy of Stewart Indian Museum

Throughout the tribes there is a rekindling of interest in Indian traditions. Older members feel the loss of the old knowledge among the young people. They would like to revive that knowledge. Many young Indians do not know about the old Indian ways of life. Very little information about modern Native Americans is contained in the textbooks of Nevada schools. However, some schools do include Indian courses. The Washo language is taught at Douglas High School, and Indian tribal government is now taught at Yerington High School. The tribes would like to see more courses dealing with Native American life today offered in other schools.

Native American tribal leaders have two main educational objectives. They want their young people to become skillful in the business world and, at the same time, to keep alive the knowledge of their native culture and heritage.

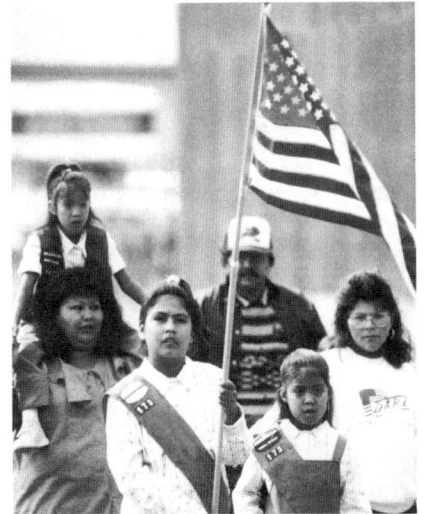

Parade at the Reno-Sparks Indian Colony. *Indians celebrating "Honoring Our Elders Day," carry an American flag to portray their role as modern Americans. The celebration was also a tribute to their ancestry as the Native Americans who were here before Columbus brought the white man.*
Courtesy of Reno Gazette Journal

Jewish People in Nevada

From it's earliest days Jewish people have played a vital role in the development of Nevada. They came into Carson Valley with the settlers that came into Nevada. They lived in Carson City before it became a city. They were merchants, miners and farmers, especially as independent business people who owned and operated many different small shops and services. They went where their shops would be especially promising and were needed.

As an example of Jewish contribution, was a Jewish tailor, named Davis making saddlebags and wagon covers in his shop in Reno, who made the world's first pair of Levi pants. In 1871, a woman asked Mr. Davis to make an especially durable pair of pants for her husband. He used the same tough material to make the overalls that he used to make saddlebags. As an afterthought he fastened the pockets with copper rivets, the same as he used on his saddlebags.

Word about the unusual pockets spread and the pants made by Davis sold rapidly. Davis asked a friend San Francisco to help him get a patent on the pants. The friend knew Levi Strauss and asked Strauss to help. Strauss got the new pants patented and Davis moved to San Francisco to supervise the making of Levi's.

The Jewish people in Nevada are actively involved in social and fraternal organizations. They also contribute generously to community charities. Flora Duncan started a service program for children with drug problems, many were runaways from all over the country.

The children and their problems cried out for help and the service minded people responded.

Edythe Katz helped to organize a prestigious board of advisors for the program. She raised funding for The Focus House and goods, which were needed.

Edythe Katz. A strong leader and one of Nevada's great people. From the time she first came to Las Vegas in 1951, her life has been an outstanding example of service to the community, the state and people of Nevada. She has been a vigorous advocate of many good causes, as well as those supported by Jewish people. She has been a leader in strong support of education and in reminding Americans to never forget the horror of the Nazi Holocaust and to see that such horror never happens again. She was the first person to receive the Nevada Humanities Committee Award. She has been chairperson of the Governor's Advisory Council on Education relating to the Holocaust. She established the curriculum guide in Holocaust education for the Las Vegas School District, a guide that has been adopted in many schools in Europe and Israel. She received the Distinguished Service Award of Southern Utah University in recognition for all her services.
Courtesy of Edythe Katz.

Portuguese

The Portuguese came to Nevada in large numbers. They did not come from mainland Portugal itself. They came from the Azores and Atlantic Islands off the coast of Portugal. Since most did not know the English language, the first work that many of them did was as sheepherders, just as the Basques did. The Portuguese settled throughout Nevada and performed all kinds of work. They came to Fallon, Yerington, Lovelock and Reno in sufficient numbers to open businesses for their own people. There was an Azores mercantile store in Lovelock and an Azores store in Fallon.

The first Portuguese Pentecostal Festival – The Feast of the Holy Ghost – a uniquely Azorian religious ceremony, was celebrated in Yerington in 1919, then in Fallon in 1929, in Reno in 1934 and in Lovelock in 1935.

In Fallon, Yerington and especially in Reno the Portuguese took up dairying, an occupation that had been familiar to them in the Azores. A study of dairying in 1925 showed that a quarter of Nevada's dairymen were Portuguese.

Everywhere the Portuguese supported community activities and served in public offices.

Current Nevada State Archivist, Guy Rocha is a prominent Portuguese Nevadan. He traces his roots to Terceira, one of nine Atlantic islands in the Azorean archipelago. Generations of his family lived in Doze Rebeiras (Twelve Rivers) on the west side of the island.

Francisco Lourenzo da Rocha, Guy's grandfather, immigrated to the United States in 1904. His port of entry was San Francisco, where he met Rose Ormande who had also immigrated from Terceria. Marrying in 1915, they moved to a farm in Los Banos, California. Guy's father, Ernest, was born there in 1920 and worked in the livestock industry.

W.F. Mendes, one of four brothers from the island of Flores in the Azores who settled and found success in central Nevada.
(Reno Evening Gazette, 4 August 1909)

Guy Rocha, prominent Portuguese Nevadan.
Courtesy of Guy Rocha

Guy, who grew up in Las Vegas, has done much to promote the study of the Portuguese in Nevada and the American west. He likes to point out that the Portuguese were significant players in the agricultural and maritime history of the Far West; after the Chinese the second largest workforce in building the Central Pacific Railroad; and sizeable numbers of them toiled in the Comstock mines.

The Portuguese name most notable in government in Nevada was that of Nancy Gomes. She was not Portuguese herself, but was married to John Gomes giving her a Portuguese name. She was known for outstanding service as a social worker and as a member of the state legislature. She is most remembered for getting the legislature to pass the enabling law that made it possible for Washoe County to build the Rancho San Rafael Regional Park.

Nevada's People Today

During the years coming up, just before and after the turn of the century, Nevada will be approximately 150 years old. Now, as in the beginning, outside forces strongly affect the makeup of Nevada. In its earliest days, the Native American style of life in Nevada was much influenced by the culture and institutions of the European immigrants. Now it is coming under the new influence of the rapidly growing. Hispanic and Asian populations.

There's an old French saying that might be applied to Nevada, "The more things change, the more they stay the same".

Verne Horton

NEVADA FACTS

STATE FLAG – Cobalt blue background; in upper left quarter is a five-pointed silver star between two sprays of sagebrush crossed to form a half wreath; across the top of wreath is a golden scroll with the words, in black letters "Battle Born". The name "Nevada" is below the star and above the sprays in golden letters. Design modified June 8, 1991, original design approved on March 21, 1929.

STATE BIRD – Mountain Bluebird
STATE ANIMAL – Desert Bighorh Sheep
STATE FLOWER – Sagebrush, adopted March 20, 1917
STATE TREE – Pinon Pine
STATE CAPITAL – Carson City; designated in July 1864; territorial capital dating back to 1861
AREA – 110,540 sq miles, 485 miles long, 315 miles wide; seventh in size

PRINCIPAL LAKES – *Natural:* Lake Tahoe, Pyramid Lake, Walker Lake, Topaz Lake, Ruby Lake
Man-Made: Lake Mead, Lake Mohave, Lake Lahontan, Rye Patch Reservoir

PRINCIPAL MOUNTAINS – Highest peak, Boundary Peak 13,145 ft., Wheeler Peak, 13,061; Mt. Charleston, 11,910; N. Schell Peak, 11,890; there are 51 peaks above 9,000 ft.

PRINCIPAL RIVERS – Longest, Humboldt River, 500 miles; Carson River, Truckee River, Walker River, Colorado River

HIGHWAYS – A total of 49,702 miles of streets and highways of which 40,519 are country roads

GOVERNORS OF NEVADA, 1864-1997

1864-71 Henry Goode Blasdel	1927-34 Frederick Bennet Balzar
1871-79 Lewis Rice Bradley	1934-35 Morley Issac Griswold
1879-83 John Henry Kinkead	1935-39 Richard Kirman, Sr.
1883-87 Jewett Williams Adams	1939-45 Edward Peter Carville
1887-90 Charles C. Stevenson	1945-51 Vail Montgomery Pittman
1890-91 Francis Jardine Bell	1951-59 Charles Hinton Russell
1891-95 Roswell K. Colcord	1959-67 (Frank) Grant Sawyer
1895-96 John Edward Jones	1967-71 Paul Dominique Laxalt
1896-1903 Reinhold Sadler	1971-79 Donald N. 'Mike' O'Callaghan
1903-08 John Sparks	1979-83 Robert Frank List
1908-11 Denver S. Dickerson	1983-89 Richard H. Bryan
1911-15 Tasker Lowndes Oddie	1989-present Robert Joseph 'Bob' Miller
1915-23 Emmet Derby Boyle	
1923-27 James G. Scrugham	

GLOSSARY

alfalfa - a type of perennial, high-quality hay crop

allotment - something given, assigned or distributed by a drawing or shares

ancestry - a line of forefathers from which one is descended

archaeologist - one who studies the life and culture of ancient peoples

archives - a place for storage of important documents

artesian wells - a deep well which has water being forced to the surface by the pressure below

artifact - a simple ancient tool, weapon, vessel, basket, etc.

assay - the analysis of an ore to determine its ingredients, the proportion of ingredients and its worth

atlatl - wooden, hand-held spear which is thrown with a special device

autobiography - a written account of one's own life

barrier - something in the way of one's movement

basin - a low, bowl-shaped area of land

bicameral - two legislative chambers, such as the senate and assembly

bilingual - to speak more than one language

bonanza - a rich vein of ore

borrasco - an unsuccessful mine

buckaroo - a cowboy

bulwark - a defensive wall or structure

claim - a demand for something, as land staked out by a miner or a settler

climate - the prevailing weather conditions of a place over a period of years

combine - a machine for threshing and harvesting grain

commerce - the business of buying and selling of goods on a large scale

conspicuous - easy to see or obvious

contaminate - to pollute

cultivate - to prepare land and care for crops

degikup - a finely-coiled and braided fiber basket of elegant design

depression - a condition of less business activity

discrimination - treating differently, usually unfairly

diversion - to turn aside from one direction to another, such as redirecting water for irrigation

ecological - a branch of biology that studies the relations between living things and their environment

emigrant - one that leaves one place to settle in another

enterprising - having a capacity for action, especially to gain wealth

erosion - the carrying away of soil by water, wind or ice

ethnic - a people who are similar in racial, language, religious and cultural ways

fertile - highly productive soil

ford - a shallow place where a river can be crossed

garments - any article of clothing

harvester - a machine used to gather crops

high-grading - stealing small amounts of gold in one's clothing

homestead - a tract of land for a home granted to a settler by the Homestead Act of 1862

immigrants - people moving into a country from another country

interstate - something between states of a federal government, such as an interstate highway

intrude - to thrust or force in without permission

ledge - a projection of rock or a vein

legalization - making something legal

long tom - a long, narrow box used to catch heavier gold particles washed from rock or ore

mainstay - a principal support

migration - moving from one place to another

mustang - a horse living in the wild, not owned or domesticated

native - one belonging to a locality or country by birth, or plants which originated in a locality; not imported or introduced

novelty - something or some action which is different

oasis - a place in the desert where there is water

ore - any natural combination of minerals from which metal can be separated

pelt - an animal skin

petition - a formal signed request, usually to a governmental body, for something to be done

plateau - an extensive level land area raised sharply above surrounding land, or at least one side

promoter - one who begins and/or helps the organization of a new activity, business or event

prospector - a person who searches for valuable metals or minerals

prosperous - financially successful

provocation - an action that causes resentment and usually anger

public land - land held by the government, often federal land

quartz - a crystal mineral occurring in colors but most often in a colorless, transparent form and sometimes containing minerals such as gold, platinum and lead

ratified - confirmed by voting

reclamation - to bring back land suitable for human use by irrigating or draining

reprisal - an injury inflicted for something done, lost or suffered, usually because of another person

reservation - public land set aside for some special use, as for Indians

roundhouse - a usually circular building with a turntable in the center for storing and repairing locomotives

rushes - plants having round and hollow stems, sometimes used for making baskets

sink - an area of sunken land, especially one in which water collects and then may evaporate or be absorbed into the ground

skirmish - an unusually brief conflict or battle, especially between military units

slaughterhouse - a place where animals are killed for market

smelting - the reduction of ore by heat

spectacular - something which attracts attention or is impressive to see

spittle - a liquid in the mouth which is helpful to digestion

stamp mill - power machinery for crushing ore

stench - to have or give off a bad odor

strike - to find valuable minerals in the process of mining

strip mining - removal of topsoil to get to the underlying ore

suffrage - the right to vote in a political election

surveyor - one who determines the location, shape or boundaries of land by using geometry

tailings - that which is left after mining and/or milling

tepee - a cone-shaped tent of poles covered with skins, used by certain American Indians

toll road - a road for the use of which a fee is charged

tourism - the business of assisting and/or promoting travel of people for pleasure

transcontinental - the crossing of a continent

unscrupulous - unprincipled or dishonest

vein - a body of minerals occupying a crack, or fissure or zone

vigilance - watching carefully or being on alert against harm

vigilantes - a group of citizens who watch and punish law breakers

vocational skills - skills required for a trade, profession or occupation

wash - a low strip of ground that is flooded part of the time and dry the rest of the time

wickiup - temporary Indian shelter made of branches covered with grass or brush

winnowing basket - a large, flat tray used for tossing a mixture of nuts and shells into the air to remove the shells

INDEX